AS

History

Michael Scaife

Contents

Contents

Specification lists

AQA History

MODULE	SPECIFICATION TOPIC	CHAPTER REFERENCE	STUDIED IN CLASS	REVISED	PRACTICE QUESTIONS
Module 1 (M1) European/ World History	Germany and Russia before the First World War 1870–1914	8.1, 8.2 10.3, 10.4			
	Russia 1855–1917	8.1, 8.2, 8.3			
	Germany 1871–1925	10.2, 10.3, 10.4, 12.1			
	The origins and consolidation of totalitarian regimes 1918–39	11.1, 12.2, 13.2			
Module 2 (M2) British History	Britain 1815–41	1.1, 1.2, 1.3, 3.1			
	Britain 1895–1918	4.1, 4.2, 4.4, 4.5			
	Britain 1929–1951	5.4, 5.5, 6.1			
Module 3 (M3) Course Essays	The Balkans 1870–1914	3.2, 10.4			
	Russia 1917–29	8.3, 13.1, 13.2			
	Germany c.1925–38	12.1, 12.2, 12.3			
	Germany 1918–1923	11.1			
	Italy 1915–20	12.1			
	The Government response to poverty 1815–41	1.2			
	The New Liberalism 1906–15	4.2			

Examination analysis

The specification comprises three unit tests. For each of Units 1 and 2 candidates choose one of the alternatives listed above. For Unit 3 two alternatives have to be studied.

Unit 1 Candidates answer two questions on their chosen alternative:
one compulsory three-part source-based question
one three-part structured question from a choice of two   *1 hr 30 min test 35%*

Unit 2 Candidates answer two questions on their chosen alternative:
one compulsory three-part source-based question
one three-part structured question from a choice of two   *1 hr 30 min test 35%*

Unit 3 Two course essays. Externally set and marked.   *30%*

For the source-based questions three sources are provided, approximately 300 words in total, and three questions are set on them. In Unit 1 the sources are largely secondary and the questions focus on explanation/ comprehension, comparison and use of the sources and own knowledge for an extended response. In Unit 2 at least one of the sources is primary and the questions focus on comprehension, assessment of utility or reliability and an extended response.

For the structured questions a brief stimulus is provided. There are three sub-questions: the first requires explanation of something in the source, and the other two focus on issues arising from it.

For Unit 3 you will have to write two course essays of 1000 words each under supervised and timed conditions. The relevant sections of this study guide will provide you with a starting point for these.

OCR History

MODULE	SPECIFICATION TOPIC	CHAPTER REFERENCE	STUDIED IN CLASS	REVISED	PRACTICE QUESTIONS
Module 1 (M1) Document Study	The condition of England 1832–53	1.2, 1.3			
	Italian unification 1848–70	9.1, 9.2			
	The Irish Question 1877–1893	2.3			
	England in a New Century 1900–1918	4.1, 4.2, 4.3 4.4, 4.5			
	Nazi Germany 1933–45	12.2, 12.3			
Module 2 (M2) British History	The age of Peel 1829–46	1.4			
	Whigs and Liberals 1846–74	2.1			
	The Conservatives 1846–1880	2.1			
	Foreign and imperial policies 1846–1902	3.1, 3.2, 3.3			
	Trade Unions and Labour 1867–1906	4.4			
	Liberals and Labour 1899–1918	4.1–4.5			
	Inter-war domestic problems 1918–39	5.1, 5.2, 5.3, 5.4,			
	Post-War Britain 1945–64	6.1, 6.2			
Module 3 (M3) European History	France 1814–1848	7.1			
	Italy 1830–70	9.1, 9.2			
	Germany 1862–90	10.2, 10.3			
	France 1848–75	7.2			
	Russia 1825–81	8.1			
	Russia 1894–1917	8.2, 8.3			
	Italy 1919–1945	11.1–11.4			
	Germany 1919–1945	12.1, 12.2, 12.3			
	The USSR 1924–1953	13.2, 13.3			

Examination analysis

The specification comprises three unit tests. For each unit test candidates choose one of the options listed above and answer one question on it. Your teacher may choose to study additional options in Modules 2 and 3 to give you a choice of questions.

Unit 1	One source-based question	1 hr test	40%
Unit 2	One question chosen from two for each option	45 min test	30%
Unit 3	One question chosen from two for each option	45 min test	30%

For Unit 1 questions, four sources are provided, approximately 300–400 words in total. Sources are mainly primary but one may be secondary. The three questions test explanation/comprehension, comparison of two sources and use of the sources and own knowledge as evidence to test an assertion.

Edexcel History

MODULE	SPECIFICATION TOPIC	CHAPTER REFERENCE	STUDIED IN CLASS	REVISED	PRACTICE QUESTIONS
Module 1 (M1)	Poverty and the British State: c.1815–50	1.2			
	Votes for women, c.1880–1918	4.3			
	Russia in revolution 1905–17	8.2, 8.3			
	The rise of national socialism in Germany to 1933	12.2			
Module 2 (M2)	Unification of Italy, c.1848–70	9.1, 9.2			
	The Liberal Governments 1905–15	4.2			
	Russia 1918–29	13.1, 13.2			
	Italy: the rise of fascism 1918–25	11.1, 11.2			
	Weimar Germany 1918–29	12.1			
Module 3 (M3)	Parliamentary reform, 1815–50	1.1, 1.2			
	Bismarck and the unification of Germany, c.1848–1871	10.1, 10.2			
	Party and policy in the age of Gladstone and Disraeli 1867–85	2.2, 2.3			
	British society between the wars 1919–39	5.2, 5.4			
	Life in Hitler's Germany 1933–39	12.3			
	Life in the Soviet Union 1928–41	13.2			

Examination analysis

The specification comprises three unit tests. For each unit test you choose one of the options listed above.

Unit 1	One source-based question on each option	1 hr 30 min test	40%
Unit 2	Two two-part structured questions on each option, of which you answer one.	1 hr test	30%
Unit 3	offers two alternatives:		
	Examination option: One single-source, three-part structured question on each option **or**	1 hr test	30%
	Coursework option: Centre-assessed coursework – 1750-3000 words		30%

For Unit 1 questions 4-6 sources are normally provided, about 500 words in total. Sources are mainly primary but one will be secondary. Five questions are set, focusing on comprehension, abstraction, cross-referencing evaluation of usefulness or reliability and use of the sources and own knowledge for explanation or analysis of an issue.

Unit 2 questions focus on identification of key issues and causation.

For Unit 3 questions one or two sources (about 150 words) are provided. There are three sub-questions, one of which focuses on extraction of information from the sources.

WJEC History

MODULE	SPECIFICATION TOPIC	CHAPTER REFERENCE	STUDIED IN CLASS	REVISED	PRACTICE QUESTIONS
Module 1 (M1) Period Study	History of Wales and England c.1815–65	1.1, 1.2, 1.3, 1,4, 3,1, 3,2,			
	History of Wales and England c.1880–1918	4.1, 4.2, 4.4, 4.5			
	History of Europe 1815–71.	9.1, 9.2, 10.1, 10.2			
	History of Europe, c. 1878–1933	11.1, 12.1			
Module 2 (M2) Period Study	Disraeli and Gladstone c.1846–93	2.1, 2.2, 2.3, 2.4			
	History of Wales and England c.1900–39	4.3, 5.2, 5.4, 5.5			
	History of Europe 1855–1914.	8.1, 10.3			
	History of Europe 1917–41: Soviet Russia, Fascist Italy, Nazi Germany	11.2, 11.3, 12.3, 13.1, 13.2			
Module 3 (M3) Depth Study	Reform and protest in Wales and England c.1830–48	1.2, 1.3, 1.4			
	Britain c.1929–39	5.3, 5.4, 5.5			
	Unification of Italy c.1856–1871	9.2			
	Nazi Germany c.1933–45	12.3			

Examination analysis

The specification comprises three unit tests. For each unit test you choose one of the options listed above.

Unit 1	One two-part structured question from a choice of three for each period.	*45 min test*	*30%*
Unit 2	One open-ended essay question from a choice of three for each period.	*45 min test*	*30%*
Unit 3	One single-source question from a choice of two **and** one multi-source question from a choice of two for each study topic.	*1 hr 30 min test*	*40%*

Unit 1 structured questions focus on explanation and assessment.

Unit 2 essay questions require candidates to discuss an interpretation of a key issue.

In Unit 3 single-source questions three questions are set, focussing on comprehension, extraction of information from the source and assessment of usefulness. In the multi-source question five sources are provided and the three questions focus on comparison, reliability and usefulness.

NICCEA History

MODULE	SPECIFICATION TOPIC	CHAPTER REFERENCE	STUDIED IN CLASS	REVISED	PRACTICE QUESTIONS
Module 1 (M1)	*Reaction and reform: England 1815–41*	*1.1, 1.2*			
	The Nazis and Germany 1919–45	*12.2, 12.3*			
Module 2 (M2)	*Re-established Monarchy in France 1824–48*	*7.1*			
	Fascism and Italy 1918–43	*11.1, 11.2 11.3, 11.4*			
Module 3 (M3)	*The condition of England 1841–65*	*1.3, 1.4, 2.1*			
	Revolutionary change in Russia 1917–41	*13.1, 13.2*			

Examination analysis

The specification comprises three unit tests. For each unit test you choose one option. In addition to the options listed above there is an Irish History option in Module 2.

Unit 1	External examination, including use of sources	*1 hr 30 min test*	*40%*
Unit 2	External examination	*45 min test*	*30%*
Unit 3	External examination	*45 min test*	*30%*

For units 2 and 3 candidates will be required to answer one two-part question on their chosen topic.

AS/A2 Level History courses

AS and A2

All History A Level courses being studied from September 2000 are in two parts, with three separate modules in each part. Students first study the AS (Advanced Subsidiary) course. Some will then go on to study the second part of the A Level course, called A2. Advanced Subsidiary is assessed at the standard expected halfway through an A Level course: i.e. between GCSE and Advanced GCE. This means that the new AS and A2 courses are designed so that difficulty steadily increases:

- AS History builds from GCSE History
- A2 History builds from AS History

How will you be tested?

Assessment units

For AS History, you will be tested by three assessment units. For the full A Level in History, you will take a further three units. AS History forms 50% of the assessment weighting for the full A Level.

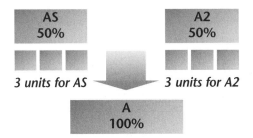

Each unit can normally be taken in either January or June. Alternatively, you can study the whole course before taking any of the unit tests. There is a lot of flexibility about when exams can be taken and the diagram below shows just some of the ways that the assessment units may be taken for AS and A Level History

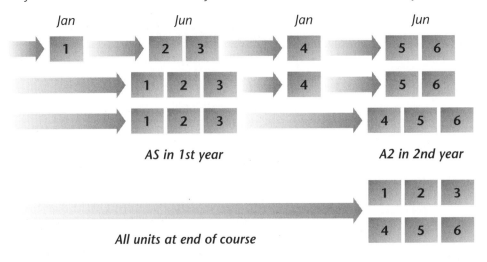

If you are disappointed with a module result, you can resit each module once. You will need to be very careful about when you take up a resit opportunity because you will have only one chance to improve your mark. The higher mark counts.

A2 and Synoptic assessment

After having studied AS History, you may wish to continue studying History to A Level. For this you will need to take three further units of History at A2. Similar assessment arrangements apply except that some units, those that draw together different parts of the course in a 'synoptic' assessment, have to be assessed at the end of the course.

Coursework

Coursework may form part of your A Level History course, depending on which specification you study. At AS Level it is an option for Edexcel candidates. If your course includes coursework, follow closely the advice of your teacher and make sure you allow yourself plenty of time to complete the assignment, especially if you have to submit coursework in other subjects.

Key skills

It is important that you develop your key skills throughout your AS and A2 courses. These are important skills that you need whatever you do beyond AS and A Levels. To gain the key skills qualification, which is equivalent to an AS Level, you will need to collect evidence together in a 'portfolio' to show that you have attained Level 3 in Communication, Application of number and Information technology. You will also need to take a formal testing in each key skill. You will have many opportunities during AS History to develop your key skills in Communication and Information technology.

It is a worthwhile qualification, as it demonstrates your ability to put your ideas across to other people, collect data and use up-to-date technology in your work.

What skills will I need?

For AS History, you will be tested by assessment objectives: these are the skills and abilities that you should have acquired by studying the course. The assessment objectives for AS History are shown below.

Historical knowledge and understanding

- recall, select and deploy historical knowledge accurately, and communicate knowledge and understanding of history in a clear and effective manner

Historical explanations

- present historical explanations showing understanding of appropriate concepts and arrive at substantiated judgements

Historical interpretation

In relation to historical context:

- interpret, evaluate and use a range of source material
- explain and evaluate interpretations of historical events and topics studied.

Assessment of your work will also take into account the quality of your written communication, including clarity of expression, structure of arguments, presentation of ideas, spelling, grammar and punctuation. This will not be awarded separate marks but will be assessed as part of the first assessment objective.

Different types of questions in AS examinations

In AS History examinations, different types of question are used to assess your abilities and skills. Unit tests mainly use either source-based questions or structured questions.

Source-based questions

The types of question you may encounter are:

- Comprehension and explanation of references or issues mentioned in the sources.

  Here is an example:

  Explain briefly what is meant by the phrase 'people of the free provinces'.

- Extraction of information from the sources.

  Here is an example:

  What can you learn from source 2 about why the Old Poor Law was often criticised in the years before 1834?

- Comparison between two sources.

  Here are two examples:

  Compare and explain the objections made in sources B and C to Lloyd George's proposals for National Insurance in 1911.

  Explain how far the statistics in source A support the view expressed in source B concerning economic growth in Russia after 1880.

- Evaluation of the reliability or usefulness of one or two of the sources.

  Use all the information available to you – the content of the source, the information given to you about it by the examiners, comparison with the other sources, your own knowledge – to decide what use a historian could make of it

  Here are two examples:

  Assess the value of these sources to a historian studying the reasons why people supported the Nazis in the 1920s and early 1930s.

  How reliable are sources B and C to an historian as evidence of the relations between France and Piedmont?

- Use of sources as evidence to answer a broader question, e.g. to construct an explanation, discuss an interpretation or assess a judgement.

  This type of question usually requires you to use your own knowledge as well as the sources. Make sure you refer to both: failure to do so is one of the commonest mistakes made by candidates.

  Here is an example:

  From source A and from your own knowledge explain why Ulster was such an important consideration in the Home Rule question in 1886.

Structured questions

Structured questions are in two or three parts. The parts are usually related to a common issue and are progressively more difficult. Typically the first part of a two-part question will ask for identification or explanation of key issues and the second part for analysis of causation or assessment of the significance of an issue. Sometimes one or two relatively short sources are provided and the first part then asks you to extract information from the source or explain a reference in it.

Here are two examples:

(a) In what ways did Lenin's economic policies, in the period to 1924, attempt to solve the problems facing the Bolsheviks in 1918?   [15]

(b) Explain why these policies aroused opposition within the Bolshevik Party and within the USSR.   [15]

Edexcel specimen question

(a) Explain briefly the main aims of British foreign policy in 1815.   [24]

(b) To what extent was British foreign policy consistent between 1815 and 1865.   [36]

WJEC specimen question

Exam technique

Advanced Subsidiary History builds on the knowledge, understanding and skills established by GCSE History but does not depend on them. If you have not studied History for some time, you should still be able to learn AS History from this text. It is more important to have an enquiring mind, an interest in the past and its relevance to current affairs and an ability to communicate ideas effectively.

It is important to remember that History is not a subject which can be learnt from a single text. This study guide will provide you with the essential knowledge and ideas you need to understand the topics you study but you will need to build on this by the wider reading suggested by your teacher.

What are examiners looking for?

History examiners indicate the length of answer expected by the mark allocation and the type of answer expected by key words in the questions.

The mark allocation tells you two things: the length of answer expected and the relative difficulty of the question. Questions allocated higher marks are not only to be answered at greater length but are more testing. In source-based questions, a question which asks you to evaluate the reliability and usefulness of two sources is more testing than one which asks you to explain a reference and would earn more marks. In structured questions, questions with lower marks will generally be narrower in focus and require a shorter answer.

Key words point you to the type of question. The most common types of question are those, which require an analysis of **cause** and **consequence**, and those, which require an **assessment** or **judgement**. You may also be required to produce a piece of descriptive writing.

Explain, Describe, Examine, In what ways?

These instructions call for a piece of descriptive or analytical writing. Be sure to focus on the issue or event required, e.g. aims, factors, policies, or results.

Why?

This asks for an analysis of causes. Make sure you do not leave out important causes and that you consider long-term causes as well as short-term ones. A good answer will consider the relative importance of causes and how they are linked together.

Assess, How far? To what extent?

These instructions require you to make a judgement. The examiners expect you to set out the main arguments on opposite sides and balance them in your conclusion. For example, you might assess the success of a statesman by explaining his successes and then his failures. Most questions which begin with the word 'how' (e.g. 'how valid', 'how serious') are of this type. Another way of setting this type of question is to offer you a judgement for assessment and ask why you agree or disagree.

Compare

If you are asked to compare two sources, look for similarities and differences. You should explain in turn each point of similarity or difference for both sources. Avoid the temptation to paraphrase the first source and then the second.

Some dos and don'ts

Dos

Do answer the question

No credit can be given for good History that is irrelevant to the question.

Do spend some time planning your answers

This is especially important for questions requiring extended writing. It will ensure that your argument is coherent and that you avoid omissions.

Do use the mark allocation to guide how much you write

A question allocated 18 marks out of 30 or 60 out of 90 requires a piece of extended writing.

Do pay attention to correct spelling, grammar and punctuation

Quality of written communication is taken into account in all assessment units.

Do write legibly

An examiner cannot give marks if the answer cannot be read.

Don'ts

Don't produce undirected narrative

Most questions require you to use your knowledge to follow the instructions given in the key words of the question. Even descriptive answers need to be ordered and directed to the requirements of the question.

Don't introduce irrelevant material

You will get no credit for it.

Four steps to successful revision

Step 1: Understand

- Study the topic to be learned slowly. Make sure you understand the logic or important concepts.
- Mark up the text if necessary – underline, highlight and make notes.
- Re-read each paragraph slowly.

GO TO STEP 2

Step 2: Summarise

- Now make your own revision note summary:
  What is the main idea, theme or concept to be learned?
  What are the main points? How does the logic develop?
  Ask questions: Why? How? What next?
- Use bullet points, mind maps, patterned notes.
- Link ideas with mnemonics, mind maps, crazy stories.
- Note the title and date of the revision notes
  (e.g. History: The Edwardian age, 3rd March).
- Organise your notes carefully and keep them in a file.

This is now in **short-term memory**. You will forget 80% of it if you do not go to Step 3.
GO TO STEP 3, but first take a 10 minute break.

Step 3: Memorise

- Take 25 minute learning 'bites' with 5 minute breaks
- After each 5 minute break test yourself:
  Cover the original revision note summary
  Write down the main points
  Speak out loud (record on tape)
  Tell someone else
  Repeat many times.

The material is well on its way to **long-term memory**.
You will forget 40% if you do not do step 4. **GO TO STEP 4**

Step 4: Track/Review

- Create a Revision Diary (one A4 page per day)
- Make a revision plan for the topic, e.g. 1 day later, 1 week later, 1 month later.
- Record your revision in your Revision Diary, e.g.
  History: The Edwardian Age, 3rd March 25 minutes
  History: The Edwardian Age, 5th March 15 minutes
  History: The Edwardian Age, 3rd April 15 minutes
  ... and then at monthly intervals.

Chapter 1

The age of reform, 1815–46

The following topics are covered in this chapter:

- Lord Liverpool and the Tories, 1815–30
- The Whigs, 1830–41
- Chartism
- Peel

1.1 Lord Liverpool and the Tories, 1815–30

After studying this section you should be able to:

- *account for the discontent in the years 1815 to 1820*
- *explain the policies of Liverpool's ministry in these years*
- *discuss whether these policies can be described as repressive*
- *explain the reforms carried out by the Liberal Tories*
- *assess how far the term 'Liberal Tories' is appropriate*
- *account for the split in the Tory party after 1827*

LEARNING SUMMARY

The post-war years, 1815–22

AQA	M2
EDEXCEL	M3
OCR	M2
WJEC	M1
NICCEA	M1

Distress and discontent

In the period after the end of the Napoleonic Wars there was widespread discontent. There were Luddite outbreaks (machine breaking) in some industrial areas from 1811 onwards. The main disturbances after 1815 were the Spa Fields Riots in London, 1816; the Derbyshire Rising, 1817; the March of the Blanketeers, 1817; Peterloo, 1819; and the Cato Street Conspiracy, 1820.

One of the main causes of discontent was **unemployment**, which was particularly high after 1815 because of the ending of wartime contracts for industry and the demobilisation of soldiers. The Industrial Revolution made some workers (e.g. many hand-loom weavers) redundant. Living and working conditions in the new industrial towns were very poor.

Conditions in the countryside were often even worse. Some rural workers responded to enclosure and population pressure by moving to the towns. Those who stayed were badly paid; in much of southern England, their wages were so low that they had to be supplemented by the Poor Law under the Speenhamland System.

The Speenhamland System is explained more fully on page 21.

Government policies added to discontent. The Corn Laws (1815) kept the price of bread high. When income tax was abolished in 1816, indirect taxes were raised, adding to the burden on the poor.

The government's response to discontent

- Liverpool and his ministers feared a revolutionary outbreak like that in France in 1789. They also believed it was the first duty of government to maintain law and order. So they followed a policy of **repression.**
- *Habeas corpus* was suspended and the Seditious Meetings Act was passed in 1817.
- Spies (e.g. Oliver) were sent into the industrial areas where discontent was greatest.
- Troops were used to disperse crowds, e.g. at Peterloo.

Not much use was made of these powers.

- The Six Acts were passed in 1819, giving magistrates increased powers of search and the power to try political cases without a jury. The stamp duty on journals was increased with the aim of making Cobbett's *Political Register* too dear for working men to buy.

The government did nothing to remedy the causes of discontent. The Tories were firmly opposed to parliamentary reform (one of the main demands of the Radicals). Ministers believed in *laissez faire,* i.e. that intervention in the economy was undesirable. Therefore they failed to introduce social or political reforms.

Try to be balanced in your assessment. The government had some justification for its attitude.

Liverpool's government may have exaggerated the danger of revolution. Discontent was at its highest when economic conditions were worst; when they improved in 1818 and again in 1820 the disturbances died down. Some of the government's policies actually increased the discontent. The Corn Laws and the tax changes were highly unpopular and government spies sometimes became *agents provocateurs.* This seems to have been the role of Oliver in the Derbyshire Rising. On the other hand, the government was undoubtedly faced by disorder and it had no effective police force. Could it have done less in the circumstances? It is worth noting also that the powers taken by the government were used sparingly.

There are differing views about Liverpool's government, 1815–22.

1 It was reactionary, acted in the interests of the landowning aristocracy and met discontent with repression.
2 In post-Napoleonic Europe the fear of revolution was understandable and the need to prevent disorder developing into revolution was paramount.

KEY ISSUES

The Liberal Tories, 1822–30

AQA	M2
EDEXCEL	M3
OCR	M2
WJEC	M1
NICCEA	M1

The suicide of the Foreign Secretary, Castlereagh, in 1822 led to the entry of Canning, Peel, Huskisson and Robinson into the Cabinet. These Liberal Tories were responsible for some important reforms.

Reform was easier after 1822 as disturbances died down.

- Peel (Home Secretary) reformed the administration of justice. The penal code was reformed and conditions in the bigger gaols were improved. He also established the Metropolitan Police (1829).
- Huskisson (President of the Board of Trade) introduced free trade measures: reduction of import duties, relaxation of the Navigation Acts, reciprocity agreements and preferential duties for the colonies. He also modified the Corn Laws in 1828 by the introduction of a sliding scale.
- The Combination Acts were repealed in 1824. This made the formation of trade unions legal, but an Amending Act (1825) made it difficult to organise strikes within the law.

The split over Catholic emancipation was a turning point in politics.

In 1827 Liverpool resigned after a stroke. His successors as Prime Minister – Canning, Goderich and Wellington – were unable to hold the Tory party together. Nevertheless, two further important reforms were passed. The Test and Corporation Acts, which excluded nonconformists from public office, were repealed. In practice, they had not been enforced for many years. Roman Catholics were still excluded, but in 1829 the Catholic Relief Act (Catholic emancipation) was passed. Wellington (Prime Minister) and Peel (Home Secretary) believed this was necessary to avert civil war in Ireland after the election of Daniel O'Connell in the County Clare by-election, even though they had previously opposed it. But it split the Tory party. The High Tories accused Wellington and Peel of betrayal. Wellington's ministry survived the general election of 1830 but fell later that year.

How liberal were the 'Liberal Tories'?
1 They introduced important reforms but would not consider parliamentary reform and upheld the Corn Laws.
2 Their most important reform, Catholic emancipation, was only introduced because of the threat of civil war in Ireland.

You should be able to explain the significance of each of these dates.

1812–27	Liverpool Prime Minister
1815	End of Napoleonic Wars; Corn Law passed
1816	Spa Fields Riots
1819	Peterloo 'massacre', followed by the Six Acts
1822	Entry of 'Liberal Tories' into the ministry
1824	Repeal of the Combination Acts
1828	Repeal of Test and Corporation Acts; County Clare by-election
1829	Catholic emancipation

1.2 The Whigs, 1830–41

After studying this section you should be able to:

- *give an account of the Reform Act crisis of 1830–32*
- *assess the significance of the Act*
- *assess the importance of the main Whig reforms*

The Great Reform Act of 1832

AQA	M2
EDEXCEL	M3
WJEC	M1, M3
NICCEA	M1

The unreformed parliament had many defects.

- Qualifications for voting were outdated, arbitrary and illogical. In the counties, 40 shilling freeholders had the vote, but in the boroughs there was a wide variety of different qualifications. In some, e.g. many of the corporation boroughs, there were fewer than fifty voters.
- The electorate was tiny – less than half a million.
- The distribution of seats did not match the distribution of population. The South of England was over-represented and the North and Scotland were under-represented.
- There were many rotten and pocket boroughs. Notorious examples were Old Sarum, Dunwich and Gatton.
- Growing industrial towns such as Manchester were unrepresented.
- There was no secret ballot, leading to bribery and intimidation of voters.

The movement for reform dated back to the eighteenth century. Pitt tried to bring about some limited reforms in 1785 but dropped the idea after the outbreak of the French Revolution. The Tories after the Napoleonic War were strongly opposed to parliamentary reform. The split in the Tory Party over Catholic emancipation opened the way for the Whigs to come to power on the fall of Wellington in 1830. Grey, who had long favoured limited reform, led the new Whig government.

It is important to understand that the opponents of reform were not acting purely out of self-interest.

There was fierce opposition to reform from Tories in the Commons and from the Lords. Some of the opposition came from people who would lose out by reform, e.g. members of the House of Lords who were able to nominate MPs for pocket boroughs. But there were also genuine arguments against reform. Some argued that the present system worked perfectly well and did not need to be changed. Pocket boroughs, they said, enabled promising young men to be brought into parliament (e.g. Pitt, who became an MP at 21 and Prime Minister at 24). They argued that all the important 'interests' in the country – e.g. landowners, merchants, the professions – were represented. Peel argued (correctly) that this would not be the end of reform, as the Whigs claimed: one reform would lead eventually to another.

The Reform Act crisis, 1830–32.

Three Bills had to be introduced before the Act was finally passed. A general election in 1831 strengthened the supporters of reform. Fear of revolution, strengthened by the 1830 revolution in France and widespread disturbances in England in 1831–32, helped the Whigs to overcome the opposition. In 1832 Grey resigned when the House of Lords rejected the third version of the Bill. Wellington tried to form a government but failed and Grey returned to office with a promise from the King to create enough peers to force it through if necessary. The House of Lords then gave way and the Bill was passed.

The terms of the Reform Act were:

- The vote was given to £10 householders in the boroughs; in the counties the 40 shillings freeholders retained the right to vote and it was also given to £50 leaseholders and £10 copyholders.
- Over 140 seats were redistributed from rotten and pocket boroughs to growing towns and the larger counties.

This was the first time parliament had been reformed. Even limited reform was a crucial step towards democracy.

In many respects the results of the Act were limited. The electorate was still only about 800,000. The working classes were not enfranchised. Constituencies still varied greatly in size. The South of England was still over-represented. MPs were still largely drawn from the landowning class. Bribery continued. But the Act did give many of the middle classes a vote; thereafter governments and political parties had to take more account of their views.

> The Reform Act set a precedent for changing the constitution and opened the way for future reforms of parliament. **KEY POINT**

The Whig reforms

AQA	M2
OCR	M1
NICCEA	M1

The most important of the Whig reforms were:

- The abolition of slavery in the British Empire, 1833.
- The Factory Act of 1833 restricted child labour in textile factories (except for silk mills). Children under 9 were not permitted to work. Those aged between 9 and 13 were only allowed to work for eight hours a day and they had to receive two hours' schooling. Young people aged 14 to 18 were limited to twelve hours a day. For the first time inspectors were appointed to enforce the law but there were only four of them. Nevertheless, this was the first effective Factory Act.

There had been previous Factory Acts but they had not been enforced.

- The first government grant for education (1833) provided £20 000, divided between two religious societies which provided elementary schools (the National Society and the British and Foreign Society). The grant was increased to £30 000 in 1839.

The beginnings of the state education system.

- The Poor Law Amendment Act of 1834 (see below).
- The Municipal Corporations Act of 1835 reformed local government in the boroughs. Councils were to be elected by ratepayers. They were obliged to set up a police force and were allowed to provide other services such as drainage and street cleaning. Because such services would be a burden on the rates, many boroughs did not use these powers at first. Nevertheless, the Act laid the foundations for later improvements in the administration of urban areas.

This helped the inspectors enforcing the Factory Act.

- Registration of births, marriages and deaths (1836).
- Church reforms: the Marriage Act and the Tithe Commutation Act.

These reforms were intended to satisfy the demands of the new middle-class electors and to tackle the problems of an emerging industrial society. They were much influenced by pressure from radicals (following the ideas of Bentham) and humanitarians. But they were limited and the most important of them, the Poor Law Amendment Act, was immensely unpopular with the working classes.

The Poor Law Amendment Act, 1834

AQA	M2, M3
EDEXCEL	M1
OCR	M1
WJEC	M1
NICCEA	M1

> The cost was probably the main spur to reform.

> Utilitarianism aimed for 'the great happiness of the greatest number'. It influenced many reforms at this time.

The Poor Law of 1601 made each parish responsible for its own poor. Poor relief was paid for by a parish rate levied by Overseers of the Poor. In much of the South of England the Poor Law operated on the Speenhamland System, which began in 1795 in Berkshire. Poorly paid agricultural labourers had their wages supplemented according to the size of their families and the price of bread. This kept many families from starvation but its effects were in the end thought to be undesirable. It kept wages low, so that labourers were unable to earn a living wage and never escaped dependence on the Poor Law. Agricultural employers did not need to pay proper wages and were being subsidised by other ratepayers. The cost of the Poor Law escalated: by 1830 it was over £7 million a year.

In 1832 a Poor Law Commission was appointed to investigate the problem. It was dominated by Edwin Chadwick. Chadwick was a Utilitarian who followed the ideas of Jeremy Bentham. His aim was to set up a system which would be both efficient and economical. The Commission's report led to the Poor Law Amendment Act.

- Outdoor relief, i.e. the payment of money to the poor, was abolished, except for the sick and aged. This meant the end of the Speenhamland system.
- For the able-bodied poor, relief was to be provided in workhouses.
- The workhouses were to be run on the principle of 'less eligibility'. This meant that life in the workhouse should be as unattractive as possible – less attractive than the condition of the poorest labourer outside it. This would ensure that the poor would only come to the workhouse as a last resort.
- Administration of the Poor Law was completely reformed. Parishes were grouped into Poor Law Unions run by elected Boards of Guardians. A central Board of Commissioners was appointed to supervise the whole system. Chadwick was its secretary.

The new Poor Law was successful in reducing costs and was therefore popular with ratepayers. In the late 1830s the annual cost was about £4.5 million. But it was very unpopular with the working classes and the humanitarians criticised it as harsh and cruel. Dickens attacked it in *Oliver Twist*.

> The workhouses.

Conditions in the new workhouses were harsh. The original intention of the Act was that there should be separate workhouses for different classes of the poor but this proved too expensive. Instead, families were separated within the workhouses. The work was back-breaking. The food was poor. It seemed to the working classes that the poor were being punished simply for being poor – hence the description of the workhouses as 'Poor Law Bastilles'. Conditions improved slightly in the 1840s. From 1842 the separation of husbands and wives was ended and parents were allowed to see their children. The Commissioners were replaced by a Poor Law Board under a government minister in 1847 and after this there was a slow improvement in the treatment of children, the sick and the old.

> The new Poor Law was designed to cope with the rural poor of southern England.

In the industrial north it proved impossible to implement the new system in full because periodic trade recessions caused more widespread unemployment than the workhouses could cope with. There was a recession in 1837–38 and there were attacks on the Guardians and the workhouses. An Anti-Poor Law Movement developed in the North of England. Hostility to the new Poor Law was one of the causes of the rise of the Chartist movement, into which the Anti-Poor Law Movement was absorbed.

1. 3 Chartism

After studying this section you should be able to:

- *explain why the Chartists gained so much support*
- *account for the failure of the movement*

LEARNING SUMMARY

The Chartists

AQA	M2
OCR	M1
WJEC	M1, M3
NICCEA	M3

These were years of high unemployment. Hence the description of Chartism as a 'knife and fork question'.

The aim of Chartism was a democratic parliament, to be achieved by the Six Points of the Charter. The years of greatest Chartist activity were 1839, 1842 and 1848, in each of which a petition was presented to parliament. All three petitions were rejected and after 1848 support dwindled.

Chartism was a movement of the industrial working class, protesting against their living and working conditions. It arose as a response to the economic depression of the late 1830s and 1840s. The Chartists sought political reform as the first step to a better society. It can therefore be seen as reflecting working-class disappointment with the 1832 Reform Act. It also reflected working-class anger at the Poor Law Amendment Act and the collapse of Owen's Grand National Consolidated Trade Union. It was a movement with much local diversity and only loosely held together by its leaders, its organisation and its press.

The main reasons for its failure were:

- Poor leadership – Lovett, Attwood and O'Connor all had their differing faults.
- Divisions over tactics – Moral Force versus Physical Force.
- Lack of co-ordination, reflecting the essentially local nature of much Chartist activity.
- Improving economic conditions from the mid-1840s (except in 1848).
- Firm action by the government.
- Lack of middle-class support; in this respect it was at a great disadvantage compared with the Anti-Corn Law League.

> The Six Points of the Charter were unacceptable to the middle classes, who had just gained the vote by the Reform Act. Without their support the Chartists were almost bound to fail.

KEY POINT

Be sure to consider why it is important even though it failed in the short term.

Although the Chartist movement failed, it was not insignificant. It drew attention to working-class grievances. Peel's aim to make Britain 'a cheap country for living' may be seen as a response. Although much Chartist activity was local, the movement achieved a higher degree of organisation than any previous working-class protest movement. Some historians would see it as an important step on the road to organising an effective working-class movement in the Labour Party.

1.4 Peel

After studying this section you should be able to:

- *explain why, by 1830, Peel was regarded as a traitor by many Tories*
- *show how he rebuilt the Tory party after the split of the late 1820s and the passing of the Reform Act*
- *evaluate the reforms of Peel's second ministry*
- *assess the achievements of Peel*

LEARNING SUMMARY

Peel's early career

OCR	M2
WJEC	M1
NICCEA	M1

The Tory Party represented the landowners and the Church. By 1829 Peel had 'betrayed' the party twice.

But in 1834 he saved it from being marginalised.

Peel first gained prominence as Chief Secretary for Ireland from 1812–1818. In 1819 he was Chairman of the Bullion Committee which recommended a return to the gold standard. This upset landowners, who blamed this decision for a sharp fall in agricultural prices. As one of the Liberal Tories, he was Home Secretary 1822–7 and 1828–30. In 1829 he played a crucial role, with Wellington, in bringing about Catholic emancipation, even though he was a staunch Anglican who had previously opposed it. Many Tories attacked him for betraying the Church.

Peel opposed the 1832 Reform Act, but then went on to re-shape the Tory Party to appeal to the new electorate. In December 1834 he issued the **Tamworth Manifesto**. This set out two basic principles for the Tory Party, which was renamed the Conservative Party:

- it accepted that the Reform Act could not be reversed;
- it would reform proved abuses while preserving what was good about the British system.

Peel was briefly Prime Minister in 1834–35. Despite the Tamworth Manifesto, the Whigs returned to power after the 1835 election, but Peel won a convincing victory in the election of 1841. By then he had won the confidence of the new electorate. The Whigs had lost their reforming impetus after 1835 and they had failed to balance the budget.

Peel's second ministry, 1841–46

OCR	M2
WJEC	M1, M3
NICCEA	M3

Make sure you understand the arguments for free trade. Remember that Britain was the leading industrial nation at the time.

Reforms

Peel's budgets of 1842 and 1845 were a major step towards free trade. Peel believed that free trade would make imports cheaper and boost exports. Industry would benefit and the cost of living would be reduced. Thus free trade would make Britain 'a cheap country for living'. The case for free trade was based on the work of Adam Smith. Huskisson had made some progress in this direction in the 1820s. By reducing duties on over 600 articles and reducing many others, Peel's budgets helped to bring about a trade revival. To make up for the revenue lost, he reintroduced income tax – for three years at first, but it was then renewed and has never been abolished.

Two other Acts were important for the economy. The Bank Charter Act (1844) stabilised the banking system and the currency under the control of the Bank of England. The Companies Act (1844) established better regulation of companies.

There were two social reforms. The Mines Act (1842) prohibited the employment of women, girls and boys under the age of ten underground. This resulted from the report of a Royal Commission which shocked public opinion. The Factory Act (1844) lowered the age at which children could be employed in textile factories to eight but also reduced hours of work to $6\frac{1}{2}$ for children aged up to 13.

Ireland

Peel had played a major role in bringing about Catholic emancipation in 1829 because he feared civil war would result if O'Connell were not allowed to take his seat after the County Clare election. By 1843 O'Connell's leadership was challenged by a new Irish organisation, 'Young Ireland'. O'Connell tried to re-establish his authority by holding a series of meetings to demand repeal of the Act of Union, culminating in a mass meeting at Clontarf in 1843. Peel banned the meeting, rightly judging that there was no real danger that the agitation would develop into rebellion. At the same time he appointed the Devon Commission to investigate problems of Irish land tenure, but was unable to act on its report before the fall of his ministry. More controversially, he increased the government grant to Maynooth College, a training college for Catholic priests, in the face of opposition from some of his own party, including Gladstone. In 1845 a more serious problem arose in Ireland: the potato famine.

> Remember that the Tory Party was the party of the Church of England.

The repeal of the Corn Laws

The Irish famine brought a new urgency to the issue of the repeal of the Corn Laws. Throughout Peel's ministry the Anti-Corn Law League had been campaigning for repeal. The League was formed in Manchester in 1839. Its sole aim was the repeal of the Corn Laws, which were the last main obstacle to free trade. It had middle-class leadership (Cobden and Bright, both of whom became MPs), and gained support from both the middle and working classes. It ran a highly organised campaign, making good use of the press.

Its arguments were that free trade would:

- reduce the price of bread and thus improve living standards;
- enable British manufacturers to expand exports, thus increasing employment;
- make agriculture more efficient by exposing it to foreign competition;
- promote international peace through trade.

Repeal was opposed by the landed interest, which dominated the Conservative Party. They argued that repeal would lead to an influx of cheap foreign corn, ruining farmers and causing unemployment in the countryside.

The campaign against the Corn Laws, therefore, had a political as well as an economic significance: it was a struggle by the industrial middle classes against the continuing influence of the landed aristocracy.

> You need to make a balanced assessment of the potato famine and other factors which influenced Peel.

Although the Anti-Corn Law League's campaign was highly effective, it was Peel himself who played the decisive role in bringing about repeal. He was already committed to free trade but knew that repeal of the Corn Laws would split the Conservative Party. The Irish famine made him decide to act. The Repeal Bill was passed with the support of the Whigs and a minority of Conservatives. Peel was accused by Disraeli of betraying his party. Shortly afterwards his ministry was defeated and he was forced to resign.

> The political results were just as important as the economic. 1846 was particularly important for Gladstone and Disraeli.

The repeal of the Corn Laws was a turning point in British politics. It was disastrous for the Conservatives, who held office for only three short periods between 1846 and 1874. Peel's followers, the Peelites, led by Gladstone, eventually joined the Whigs to form the Liberal Party. The Whigs held office for most of the next twenty years. British agriculture, contrary to the landowners' fears, entered a period of prosperity – until the depression of the 1870s.

> The repeal of the Corn Laws was the decisive step in Britain's development into a free trade country.
>
> **KEY POINT**

Assessment of Peel

There are two main points of view about Peel. On the one hand, some historians argue that he was a great statesman because he put the national interest before the Conservative Party. They claim that his free trade policies and the repeal of the Corn Laws brought economic prosperity and probably saved the country from revolution in 1848. The alternative view is that he was a poor party leader, failing to win support for his policies and accused of betraying the party on the issues of corn, cash and Catholics.

You should be able to explain the significance of each of these dates.

		KEY DATES
1830–41	Whig ministries	
1832	Reform Act	
1834	Poor Law Amendment Act; Tamworth Manifesto	
1839	First Chartist Petition; Anti-Corn Law League founded	
1841–6	Peel's second ministry	
1842	Free trade budget; Second Chartist Petition	
1845	Irish potato famine	
1846	Repeal of the Corn Laws	

Sample question and model answer

The New Poor Law

Study the following sources and then answer the questions which follow.

source 1

From the Report of the Royal Commission on the Poor Laws, 1834

The first and most essential of all conditions is that the pauper's situation shall not be made as eligible as the situation of the independent labourer of the lowest class.

The chief measures which are recommended are:
First, that except as to medical attendance, all relief whatever to able-bodied persons or to their families, otherwise than in well-regulated workhouses, shall be declared unlawful and shall cease. All who receive relief from the parish should work for the parish exclusively, as hard and for less wages than independent labourers work for individual employers.

source 2

From the Second Annual Report of the Poor Law Commissioners, 1836

It could not be expected that the new Poor Law could possibly be carried into effect without difficulty and resistance. That the pauper labourers themselves should adopt this course was naturally to be anticipated. In many districts they set themselves without much delay, fairly and honestly, to seek a livelihood by their own industry. In other places, where a reliance on the poor rate had become engrafted in the manners and habits of the labouring population, every method has been resorted to for the purpose of impeding the operation of the law.

source 3

From *An Article on the Principles and Progress of the Poor Law Amendment Act* by Edwin Chadwick, 1837

When the overseers of Uckfield Poor Law Union in Sussex met for the purpose of making a poor rate, it was found that instead of 5 shillings or 6 shillings [25 or 30p], as had hitherto been the case, a rate of 1s 6d [7p] would be amply sufficient. Here, then, was upwards of £1000 left in the hands of the ratepayers to meet the demands of such labourers as were willing to earn it; on the other hand there were two workhouses for able-bodied men who were out of employment, with regular hours, regular diet, no beer, no tobacco, strict supervision and the irksome task of picking oakum.

The effect was almost magical. The labourers began to think, to use their own expression, it was high time to 'look out'. Employment was now sought after.

source 4

From *Essays on Poor Relief* by Nassau Senior, 1841

The total amount of the poor rates for 1834 was £7.5m., that for 1840 was £5.1m. We attach, however, comparatively little importance to the financial results of the Poor Law Amendment Act. We are grateful to the Commissioners not for having saved £2.4m. a year, but for having stopped the progress of the plague of destitution and improved the morals of the people. The general result is that the labourer, finding himself no longer entitled to a fixed income, whatever his idleness or misconduct, becomes stimulated to work and honesty by the double motivation of hope and fear.

source 5

From *The Condition of the Working Classes* by Friedrich Engels, 1844

Since the rich have all the power, the working classes must submit to have the law declare them as not required. This has been done by the New Poor Law. The regulation of these Poor Law Bastilles is such as to frighten away everyone who has the slightest prospect of life without this form of public charity. The workhouse has been made the most repulsive residence which man can invent.

(a) Study source 1. What can you learn from this source about the objectives of the New Poor Law? [3]

You should link this to abolishing Speenhamland.

The main aim is to ensure that paupers are worse off than the poorest labourers who are not being assisted by the Poor Law. They should earn 'less wages' than men in work. This is to ensure that the Poor Law is the last resort for the poor.

(b) Study source 2. Use your own knowledge to explain what is meant by 'every method has been resorted to for the purpose of impeding the operation of the law'. [4]

There were isolated instances of resistance in the south, but in the industrial midlands and north there were demonstrations and riots. Enforcement in these areas was made more difficult by widespread unemployment resulting from the depression of 1837–42. Attempts to build workhouses sometimes met with physical resistance. An Anti–Poor Law movement grew up. In parts of the north outdoor relief remained the norm.

(c) Study source 3. How useful is this source as evidence for the working of the New Poor Law? [5]

Assessing usefulness means 'What does it tell me?' and 'Is it reliable?'

You can add other quotations, but they should be brief.

There is no reason to doubt the figures but since Chadwick was the driving force behind the New Poor Law, he has probably chosen an example to show its benefits. His evident approval of the workhouse regime ('regular hours picking oakum') betrays his point of view. He clearly thinks it is good that the work is 'irksome'. Chadwick's satisfaction ('the effect was almost magical') and the reasons for this satisfaction are useful in showing what purposes lay behind the new law: workhouses were to act as deterrents and provide an incentive to the poor to seek work.

(d) Study sources 4 and 5. Compare the views of Nassau Senior and Engels about the effects of the New Poor Law on the working classes. [6]

Use quotations and paraphrases of the sources to amplify these ideas.
Be sure to compare.

Senior approves: the New Poor Law has improved the 'morals of the people'. It has provided an incentive to men to seek work, whereas previously even the idle could expect a 'fixed income'. Engels strongly disapproves. The New Poor law has set up workhouses the aim of which is to frighten people away. Thus the law regards the working classes as 'not required'. The two views are diametrically opposed.

(e) Use all the sources and your own knowledge. How far do you agree that the New Poor Law was successful in achieving its objectives? [12]

Objectives are:
- to abolish the Speenhamland system and substitute a workhouse system (source 1);
- to make the working classes more self–reliant and reduce the cost of the Poor Law (implied in sources 3 and 4).

Amplify the references to sources by appropriate, but brief, quotations.

Own knowledge.

Own knowledge.

Sources 3 and 4 show that both locally and nationally the last objective was achieved. The new law was largely successful in abolishing the Speenhamland system in the south (source 3). But there was resistance to the new law (source 2). This was mainly in the north and midlands. The cyclical unemployment of industrial areas could only be dealt with by outdoor relief. As for the deterrent effect of the workhouse test, both supporters (sources 3 and 4) and opponents (source 5) agree that the new law achieved this. The workhouse 'stimulated' labourers to work by the 'motivation of fear' (source 4). One aim which was not achieved was providing separate workhouses for different categories of the poor (abandoned on grounds of cost). An aim not mentioned in the sources but successfully achieved was the overhaul of the administration of the Poor Law.

Practice examination questions

1 Read the following source and then answer the questions which follow.

From *Britain since 1789* by Martin Pugh, 1999

Although the revolution had been defeated on the battlefield, its legacy in the form of a domestic radical movement [was] more tenacious. Indeed, the chaotic economic conditions prevailing between 1815 and 1820 gave it fresh momentum.

  (a) What is meant by describing the domestic radical movement as a 'legacy' of 'the revolution'? [3]

  (b) Why were economic conditions between 1815 and 1820 'chaotic'? [7]

  (c) How serious a threat to the government were radical movements in the years 1815–20? [15]

2 Read the following source and then answer the questions which follow.

From *Britain since 1789* by Martin Pugh, 1999

As circumstances changed, the government grew less authoritarian … Parliament became a little more relaxed in its attitude towards the working classes … The other change that lends some credence to the idea of a more liberal approach is the rise of some younger and more reformist ministers into high office.

  (a) What is meant by a 'more relaxed … attitude towards the working classes'? [3]

  (b) In what ways did 'younger ministers' show themselves to be 'reformist'? [7]

  (c) How far do the policies of the Tory governments between 1822 and 1830 justify describing them as 'Liberal Tories'? [15]

3 Study the following source and answer the questions which follow.

From a report of a speech by Lord Palmerston in the House of Commons, 3 March 1831

[The government] disclaimed any intention to sever the ties which bind together the middle classes and the aristocracy. On the contrary, it was their earnest desire to increase rather than diminish that influence … He looked on the increase of the Members for counties as the surest and most stable basis of representation …The great merit of the Bill, in his opinion, was that it altered the distribution of political power, and restored the constitution, by placing the middle classes in that situation to which they were entitled, and which was most likely to prove advantageous to themselves and the community.

  (a) What, according to the source, was Palmerston's attitude towards the proposals in the Reform Bill? [5]

  (b) What defects in the existing system of representation did the Reform Act seek to rectify? [7]

  (c) What factors enabled the Whigs between 1830 and 1832 to overcome the opposition to reform of parliament? [18]

4 (a) Explain the reasons for the revival of the Conservatives in the 1830s. [10]

  (b) Assess the success of the main domestic policies of Peel's second Ministry, 1841–46. [20]

Chapter 2

England, 1846–86

The following topics are included in this chapter:

- Politics 1846–68
- Gladstone
- Gladstone, Parnell and Ireland
- Disraeli

2.1 Politics 1846–68

After studying this section you should be able to:

- *explain the changes in the political parties between 1846 and 1868*
- *account for the Reform Act of 1867 and assess its significance*

LEARNING SUMMARY

The age of Palmerston and Russell

OCR	M2
WJEC	M2
NICCEA	M3

The Conservatives.

The Whigs.

The emergence of the Liberal Party. This was the most important development in the political parties in the period.

There is a fuller discussion of Palmerston's foreign policy on pages 42–43.

The political parties

The crisis over the repeal of the Corn Laws in 1846 cast its shadow over the politics of the next twenty years. The split in the Conservative Party produced a confused situation in which no party won an overall majority in the elections of 1847 and 1852. The Conservatives, however, were clearly the losers and they did not win a general election until 1874. There were three short Conservative ministries under Lord Derby in 1852 (Feb.–Dec.), 1858–59 and 1866–68. All three were minority governments.

Because of the weakness of the Conservatives, the Whigs dominated politics. There was a Whig Prime Minister (either Russell or Palmerston) in 1846–52, 1855–58 and 1859–66. By the end of the period, however, the Whig Party had evolved into the Liberal Party, consisting of Whigs, Peelites and Radicals. The **Peelites** – those Conservatives who had supported Peel over the repeal of the Corn Laws – gradually moved towards the Whigs. In 1852–55 they joined a coalition with the Whigs with the Peelite Aberdeen at its head. The decision of Gladstone, the outstanding figure among the Peelites, to accept office as Chancellor of the Exchequer under Palmerston in 1859 was the turning point. From this point it is customary to describe the Whig–Peelite–Radical alliance as the Liberals.

Personalities

Because of the confused party situation, personalities were important.

Palmerston held office as either Foreign Secretary or Prime Minister for most of the period 1846–65. His willingness to stand up for British interests made him popular and helps to explain the political dominance of the Whigs. But he offended Queen Victoria by his high-handed conduct as Foreign Secretary between 1846 and 1851 and she secured his dismissal by Russell in 1851. In 1855 public pressure for him to take charge during the Crimean War forced the Queen to appoint him as Prime Minister, an office which he held (except for a short period in 1858–59) until his death in 1865. Foreign affairs continued to be his main concern and much public attention was focused on foreign issues, especially Italian unification. Palmerston had little interest in domestic affairs and saw little need for reform. He opposed the renewed demand for parliamentary reform in the 1860s.

Russell was the other main Whig leader. During his 1846–52 ministry there were two Factory Acts, a Public Health Act (1848) and an increase in the government grant for education. His ministry also dealt effectively with the third Chartist petition. At the end of his career in 1866 he accepted the need for further parliamentary reform.

It was during this period that Gladstone and Disraeli came to the fore. Gladstone had entered Parliament in 1832 as a Tory and had soon become noted for his strong views on the role of the Church of England in national life. From 1843 to 1845 he was President of the Board of Trade under Peel: this gave him his interest in financial and economic affairs. In 1845 he resigned in protest against the increased grant to Maynooth College in Ireland, where Catholic priests were trained. In 1846, however, he supported Peel over the repeal of the Corn Laws. He was Chancellor of the Exchequer from 1852 to 1855 in Aberdeen's coalition and from 1859 to 1866 in Palmerston's and Russell's Liberal governments. As Chancellor he completed Britain's move to free trade. He also tried (but failed) to abolish income tax. His acceptance of office under Palmerston marked the emergence of the Liberal Party from the Whigs and Peelites.

> Religion was always very important to Gladstone.

> Palmerston supported the unification of Italy, which Gladstone passionately advocated.

Disraeli led the attack on Peel by Protectionist Conservatives over the repeal of the Corn Laws. Although he was the outstanding figure in the Conservative Party over the next twenty years, he was mistrusted. This was partly because of his background: he came from a Jewish family which had converted to Christianity and he lacked influential connections. But he was also regarded as eccentric, ambitious and unscrupulous. He had good reason to describe his rise to be leader of the Conservative Party as 'climbing the greasy pole'. In the three Derby ministries of 1852, 1858–59 and 1866–68 he was Chancellor of the Exchequer. He was largely responsible for the 1867 Reform Act (see below). On the retirement of Derby in 1868 he became Prime Minister but was defeated in the election at the end of the year.

Mid-Victorian prosperity and free trade

From the mid-1840s to 1873 Britain enjoyed great prosperity. Free trade played an important part in this. Gladstone's budgets of 1853 and 1860 abolished nearly all remaining duties. The Cobden Treaty with France (1860) boosted Anglo-French trade. Free trade became one of the fundamental principles of the Liberal Party.

> **KEY POINT**
>
> The split in the Conservative Party in 1846 led to a realignment of the political parties by 1868.

The Second Reform Act, 1867

EDEXCEL	M3
OCR	M2
WJEC	M2

Pressure for further parliamentary reform built up in the 1860s. In 1864 Gladstone was converted to the idea. The death of Palmerston in 1865 removed an obstacle.

Both parties were divided on the issue. A Liberal reform bill was defeated in 1866 when Liberal opponents of reform voted against it. The Conservatives came to office. Public pressure for reform was growing; there was a massive demonstration in Hyde Park. Disraeli introduced a more far-reaching bill in the hope of winning support for the Conservatives, and a series of amendments made the final Act still more radical.

The terms of the Act were:

> This meant working-class men.

- In the boroughs the vote was extended to male householders with one year's residence and £10 lodgers.
- In the counties the vote was extended to £12 leaseholders.
- Seats were redistributed from small boroughs to large counties and growing towns.

The working class in the counties were still unable to vote.

As a result of the Act the electorate doubled to 2.5 million. Since most of the new voters were from the urban working class, it was an important step towards democracy. The Act also marked an important stage in the development of political parties because in the larger boroughs the electorate was too big to bribe. It was therefore necessary to have an efficient local organisation.

Although Disraeli was mainly responsible for this Act, Gladstone won the 1868 election, mainly because he and Bright conducted a nationwide campaign to win the support of the new voters.

> **KEY POINTS**
>
> 1 The 1867 Reform Act was 'a leap in the dark' – a major step towards democracy, though still far short of full democracy .
> 2 It was Disraeli's greatest parliamentary triumph but the immediate benefit went to Gladstone.

You should be able to explain the significance of each of these dates.

> **KEY DATES**
>
> | | |
> |---|---|
> | 1846 | Repeal of the Corn Laws; split in the Conservative Party |
> | 1852–55 | Aberdeen ministry; Gladstone Chancellor of the Exchequer |
> | 1859–65 | Palmerston's Second Ministry (Liberal); Gladstone accepts office as Chancellor of the Exchequer |
> | 1867 | Second Reform Act |
> | 1868 | Liberal election victory |

2.2 Gladstone

After studying this section you should be able to:

- *explain the meaning of Gladstonian Liberalism and its practical application in Gladstone's first ministry*
- *assess the success of Gladstone's first ministry*
- *discuss the domestic policies of Gladstone's second ministry*

LEARNING SUMMARY

Gladstonian Liberalism

EDEXCEL	M3
OCR	M2

Try to link these principles to the phrase 'peace, retrenchment and reform'.

The chief characteristics of the Liberal Party under Gladstone were:

- Commitment to free trade.
- *Laissez faire* – the view that the government should not intervene in the economy.
- Strict economy in government finance, which meant a restricted role for government and a high degree of efficiency.
- Equality of opportunity and hostility to privilege; this meant an emphasis on institutional reform rather than social reform.
- A peaceful foreign policy based on respect for other countries.

The Gladstonian Liberal Party was an uneasy alliance of Whig landowners, former Peelites, Benthamite radicals and nonconformists. Gladstone added a strongly moralistic flavour, derived from his strong religious beliefs. This is shown, for example, in his opposition to Disraeli's policy on the Balkans and his growing obsession with the Irish problem.

Gladstone's first ministry, 1868–74

EDEXCEL ▸ M3
OCR ▸ M2
WJEC ▸ M2

As well as two Acts concerning Ireland (see below), Gladstone's first ministry was responsible for an important series of domestic reforms.

- Forster's Education Act (1870) provided for elementary schools to be established wherever the existing provision by the two religious societies was inadequate. Local School Boards elected by ratepayers were to provide Board Schools funded from the rates. Grants for church schools were increased (which angered the nonconformists). Attendance was not to be compulsory or free, though the Boards had the power to pay the fees for poor children.
- The University Tests Act (1871) opened teaching posts at Oxford and Cambridge to nonconformists.
- The civil service reforms (1870) provided that posts were to be filled by competitive examination rather than by recommendation by an MP or a peer.
- The Trade Union Act (1871) gave unions legal recognition, allowing them to protect their funds in the courts, but the Criminal Law Amendment Act made picketing – even peaceful picketing – illegal. This made strikes almost impossible to organise and antagonised union members.
- The Ballot Act (1872) instituted secret ballot in elections, thus reducing bribery and intimidation.
- Cardwell's army reforms reorganised the regiments and the administration of the army, abolished flogging and the purchase of commissions and reduced the length of service to six years overseas and six years in the reserves.
- The Licensing Act (1872) gave magistrates the power to reduce the number of pubs and imposed closing times.
- The Judicature Act (1872) reorganised the law courts.

This added up to a remarkable record of reforms. They did a great deal to reduce privilege and to make Britain a more efficiently run country. Many of the reforms, however, provoked opposition, especially the Education Act, the Criminal Law Amendment Act and the Licensing Act. Moreover, to the disappointment of the working classes, Gladstone failed to bring in social reforms in areas such as public health (the Public Health Act of 1872 was a failure). As a result, Gladstone lost the election of 1874.

Think about the reforms. Which promoted equality of opportunity? Which reflected the views of the nonconformists? Which aroused opposition, and from whom?

> Gladstone's first ministry was a great reforming ministry but failed to tackle social reform. Many of its reforms created enemies.
>
> **KEY POINT**

Gladstone's foreign policy was also unpopular. He was unable to do anything when Russia denounced the Black Sea clauses of the Treaty of Paris of 1856. These had been imposed on Russia by Britain and France at the end of the Crimean War, but in 1870 France was engaged in the Franco-Prussian War and Britain could not act alone. In 1872 Gladstone agreed to pay compensation to the USA for the damage caused to shipping in the American Civil War by the *Alabama*, a warship built in Britain. The public believed Palmerston would have acted differently.

Gladstone's second ministry, 1880–85

EDEXCEL M3
OCR M2
WJEC M2

This brought the franchise in the counties into line with the boroughs.

There was comparatively little reform in Gladstone's second ministry. The Married Women's Property Act (1882) and the Corrupt Practices Act (1883) are worth noting. There was, however, one important achievement: a further instalment of parliamentary reform in the Reform and Redistribution Acts (1884–85). These gave the vote to all male householders in the counties and redistributed 147 seats from smaller boroughs to more populous areas. They marked an important step towards full democracy, but women and about 40 per cent of men (mainly those who were not householders) were still without the vote.

Look back to the section on Gladstonian Liberalism to explain this.

The sparse record of the ministry in reforms was partly because of Gladstone's involvement with the Irish problem and partly because the Liberal Party was divided about the need for social reform. The Radicals were keen on it, as shown by Joseph Chamberlain's Unauthorised Programme (1885), but the aristocratic Whigs opposed it and Gladstone was unenthusiastic.

You should be able to explain the significance of each of these dates.

1868–74	Gladstone's first ministry	
1870	Forster's Education Act	
1871	Trade Union Act; Criminal Law Amendment Act	**KEY DATES**
1872	Ballot Act; Licensing Act	
1880–85	Gladstone's second ministry	
1884	Third Reform Act	

2.3 Gladstone, Parnell and Ireland

After studying this section you should be able to:

- *explain Irish grievances in the mid-nineteenth century*
- *explain the development of Gladstone's policies towards Ireland*
- *assess the role of Parnell in the struggle for Irish Home Rule*
- *discuss the reasons for Gladstone's failure to 'pacify Ireland'*

LEARNING SUMMARY

'My mission is to pacify Ireland'

EDEXCEL M3
WJEC M2

Ireland had little industry, so most people lived by farming.

The Irish had three main grievances in the 1860s:

- The established church, which was supported by the state, was the Protestant Church of Ireland. The majority of the Irish were Roman Catholics.
- Much of the land was divided into small plots, which the Irish rented from English absentee landlords. They had no security of tenure and no incentive to improve their holdings. If they did, their rents would be raised and they would receive no compensation if they were evicted. There were frequent outbreaks of agrarian violence.
- The Act of Union (1800) had abolished Ireland's parliament. The Irish felt that Ireland was being ruled from London by an unsympathetic English government. Hence a demand arose for Home Rule. In 1870 Isaac Butt founded the Home Rule League.

English politicians were generally ignorant about Ireland. It was unusual to give it such a high priority.

In 1867 the Fenian brotherhood, a revolutionary Irish-American organisation, was responsible for a number of terrorist outrages in Britain. This drew attention to the grievances of Ireland. When Gladstone came to power in 1868, he was determined to try to 'pacify Ireland'. He aimed to do this by tackling the first two grievances. In 1869 the Irish Church Act disestablished the Church of Ireland. In 1870 the First Irish Land Act was passed: evicted tenants were to be compensated for improvements, unless evicted for non-payment of rent. The Act failed to stop evictions because there was no effective provision to stop landlords raising rents to unaffordable levels.

Later in the 1870s the situation in Ireland deteriorated. In 1873 an agricultural depression began. Evictions increased as landlords sought to consolidate small farms into larger, more efficient units. In 1877 Parnell, who was willing to use more militant tactics than Butt, took over leadership of the Home Rule League. In 1879 Michael Davitt founded the Irish Land League. The Home Rule League, the Land League and the Fenians came together in the New Departure – using militant tactics to pressurise the government into giving way to nationalist demands.

Gladstone and Parnell

EDEXCEL	M3
OCR	M1
WJEC	M2

Compare this with the First Land Act and consider the charge that Gladstone's policy offered Ireland 'too little, too late'.

The Kilmainham Treaty and the Phoenix Park murders.

When Gladstone returned to power in 1880, the Land League was carrying out a campaign of rent strikes and boycotts of anyone who took over a farm from which a previous tenant had been evicted. Outbreaks of violence were becoming more frequent. In parliament Parnell's 60 Irish Nationalist MPs were mounting a campaign of deliberate obstruction. Gladstone's response was the Second Land Act (1881). This granted Irish tenants the three Fs: fair rents, fixity of tenure and free sale of the lease. At the same time a Coercion Act was passed to control the violence.

Parnell hoped that, if he kept up the pressure, Gladstone would grant Home Rule. The Land League therefore organised a campaign of non-payment of rent. Gladstone then ordered the arrest of Parnell but after six months made an agreement with him, the Kilmainham Treaty. Parnell called off the rent strike and Gladstone promised an Arrears Bill. Four days later the Phoenix Park murders took place. This act of terrorism convinced many people in England that the Irish were not fit to govern themselves. A more severe Coercion Act was passed. Gladstone, however, reached a different conclusion – that only Home Rule would pacify Ireland. He also realised that he would need to move cautiously to win support and to avoid a split in the Liberal Party.

The Home Rule Bills of 1886 and 1893

| OCR | M1 |
| WJEC | M2 |

Don't confuse this with the Second Home Rule Bill. The First Home Rule Bill never reached the Lords.

This was a crucial moment in the development of the parties. By 1895 a realignment had taken place.

The 1885 general election gave Parnell's Irish Home Rule party the balance of power in the House of Commons. Gladstone's son then revealed his father's conversion to Home Rule. Parnell therefore gave the support of the Irish MPs to Gladstone, who formed his third ministry in 1886 and introduced the First Home Rule Bill. This proposed a parliament in Dublin to deal with Irish domestic affairs, and that there would be no Irish MPs at Westminster.

The Home Rule Bill split the Liberal party: 93 Liberals, led by Joseph Chamberlain and Hartington, voted against it and it was defeated in the Commons. The split in the Liberal party ushered in 20 years of largely Conservative government, during which the Liberal Unionists (those Liberals who had voted against Home Rule) moved over to become allies of the Conservatives.

In 1892 Gladstone, with Irish support, formed his fourth ministry. The Second Home Rule Bill (1893) differed from the first in that it proposed that there should be Irish MPs at Westminster. The Bill passed the Commons but was heavily defeated in the Lords, where there was a Conservative majority. Gladstone then retired.

Despite the failure of Gladstone's Home Rule Bills, Ireland in 1894 was relatively quiet. The Conservatives had introduced a scheme to help Irish tenants to buy their land (Ashburne's Land Purchase Act, 1885). This, together with Gladstone's Second Land Act, took some of the heat out of the land question. Balfour, as Irish Secretary, had introduced in 1887 a Crimes Act which succeeded in suppressing some of the violence in Ireland.

Perhaps more importantly, Parnell's authority was undermined by the O'Shea divorce in 1890. Immediately before this, he was at the peak of his power when it was revealed that letters alleged to incriminate him in the Phoenix Park murders had been forged by Pigott. His downfall and his death a year later left the Irish nationalists divided and weak.

> Look back over Parnell's career to assess what he had achieved for Ireland.

Why did Gladstone fail to achieve Home Rule for Ireland?

- The Liberal Party split over the issue.
- The House of Lords, dominated by landowners, many with land in Ireland, was overwhelmingly opposed.
- There was opposition in Ulster (though this was probably not as strong at this time as some Conservatives claimed, or as it was to be later).
- Many people, e.g. Chamberlain, believed that Home Rule would stir up demands for independence in other territories in the British Empire.
- The Irish Nationalists were weakened by the downfall of Parnell

> You should be able to explain the significance of each of these dates.

1800	Act of Union	**KEY DATES**
1869	Disestablishment of the Irish Church	
1870	First Irish Land Act	
1877	Parnell leader of the Home Rule League	
1879	Foundation of Irish Land League	
1881	Second Irish Land Act	
1882	Kilmainham Treaty; Phoenix Park murders	
1886	First Home Rule Bill	
1890	O'Shea Divorce Case – Parnell named as co-respondent	
1891	Death of Parnell	
1893	Second Home Rule Bill	

2.4 Disraeli

After studying this section you should be able to: **LEARNING SUMMARY**

- *explain the nature of Disraelian Conservatism*
- *assess the success and popularity of Disraeli's second ministry, 1874–80*

Tory democracy

EDEXCEL   M3
OCR   M2
WJEC   M2

> Disraeli realised that the Conservatives needed working-class support.

'Tory democracy' is the phrase used to describe Disraeli's political philosophy. It was developed from the ideas he put forward in his novels *Coningsby* and *Sybil* in the 1840s. Disraeli set out his ideas in his Crystal Palace and Manchester speeches in 1872. 'Tory democracy' was intended to appeal to the new electorate created by the 1867 Reform Act. It helped Disraeli to win a handsome victory in the 1874 election. The main ideas were as follows.

- Disraeli stressed the central role of the monarchy, the aristocracy and the Church in national life.
- A Conservative government would pursue a policy of social reform on the paternalist ground that the rich should help the poor. This would strengthen the loyalty of the unprivileged to the monarchy and the aristocracy.
- The Conservative Party would develop the Empire (imperialism).

Disraeli's second ministry, 1874–80

EDEXCEL ▶ M3
OCR ▶ M2
WJEC ▶ M2

Compare Disraeli's reforms with Gladstone's.

'Tory democracy' can be seen in action in the reforms passed in Disraeli's second ministry.

- The Public Health Act (1875) imposed a range of duties on local authorities, e.g. supply of clean water, sewage, removal of nuisances.
- The Artisan's Dwellings Act (1875) gave the local authorities power to clear slums, though they were not compelled to do so.
- The Factory Act (1874) reduced the working day to ten hours and raised the minimum age for the employment of children to ten.
- The Conspiracy and Protection of Property Act made peaceful picketing legal.
- The Employers and Workmen Act made breach of contract by a worker a civil offence, as it was for an employer.
- The Education Act (1876) set up School Attendance Committees to encourage attendance, though it was still not compulsory.
- Other reforms were the Sale of Food and Drugs Act, the Rivers Pollution Act and the Merchant Shipping Act.

> Disraeli's second ministry produced a substantial record of social reform, much of which was the work of the Home Secretary, Cross. The weakness was that many of the Acts were permissive.
>
> **KEY POINT**

A fuller account of this is given on page 45.

Public opinion played an important part, first supporting Gladstone, then Disraeli.

Disraeli claimed that he had obtained 'peace with honour'.

In foreign affairs, the ministry was dominated by the Balkan crisis of 1875–78. Disraeli wished to follow the traditional British policy of supporting Turkey as a bulwark against Russian expansion. Turkish brutality, which provoked a savage denunciation by Gladstone, made this difficult. But when Russia intervened and threatened Constantinople, Disraeli sent the British fleet and threatened war. In the end he was able, in co-operation with Bismarck, to put pressure on Russia to agree to the Congress of Berlin. This was a triumph for Disraeli. The settlement which Russia had imposed on Turkey was considerably modified and Britain gained Cyprus.

Disraeli was also very active in imperial affairs. His policies were popular at first. In 1875 he purchased the Suez Canal shares and in 1876 he created the title Empress of India for Queen Victoria. But in 1878–79 his 'forward' policies led to the outbreak of the Afghan and Zulu Wars, in both of which British troops suffered defeats before they were eventually successful. Public opinion began to see Disraeli's imperialism as dangerous, and this contributed to his defeat in 1880.

You should be able to explain the significance of each of these dates.

1867	Second Reform Act	
1874–80	Disraeli's second ministry	
1875	Public Health Act; Artisans' Dwellings Act; Conspiracy and Protection of Property Act; purchase of Suez Canal shares	**KEY DATES**
1878	Congress of Berlin; Afghan War	
1879	Zulu War	

Sample question and model answer

Gladstone's first ministry

Study source 1 and then answer the questions which follow.

source 1

From a speech in 1873 by John Bright, a Cabinet Minister in Gladstone's first ministry

[The government's] measures will bear comparison with those of any government which has ever preceded it. A few years ago it was thought an impossible thing to remove an Established Church, and yet an Established Church has been removed. Another great principle has been established – that office, authority and dignity in service of the State shall not henceforth be bought by the rich to the exclusion of those that are less rich, or are poor. The corruption market is closed for ever in departments of public service. Another principle that has been established is that the franchise is the right of the electors; whether we win elections or lose them, I am for the ballot. I ask you to look at these various points and then you will see what is the character of the work that has been accomplished by one Administration.

(a) Study source 1. What, according to source 1, is 'the character of the work' accomplished by Gladstone's first ministry? [5]

Bright is proud of its achievements – three in particular:
• Disestablishment of the Church of Ireland. (N.B. Bright was a nonconformist).
• Opening up public employment and establishing equality of opportunity.
• The secret ballot, giving electors freedom to vote as they wish.

(b) What were the main characteristics of 'Gladstonian liberalism'? [7]

These are the main points. Expand them into continuous prose.

Commitment to free trade. Strict economy in government finance, which meant a restricted role for government and an emphasis on efficiency. Laissez faire – a non-interventionist government. Equality of opportunity and hostility to privilege. Belief in self-help. A peaceful foreign policy based on respect for other countries.

(c) Did the domestic reforms of Gladstone's first ministry alienate more people than they pleased? Explain your answer. [18]

Each reform should be described but the essential requirement is to comment on them.

They alienated many people – a major reason for the defeat of the Liberals in 1874.
• Disestablishment of the Irish Church – pleased Irish Catholics but alienated English Anglicans.
• First Irish Land Act – disappointing to Irish tenants because it failed to provide adequate ways of setting fair rents. Alienated Anglo-Irish landowners.
• Education Act – pleasing to broad mass of opinion which recognised the need for education for the masses, but alienated nonconformists because Anglican schools got increased government grants.
• University Tests Act – pleased nonconformists but resented by some Anglicans.
• Civil Service reforms – pleased middle classes but alienated the aristocracy who lost patronage.

Sample question and model answer (continued)

> - Army reforms – abolition of purchase of commissions alienated the aristocracy.
> - Trade union reforms. Trade Union Act pleased trade unionists but Criminal Law Amendment Act, which forbade all forms of picketing, lost Gladstone much working-class support.
> - Ballot Act – popular with the electorate but opposed by landlords and employers, who lost their power to control the way their tenants and workers voted.
> - Licensing Act – to Gladstone a necessary reform on moral grounds, but unpopular with the working classes. Also alienated brewers who used their funds to support the Conservatives.
>
> Conclusion. Most of the reforms pleased many people but alienated minorities. But the Criminal Law Amendment Act and the Licensing Act offended large groups. The cumulative effect of alienating a number of different minorities was to alienate a large part of the electorate.

Draw together the ideas of pleasing and alienating.

Practice examination questions

1 (a) Identify and explain the reasons for the political dominance of Palmerston in the period 1855–65. [10]

   (b) Compare the importance of **at least three** factors which explain why the Conservatives were out of power for most of the period 1846–74. [20]

2 (a) What were the main characteristics of Disraelian Conservatism? [10]

   (b) Assess the success of the foreign and imperial policies pursued by Disraeli during the ministry of 1874–80. [20]

3 Study the following sources and then answer the questions which follow.

The First Home Rule Bill

source 1

From Gladstone's speech in the House of Commons during the debate on the First Home Rule Bill, 8 April 1886

Our ineffective coercion is morally worn out. Something must be done to restore to Ireland the first conditions of civilised life – the free course of law, the liberty of every individual in the exercise of every legal right, the confidence of the people in the law. We stand face to face with what is termed Irish nationality, which demands complete self-government in Irish affairs. Is this an evil in itself? I believe that it is not.

source 2

From a letter from John Bright to Gladstone, 13 May 1886. Bright had been a minister in Gladstone's first ministry, 1868–74

I cannot consent to a measure which is so offensive to the whole protestant population of Ireland, and to the whole sentiment of the province of Ulster so far as its loyal and protestant people are concerned. For thirty years I have preached justice to Ireland. I am as much in her favour now as in past times, but I do not think it justice or wisdom for Great Britain to consign her population, including Ulster and all her protestant families, to what there is of justice and wisdom in the Irish party now sitting in the parliament in Westminster.

Practice examination questions (continued)

source 3

From *Perverted Politics* by J. Tyndall, published in 1887

In relation to Ireland, Mr Gladstone has proved an evil-doer. The predicted friendship between England and Ireland is pure moonshine. Give her Mr. Gladstone's Home Rule and disloyal Ireland will hit befooled England with redoubled strength and bitterness. She will work for complete separation, and will win it. The hatred which has been nursed so long has only been intensified by untimely concession.

source 4

From *The Life of Gladstone* by J. Morley, 1903. Morley was Chief Secretary for Ireland in Gladstone's third and fourth ministries.

No one knew better than [Mr Gladstone] how formidable were the difficulties that lay in his path. The giant mass of English prejudice against Ireland frowned like a mountain chain across the track. A strong and proud nation had trained itself for long courses of time in habits of dislike for the history, the political claims, the religion, the temperament, of a weaker nation. The violence of the Irish members in the last parliament, sporadic barbarities in some of the wilder portions of the island, the hideous murders in the Park, had all deepened the scowling impressions nursed by large bodies of Englishmen for many ages past about unfortunate Ireland.

(a) Study source 1. From this source, and from your own knowledge, what can you learn about British policies towards Ireland in the 1880s? [3]

(b) Study source 3. How useful is this source as evidence of the reasons for opposition to the Home Rule Bill? [5]

(c) Study sources 1 and 2. Compare and explain the arguments advanced in these two sources concerning Home Rule for Ireland. [5]

(d) Using your own knowledge and these sources, how far do you agree with the view that the cause of Home Rule was harmed more than it was advanced by the tactics of Parnell and the Irish nationalists? [12]

Chapter 3

Foreign affairs, 1815–1902

The following topics are covered in this chapter:

- Castlereagh, Canning and Palmerston
- Imperialism
- The Eastern Question

3.1 Castlereagh, Canning and Palmerston

After studying this section you should be able to:

- explain how Castlereagh and Canning protected British interests abroad
- assess the success of Castlereagh in securing an effective peace in the Vienna settlement and through the Congress System
- assess how effectively Canning and Palmerston secured British interests between 1822 and 1841

LEARNING SUMMARY

Castlereagh

AQA	M1
OCR	M2
WJEC	M1

 Understanding these principles is crucial for a study of foreign policy.

 Don't forget the period 1812–15 when assessing Castlereagh.

The aim of foreign policy is to protect the national interest. For Castlereagh this meant, firstly, promoting trade, which in turn depended on a powerful navy. Secondly, it meant maintaining the balance of power in Europe. This would preserve peace, which was beneficial to trade. Thirdly, it meant keeping a close watch on Russia and France, which Castlereagh saw as the main threats to the balance of power. The principles followed by Castlereagh became the basis for British foreign policy in the nineteenth century.

Castlereagh became Foreign Secretary in 1812, so his first task was to build up and hold together the Fourth Coalition, which overthrew Napoleon in 1814. When Napoleon escaped from exile, he played a big part in reviving the coalition. This brought about Napoleon's final defeat at Waterloo. He also ended the war of 1812–14 with the USA, which had been caused by the British navy's enforcement of the Orders in Council.

The Vienna Settlement

Castlereagh played a leading role in shaping the Peace of Vienna (1815). His aim was a peace that would last. It was largely because of him that the peace embodied three important principles.

- France was treated firmly but not vindictively.
- A balance of power in Europe was maintained.
- Buffer states were built up around France to guard against future aggression.

At the same time he did not neglect Britain's national interest. Britain's gains were colonies which were valuable for trade or as naval bases: Heligoland, Malta, Mauritius, Trinidad, Tobago, St Lucia, and the Cape of Good Hope. The treaty thus confirmed Britain's naval supremacy.

The Congress System

To ensure lasting peace Castlereagh and Metternich, the Austrian Chancellor, wanted to set up a permanent system of consultation between the great powers – a Concert of Europe. In the Quadruple Alliance of 1815 Britain, Austria, Prussia and Russia agreed to meet regularly to discuss threats to peace. These meetings were known as the Congress System, though some historians dispute whether 'system' is an appropriate word. The aims of the Congress System were muddled by the creation by Tsar Alexander I of Russia of the Holy Alliance, the members of which were supposed to guarantee the existing frontiers and monarchs. Castlereagh disapproved of this, describing it as 'a piece of sublime mysticism and nonsense', and King George III did not sign it.

> The problem was that this could mean interfering in the internal affairs of other countries.

There were four congresses.

- The first, at Aix-la-Chapelle in 1818, was successful: France was admitted to the Quintuple Alliance and the army of occupation was withdrawn.
- The Congress of Troppau (1820), however, revealed an important difference of outlook between Britain and the continental powers. Revolutions had broken out in Spain, Portugal, Naples and Piedmont. The continental powers issued the Troppau Protocol asserting their right to intervene. Castlereagh in his State Paper of 1820 opposed intervention in the internal affairs of other countries. He was particularly suspicious of the motives of the Tsar, who was keen to march the Russian armies across Europe to suppress the revolution in Spain.

> An example of Castlereagh's fear that Russia would upset the balance of power.

- Castlereagh was so worried by this turn of events that he only sent an observer to the Congress of Laibach in 1821. Despite British opposition, Austrian troops were sent to suppress the revolts in Naples and Piedmont.
- The fourth congress is described below.

> By the time Castlereagh died in 1822 Britain was on the verge of dropping out of the Congress System.
>
> **KEY POINT**

Canning

AQA ⟩ M2
OCR ⟩ M2
WJEC ⟩ M1

Canning succeeded Castlereagh in 1822. He shared many of his predecessor's aims but his style was different. Both aimed to promote British trade and to maintain a European balance of power. Both were wary of the motives of France and Russia. But Canning appeared more favourable to liberal movements and he was better at winning public support for his policies. Like Castlereagh, Canning disapproved of intervention in the internal affairs of other countries; unlike him, he did not have a founder member's desire to make the Congress System work. Nevertheless, in distancing Britain from it, he was only following the policy set out by Castlereagh in his State Paper.

> Canning's disapproval of the Congress System was summed up in his remark, 'Each nation for itself and God for us all'.

The last Congress, which met at Verona in 1822, gave its approval to a French invasion of Spain to support the king against the liberals. Wellington, the British delegate, therefore withdrew. The French invasion nevertheless went ahead in 1823. But Canning did prevent Spanish intervention in Portugal by sending a naval squadron to help the Portuguese liberals to win control. This reinforced the impression that he followed a liberal foreign policy. He also stopped France and Spain reasserting Spanish authority over the former Spanish colonies in South America. In 1824 he recognised the independence of Mexico, Colombia and Argentina and in 1825 Chile, Bolivia and Peru. The Monroe Doctrine, issued by the USA, also helped in bringing about this result. A prime motive behind Canning's policy was the importance of this area for British trade.

> Canning claimed, 'I called the New World into existence to redress the balance of the old'.

Canning's biggest problem was the **Greek Revolt**, which broke out in 1821. The Greeks sought independence from Turkey. Canning wanted to uphold Turkey as a bulwark against Russian expansion into the Mediterranean area, but there was much sympathy for the Greeks in Britain. In 1825 Turkey called in help from Mehemet Ali, the ruler of Egypt. It seemed likely that Russia would help the Greeks, which Canning thought would be dangerous to British interests. To prevent Russia acting alone, he acted jointly with Russia and France with the aim of forcing Turkey to grant self-rule to Greece. In 1827 an allied fleet sank the Turkish and Egyptian fleets at Navarino.

> Canning appeared to be supporting liberalism in Portugal, South America and Greece, but his real motive was British interests.

Unfortunately, after Canning's death in 1827, Wellington failed to continue joint action with Russia. Russia declared war on Turkey and forced it to grant full independence to Greece. Russia's influence in the Balkans was substantially increased, which was what Canning had tried to prevent.

1 Canning followed the same principles in foreign policy as Castlereagh, but his style was different.

2 Castlereagh was pulling out of the Congress System when he died. Canning was happy to kill it.

You should be able to explain the significance of each of these dates.

1815	Peace of Vienna
1820	Congress of Troppau; Castlereagh's State Paper
1822	Death of Castlereagh; Congress of Verona
1824–25	Independence of former Spanish colonies in South America recognised
1827	Death of Canning; Battle of Navarino
1830	Greek Independence

Palmerston, 1830–41

OCR	M2
WJEC	M1

Differences between Castlereagh, Canning and Palmerston were more personality and style than aims.

Palmerston's main aims in foreign policy were similar to those of Castlereagh and Canning: to protect Britain's trading interests and to maintain the balance of power. Like Canning, he was prepared to support liberal and national movements, unless they conflicted with British interests. He was very conscious of the need to uphold British prestige. He wanted to maintain peace by diplomacy if possible but was prepared to use force if necessary. In this respect Britain's naval supremacy was a great aid to his diplomacy. His outlook on foreign affairs was coloured by suspicion of Russia, especially in the Eastern Mediterranean area, and of France.

Palmerston dealt with four main issues as Foreign Secretary between 1830 and 1841.

Note Palmerston's suspicion of France –

- In **Belgium**, where there was a revolt in 1830, Palmerston's aim was to prevent France gaining too much influence. Working with Louis Philippe, he ensured that Belgium would be genuinely independent and neutral. Leopold of Saxe-Coburg, Queen Victoria's uncle, became king. In 1839 the Treaty of London guaranteed Belgium's neutrality.

– and again France –

- In **Spain** and **Portugal**, there were disputes between rival claimants to the throne. Palmerston, fearing that France might intervene, arranged the Quadruple Alliance of Britain, France, Spain and Portugal. By this means he succeeded in preserving constitutional governments in Spain and Portugal while preventing France from gaining too much influence.

– of Russia –

- In the **Near East** Palmerston feared the growth of Russian power at the expense of a weak Turkey. This would endanger Britain's trading interests in the Eastern Mediterranean and threaten her route to India. The Treaty of Unkiar Skelessi (1833) particularly worried him, because it gave Russia control over the Dardanelles and excessive influence in Turkey. Palmerston was unable to do anything until 1839, when a war broke out between the Sultan of Turkey and Mehemet Ali, the ruler of Egypt. The Sultan looked to Russia for help, while Mehemet Ali was backed by France. These were the two powers Palmerston regarded with most suspicion. By working together with Russia, Austria and Prussia and threatening France with war, he resolved the situation in Britain's interests. French ambitions in the Eastern Mediterranean were checked. Russian influence over Turkey was curbed by the Straits Convention (1841), by which the Dardanelles was closed to warships of all nations in peacetime.

– and also France.

- In **China** Palmerston took advantage of a dispute over the import of opium into China to provoke the Opium War. By the Treaty of Nanking, signed in 1842 after the Whigs had fallen from power, five Chinese ports were opened to British trade and Hong Kong was leased to Britain until 1997.

Palmerston, 1846–65

OCR ▶ M2
WJEC ▶ M1
NICCEA ▶ M1

Suspicion of Russia again. ▶

Between 1846 and 1851, Palmerston's record was mixed. In the affair of the Spanish marriages (1846) he was outwitted by Louis Philippe. When the 1848 revolutions broke out, he faced a dilemma. He sympathised with the revolutionaries, especially in Italy, but he also regarded the survival of a strong Austria as important to act as a counter balance to Russia. He therefore, took no action except to protest against the brutality of the suppression of the Hungarian rebels by the Austrians. His handling of the visit of Haynau to London and the Don Pacifico affair both won popular approval but brought him into conflict with the queen. His approval of Louis Napoleon's *coup d'état* in 1851 so angered her that she demanded that Russell dismiss him.

Palmerston returned to office as Prime Minister in 1855 in the middle of the Crimean War, which he brought to a successful end for Britain. By the Treaty of Paris, the Black Sea was neutralised (see below).

This gained him the support of liberal opinion in Britain and won over Gladstone. ▶

In the period 1855–65 Palmerston suffered his greatest failures, as well as gaining some further successes. In the Chinese Wars of 1856–60, in co-operation with the French, he forced the Chinese to open several more ports to European trade, though his methods were questionable. With Russell, he played an important role in the unification of Italy in 1859–60. They put pressure on the Austrians in 1859 to prevent them intervening in Parma, Modena and Tuscany, which then united with Piedmont. The following year they gave moral support to Garibaldi's expedition to Sicily and southern Italy.

Palmerston's handling of the problems created by the American Civil War was clumsy. His protest when a Northern cruiser seized two Confederate agents from a British ship, the *Trent*, was needlessly provocative and war was only averted by the intervention of Prince Albert. There was further friction with the North when Palmerston and Russell, his Foreign Secretary, failed to act quickly enough to prevent the *Alabama*, a warship built in Britain for the Confederates, from slipping out to sea and inflicting considerable damage on Northern shipping. Palmerston refused to pay compensation and the issue was not settled until 1872, when Gladstone agreed to pay £3.25 million.

Britain's naval power was of no help in these. ▶

Palmerston's two greatest failures arose from the Polish Revolt of 1863 and the Schleswig-Holstein question. In the first he unwisely led the Poles to expect British help. Faced by the determination of Russia, supported by Prussia, he had to back down and leave the Poles to their fate. Over Schleswig-Holstein, he threatened war in support of Denmark but was outmanoeuvred by Bismarck, who realised that he was bluffing.

You should be able to explain the significance of each of these dates. ▶

KEY POINTS

1. Over a long career Palmerston pursued British national interests and prestige and asserted Britain's influence in Europe with great success.
2. His high-handed methods won him enemies among the statesmen of Europe, but popularity at home.
3. He has been described as a master of improvisation, i.e. he reacted to situations as they arose.
4. By the 1860s, however, he was increasingly out of his depth in a changing Europe.

KEY DATES

1830–39	Belgian Independence issue, ending with Treaty of London	1841	Straits Convention
		1854–56	Crimean War
1833	Treaty of Unkiar Skelessi	1859–60	Italian Unification
1834	Quadruple Alliance of Britain France, Spain and Portugal	1862	'Alabama' incident
		1863	Polish Revolt
1839–42	Chinese Opium War	1864	Schleswig-Holstein War

3.2 The Eastern Question

After studying this section you should be able to:

- *explain the significance of the 'Eastern Question'*
- *analyse the causes and results of the Crimean War*
- *explain the development of the Balkan Crisis of 1875–78*

LEARNING SUMMARY

The Crimean War, 1854–56

OCR   M2
WJEC   M1

Underlying causes.

Suspicion of Russia again: the issue of Russian access to the Mediterranean was a constant concern of British foreign policy in the nineteenth century.

Immediate causes.

The Eastern Question was perhaps the most important international issue in the nineteenth century and was eventually to spark off the First World War. It arose from the decline of the Turkish (or Ottoman) Empire, which in 1815 still ruled Greece, Bulgaria, Romania, Serbia, Bosnia and Albania. If it collapsed, the balance of power would be upset. Consequently all the great powers had an interest in events in the Balkans. Most of them also had their own specific interests.

Britain's concern arose from its suspicion of Russian ambitions. Russia not only had racial (Slav) and religious (Orthodox) sympathies with the peoples of the Balkans, but also wanted access to the Mediterranean from the Black Sea for its fleet. But if Russia gained control of the Balkans this would endanger Britain's trading interests in the Eastern Mediterranean and could even make Russia a threat to Britain's Indian Empire.

The Eastern Question had already caused problems for Canning and Wellington in the 1820s (the Greek War of Independence) and for Palmerston in the 1830s (over the Treaty of Unkiar Skelessi). It was the underlying cause of the Crimean War.

The immediate cause of the war was a dispute between France and Russia over the guardianship of the Holy Places in Jerusalem and Bethlehem. The Russians demanded the right to protect all Christians in the Ottoman Empire, which amounted to a general right of interference in Turkey. When this demand was rejected, they invaded Moldavia and Wallachia (modern Romania). A war between Russia and Turkey ensued, in which part of the Turkish fleet was sunk at Sinope. Public opinion in Britain and France was outraged and demanded war.

Soon after the war began, the Russians evacuated Moldavia and Wallachia. The British and French therefore concentrated their efforts in the Crimea with the aim of capturing the Russian naval base at Sebastopol. After victories at the battles of the Alma, Balaclava and Inkerman, the allies achieved this objective in 1855. By the Treaty of Paris (1856) the Black Sea was neutralised, which meant that Russia was not allowed to have a navy there. Russia's claim to protect Christians in Turkey was rejected and Moldavia, Wallachia and Serbia gained a large degree of independence. Thus Britain's aim of checking the Russian threat to Turkey was achieved, though not for long: Russia repudiated the Black Sea clauses in 1870.

---

1 Russian influence in the Balkans had been checked but at the cost of 22 000 British dead.
2 The war did not solve the Eastern Question: Turkey failed to carry out its promise to reform and remained weak.

KEY POINTS

The Balkan Crisis, 1875–78

OCR ▶ M2

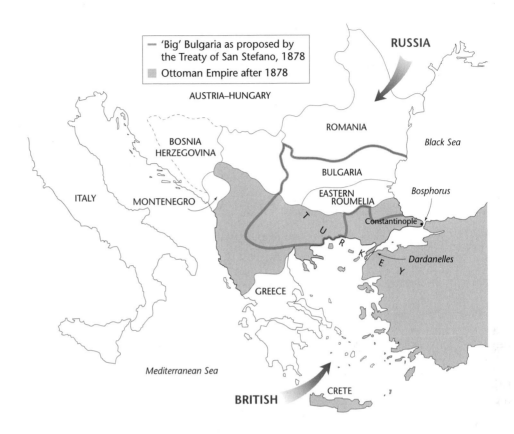

- ── 'Big' Bulgaria as proposed by the Treaty of San Stefano, 1878
- ▨ Ottoman Empire after 1878

The Balkans at the time of the 1878 Congress of Berlin

> Be clear about the difference between Gladstone and Disraeli. For Disraeli the key issue was preventing Russian expansion, even if it meant ignoring Turkish brutality.

Turkey's failure to carry out reforms, as it had promised after the Crimean War, caused revolts in Bosnia, Herzegovina and Bulgaria in 1875–76. Disraeli, suspicious of Russian and Austrian ambitions, wished to support Turkey but Turkish brutality in suppressing the revolts made this difficult. Gladstone's savage denunciation of the Turks in his pamphlet *The Bulgarian Horrors* turned public opinion against the Turks. This may have played a part in encouraging Tsar Alexander II to declare war on Turkey (1877).

> Disraeli and Bismarck agreed that 'big' Bulgaria would upset the balance of power.

When Russian troops approached Constantinople, however, the traditional British fear of Russian expansion into the Mediterranean was aroused and Disraeli sent a fleet to Constantinople. Russia then made peace with Turkey (the Treaty of San Stefano); this set up a 'big' Bulgaria, which Disraeli feared would be under Russian control. Working with Bismarck, he put pressure on Russia to agree to the Congress of Berlin, as a result of which Bulgaria was reduced in size. An area known as Eastern Roumelia was given autonomy within the Turkish Empire and Macedonia was returned to Turkey. Britain gained Cyprus.

> **KEY POINT**
>
> The Congress of Berlin was regarded as a triumph for Disraeli. He had checked Russian ambitions without a war and had bolstered Turkey.

3.3 Imperialism

After studying this section you should be able to:

- *explain the reasons for, and the nature of, the 'New Imperialism' in Britain*
- *explain the part Britain played in the 'Scramble for Africa'*
- *account for the outbreak of the Second Boer War*

'New Imperialism'

 M2

> Don't be cynical about imperialism. It must be understood in the context of its time.

The desire to build up an empire was a marked feature of the policies of the European powers in the late nineteenth century. The distinctive feature of the 'New Imperialism' was a new enthusiasm for the acquisition of colonies. There was a sense of mission and theories were developed to justify imperialism. The newly emerging popular press played an important part in arousing enthusiasm for the empire. Expansion of the empire, it was claimed, would:

- help the economy by providing markets for exports, outlets for investment and sources of raw materials for industry
- help to reduce over-population by emigration
- bring the benefits of European civilisation to 'backward' peoples
- spread Christianity.

> **KEY POINT**
>
> The motives behind 'New Imperialism' were mixed: economic self-interest, rivalry with other European powers and a genuine belief in a mission to spread European civilisation and religion.

The imperial ambitions of Britain and other European powers in the last quarter of the nineteenth century focused above all on Africa. The 'scramble for Africa' which developed added an important competitive motive for imperialism: national prestige demanded that each major imperial power should not allow its rivals to gain more than it did itself. Some historians argue that the Scramble for Africa was essentially the means by which European powers worked out their rivalries without going to war in Europe.

> Disraeli's imperial policies are explained on page 36.

> Chamberlain was worried about Britain's economic decline: his solution was his vision of the empire.

The two British statesmen most involved with imperialism were Disraeli and Chamberlain. Disraeli made the development of the empire a key part of 'Tory democracy'. Chamberlain deliberately took the post of Colonial Secretary in preference to any other in Salisbury's second ministry in 1895 because he regarded it as so important. In this office he played a key role in the events leading to the Boer War. He encouraged investment in the colonies, for example in the development of railways. He wanted to develop the empire into a single economic and political unit. At the Colonial Conference of 1897 he put forward ideas for an imperial customs union but was unable to bring it about. He later incorporated this idea into his tariff reform campaign. He envisaged a system of imperial preference as well as protective duties on imports into Britain.

> Tariff reform is explained on page 52.

The Scramble for Africa

M2

Egypt and the Sudan

The Scramble for Africa began with the French occupation of Tunisia in 1881, followed by the British occupation of Egypt in 1882. Britain's involvement in Egypt resulted from Disraeli's purchase of seven-sixteenths of the Suez Canal shares for the British government in 1875. Growing disorder in Egypt culminating in a revolt against the Khedive led Gladstone to order its occupation. Egypt became effectively a British colony, although it was not annexed.

The occupation of Egypt led Gladstone into difficulties in the Sudan, which was nominally ruled by Egypt but in a state of rebellion. Gladstone decided to abandon it but in the course of withdrawing the garrisons, General Gordon was besieged and killed in Khartoum. Public opinion was outraged. In 1896 Chamberlain sent an expedition under Kitchener to reconquer the Sudan. His victory at Omdurman (1898) brought it under British control but led to a confrontation with the French at Fashoda. In the end the French withdrew and in 1904 they recognised Egypt and the Sudan as a British sphere of influence.

This was the nearest Britain came to war with a European power over Africa.

The Berlin Conference of 1884–85

Meanwhile France, Germany and Italy all acquired colonies in Africa. Inevitably disputes arose. The Berlin Conference of 1884–85, which was called to settle some of the difficulties, agreed that any power which effectively occupied African territory would thereby become its possessor. This gave the green light for Africa to be carved up. Between 1884 and 1896 Britain acquired Somaliland, Nigeria, the interior of the Gold Coast, Kenya, Uganda, Bechuanaland, Nyasaland and Rhodesia. There was clearly a danger that colonial expansion would lead to conflicts. To prevent this, Salisbury negotiated a series of important agreements in 1890 with France, Germany and Portugal.

Cecil Rhodes played an important part.

> 1 Britain acquired extensive colonial territories in the 'scramble for Africa'.
> 2 Colonial disputes with other powers seeking colonies were settled without war.
>
> **KEY POINT**

The Second Boer War, 1899–1902

OCR ▸ M2

The Second Boer War

Background

The Boer republics of Transvaal and the Orange Free State had their origin in the desire of the Boers to escape from British rule (the Great Trek, 1835–37). Nevertheless in 1877, during Disraeli's second ministry, the Boers of the Transvaal accepted a British protectorate. This was because they faced a serious threat from the Zulus. War broke out with the Zulus in 1879. This was really the responsibility of Frere, Disraeli's High Commissioner in South Africa, rather than Disraeli himself. The British were at first defeated at Isandhlwana but were eventually victorious. With the removal of the Zulu threat, the Boers demanded the restoration of their independence. After a short war (the First Boer War, 1881) Gladstone, who was not an imperialist, agreed to this.

Causes of the Second Boer War

The situation changed dramatically between 1881 and 1895. In 1886 gold was discovered in the Transvaal. Thousand of foreigners, mainly British, flocked to the Transvaal. By 1895 these 'uitlanders' outnumbered the Boers, but they had no political rights and were heavily taxed. They had genuine grievances which the Boers, who resented their presence, did little to meet.

> The map illustrates this.

At the same time the scramble for Africa left the Boer republics almost encircled. In 1884 Cecil Rhodes set up a British protectorate over Bechuanaland and in 1887 he formed the British South Africa Company to develop colonies in Rhodesia (modern Zimbabwe and Zambia). Rhodes envisaged British colonies from southern Africa to Egypt (the Cape to Cairo Railway). His activities aroused deep suspicion among the Boers. In 1890 he became Prime Minister of Cape Colony.

> This was a provocative attack to exploit 'uitlander' grievances.

Tensions between the British and the Boers were heightened by the Jameson Raid (1895), for which Rhodes was responsible (and in which Chamberlain was implicated). Talks between Milner, the British High Commissioner, who completely mistrusted the Boers, and Kruger on the Uitlander question in 1899 broke down. War broke out when the Boers attacked Natal.

> **KEY POINT**
> Although Chamberlain tried to avoid war after the breakdown of the Kruger–Milner talks, he, along with Rhodes and Milner, must bear a large share of the responsibility for it. But Kruger was also intransigent.

The war

In the war itself, after initial setbacks the British gained military superiority by 1900 but it took two more years to wear down resistance by Boer guerilla groups. One of the methods used by the British in this phase of the war was the establishment of concentration camps.

By the Treaty of Vereeniging (1902) Transvaal and the Orange Free State were annexed but were promised eventual self-government, which was granted in 1906. In 1910 they were joined with Cape Colony and Natal in the Union of South Africa.

> **KEY POINT**
> The war exposed Britain's diplomatic isolation. All the other great powers sympathised with the Boers.

> You should be able to explain the significance of each of these dates.

		KEY DATES
1875	Purchase of Suez Canal shares	
1876	Queen Victoria Empress of India	
1879	Zulu War	
1881	First Boer War	
1882	Occupation of Egypt	
1885	Berlin Treaty defines 'spheres of influence' in Africa	
1886	Discovery of gold in Transvaal	
1895	Chamberlain Colonial Secretary; Jameson Raid	
1898	Conquest of Sudan; Battle of Omdurman; Fashoda Incident	
1899–1902	Second Boer War	

Sample question and model answer

source

Castlereagh's Foreign Policy

Study this source and answer the questions which follow.

From *The Age of Improvement* by Asa Briggs, 1959

Castlereagh managed to steer clear of the Holy Alliance and refused to identify Britain too closely with the policies of the European powers. Before he committed suicide in1822 Britain had begun to part company with the other great powers on the question of intervention to maintain autocratic government.

(a)   What is meant by 'steering clear of the Holy Alliance'?   [3]

Explain what it was and why Castlereagh kept out.

The Holy Alliance, the brainchild of Tsar Alexander I, guaranteed all European frontiers and rulers. Castlereagh kept Britain out because such a pledge would mean intervening in other countries to suppress revolutions.

(b)   How did Castlereagh attempt to create a lasting peace at the Congress of Vienna, 1814–15?   [7]

Use your knowledge of the peace settlement to add further examples.

• He tried to ensure that the terms imposed on France were not so harsh as to create bitterness and lead to a war of revenge.

• He tried to guard against future French aggression by strengthening states on its borders, e.g. Holland and Belgium were joined together.

• He tried to ensure a balance of power. Austria's gains in Italy were balanced by Prussia's in the Rhineland and Saxony and Russia's in Finland and Poland.

• With Metternich he established the Congress System.

(c)   With reference to the period 1815–22, how far do you agree that 'Castlereagh conducted British foreign affairs with considerable skill'?   [15]

• He played a major role in the Vienna settlement, as a result of which there was no war between Great Powers until 1854.

Give details.

• British gains at Vienna strengthened its naval supremacy and control over trade routes to Asia and the West Indies.

• The Congress of Aix-la-Chapelle restored France to its position among the Great Powers.

• He avoided being drawn into the Holy Alliance.

Explain this issue fully.

• Faced by the prospect of the continental powers intervening to suppress the 1820 revolutions in Spain, Portugal, Naples and Piedmont, he issued the State Paper of 1820, in which he laid down the basic principles of British foreign policy, including non-intervention in the internal affairs of other states.

• He followed this up by merely sending an observer to the Congresses of Troppau and Laibach. This did not prevent the other powers issuing the Troppau Protocol or Austria intervening in Naples and Piedmont. Thus by the end of his life, Britain was drawing out of the Congress System.

Use the conclusion to balance favourable and critical comments.

Conclusion. His foreign policy did much to promote British interests through colonial gains and the achievement of a stable post-war settlement. He showed skill in judging when it was not in British interests to go along with the other great powers, though he could not quite bring himself to break away completely from the Congress System. Although he was criticised for aligning Britain with continental autocracies, he did not go along with them when it was not in British interests.

Practice examination questions

1 (a) Explain the principles which guided British foreign policy between 1815 and 1830. [10]

(b) Assess how far these principles were successfully applied by Canning from 1822 to 1827. [20]

2 (a) Explain the aims of Palmerston in foreign policy. [10]

(b) Compare the success of Palmerston's policies from 1855 to 1865 towards Italy, the USA and Schleswig-Holstein. [20]

Chapter 4

The Edwardian age

The following topics are covered in this chapter:

- *The Conservatives, 1895–1905*
- *The Liberals, 1905–15*
- *Votes for women*
- *The rise of the Labour Party*
- *The First World War and British politics*

4.1 The Conservatives, 1895–1905

After studying this section you should be able to:

- *assess the achievements of the Conservatives, 1895–1905*
- *explain Britain's retreat from 'splendid isolation' to 1904*
- *discuss the reasons for the Liberal victory in 1906*

LEARNING SUMMARY

The ministries of Salisbury and Balfour

AQA ▶ M2
OCR ▶ M2

Salisbury's third ministry

For Chamberlain's imperialism, see pages 46–48.

The formation of Salisbury's third ministry in 1895 marked an important step in the development of the political parties: the Liberal Unionists joined the Conservatives. Apart from the Prime Minister, the outstanding figure in the cabinet was the Liberal Unionist Joseph Chamberlain. His decision to take the post of Colonial Secretary rather than Chancellor of the Exchequer showed the importance he attached to the Empire. His period at the Colonial Office was marked by the conquest of Sudan, which nearly led to war with France in the Fashoda Incident (1898), and the Second Boer War (1899–1902). This marked the high point of British imperialism. Despite his radical past, Chamberlain failed to persuade Salisbury to introduce social reforms apart from the Workmen's Compensation Act of 1897. He wanted to introduce old age pensions but failed to get his way.

The retreat from 'splendid isolation'

The Boer War aroused patriotic fervour in Britain, which Salisbury exploited to win the 'Khaki' election of 1900. But the war took longer to win than was expected and exposed Britain's diplomatic isolation. This was one reason for a retreat from the 'splendid isolation' which had characterised Salisbury's foreign policy.

A second reason was friction with Germany. In the early 1890s Anglo-German relations were good and it seemed likely that, if Britain sought allies, it would join the Triple Alliance. However, relations began to deteriorate in 1896, when the German Emperor William II congratulated Kruger, the President of Transvaal, on repelling the Jameson Raid. Pro-Boer attitudes in Germany during the Boer War did nothing to improve relations. Even more important, however, was the fact that Germany embarked upon the expansion of its navy with the Naval Laws of 1898 and 1900. The basis of British foreign policy was reliance upon naval supremacy. The 'two power standard' required that the British navy should equal the combined strength of the next two navies in the world. This now seemed to be threatened.

The British wondered why Germany, a land power, needed a powerful navy.

By 1900, increasing friction with Germany, Britain's lack of friends during the Boer War and the realisation that the Fashoda Incident had nearly caused a war with France all highlighted the dangers of 'splendid isolation'. Britain began to seek allies.

- In 1902 she made an alliance with Japan, which provided a safeguard against Russian expansion in the Far East.
- In Europe, Britain sought an agreement with Germany, but was rebuffed in 1898–99.
- Britain turned to France and in 1904 signed the Entente Cordiale: France recognised British control in Egypt, while Britain accepted France's ambitions in Morocco.

The turning point in relations between Britain, France and Germany

> **KEY POINTS**
>
> 1 By 1900 isolation had come to seem dangerous rather than splendid.
> 2 German policies pushed Britain towards an understanding with France.

Balfour's ministry, 1902–05

A major step in the development of state education, comparable with 1870 and 1944.

Salisbury retired in 1902 and was succeeded as Prime Minister by his nephew Balfour. Like his uncle, Balfour had little interest in social reform but his ministry did produce one major domestic reform: the Education Act of 1902. This transferred responsibility for the Board Schools to county councils and county boroughs. The voluntary schools – mostly church schools – were brought under the control of the local authorities in return for financial assistance from the rates. Nonconformists were outraged that money from the rates was to go to church schools.

Tariff reform.

The dominant political issue in Balfour's ministry was Chamberlain's tariff reform campaign. Chamberlain was very much aware of the challenge to British industry and trade from Germany and the USA, both of which protected their industries with tariffs. He wanted Britain to abandon free trade and impose protective duties. He also envisaged linking this with a system of imperial preference. In 1903 he resigned from the government to conduct a campaign for the introduction of tariffs. This split the Conservative Party. Balfour's attempts to produce a compromise were ineffective.

The 1906 election

This split was the main reason for the downfall of the Conservatives. In December 1905 Balfour resigned. Campbell-Bannerman formed a Liberal government and in the general election of January 1906 the Liberals won a landslide victory. The centrepiece of the Liberal campaign was an attack on tariff reform on the ground that it would lead to dearer food. But there were several other reasons for the Liberal victory.

Both carried out a survey of the poor. Booth investigated London and Rowntree investigated York. Both estimated that one-third of the working class were in serious poverty.

- There was a growing demand for social reform, which the Conservatives had failed to meet. The investigations of Charles Booth and Seebohm Rowntree had shown that there was serious poverty among the urban population.
- There was a reaction after the Boer War, especially when the public became aware of the conditions in the concentration camps.
- The Taff Vale case alienated trade unionists.
- Nonconformists were angry about the 1902 Education Act.
- There was public indignation about the Chinese labour scandal.
- The Liberals were united around the principle of free trade.

This is explained on page 59.

> **KEY POINT**
>
> Chamberlain's tariff reform campaign was probably the crucial reason for the defeat of the Conservatives. He is the only politician to have split two major parties (the Liberals in 1886 over Irish Home Rule, the Conservatives in 1903 over tariff reform).

You should be able to explain the significance of each of these dates.

4.2 The Liberals, 1905–15

After studying this section you should be able to:

- explain the meaning of 'New Liberalism' and show how it was put into practice
- assess how far the Liberal reforms created a modern welfare state
- account for the struggle with the Lords and assess its constitutional significance
- discuss the development of the Irish problem down to 1914
- explain why Britain became involved in war against Germany in 1914

LEARNING SUMMARY

New Liberalism

AQA M2, M3
EDEXCEL M2
OCR M2
WJEC M1

The policies of the Liberal ministries were much influenced by 'New Liberalism'. Gladstonian Liberalism placed great emphasis on individual liberty and self-help. It took a *laissez-faire* view of the role of the state and sought to make government as cheap and efficient as possible by limiting its activities. New Liberalism advocated social reform, financed by higher taxes on the wealthy. The social surveys of Booth and Rowntree had revealed the extent of poverty. The New Liberals argued that individual liberty had little meaning for the very poor, since their poverty restricted what they could do, and self-help could not lift them out of poverty. State intervention was necessary in the interests of both national efficiency and social justice. Their political outlook was thus collectivist rather than individualist. There was also a political motive: the New Liberals saw social reform as the way to attract working-class votes and to avoid being outflanked by the recently formed Labour Party.

Note the differences between Gladstonian Liberalism and New Liberalism.

By 1905 the New Liberals had probably won over the majority of the party but there was still a minority which stood for Gladstonian Liberalism. This was to be a source of weakness later but between 1906 and 1914 New Liberal policies were pursued. The outstanding New Liberal ministers were Lloyd George and Churchill.

> 'New Liberalism' advocated collectivist solutions to social problems. This was the basic difference from Gladstonian Liberalism, which was individualist.

KEY POINT

The Liberal reforms

AQA M1, M3
EDEXCEL M2
OCR M1, M2
WJEC M1

The Liberals were responsible for a notable series of social reforms. There were two measures affecting **trade unions**. The Trade Disputes Act (1906) reversed the Taff Vale judgement and freed unions from liability to pay damages for employers' losses in a strike. The Trade Union Act (1913) gave them the right to add a 'political levy' to their members' subscriptions, though members were allowed to 'contract out'.

53

Note how the principles of New Liberalism were carried out in these reforms.

The reforms helped vulnerable groups in society – poor children

– the unemployed

– workers in the sweated industries

– the elderly poor

– workers who were sick or unemployed.

The so-called **Children's Charter** comprised several measures to help the children of the poor. There were to be compulsory medical inspections in schools and local authorities were allowed to provide free medical treatment and free school meals for poor children. Juvenile courts and special corrective schools (borstals) were set up in order to keep child offenders out of adult law courts and prisons. Free places were provided at fee-paying grammar schools.

A number of measures were introduced to help **working people**. In 1909 Churchill set up employment exchanges to help the unemployed find jobs. The Trade Boards Act of the same year set up boards to fix minimum wages in the 'sweated' industries, where there were no trade unions. Acts were also passed to regulate hours of work and wages in the coal mines and to give shop assistants a weekly half-holiday.

The **Old Age Pensions Act** (1908) provided pensions of 5 shillings a week at 70, but only for the very poorest old people – those whose income was below £21 p.a. The pensions were financed out of taxation. The measure was very popular, as it kept old people out of the workhouse. Lloyd George gained great credit for it.

The most important reform was the **National Insurance Act** of 1911. This provided insurance against sickness for all workers earning less than £160 p.a., though not for their wives or families. It was a contributory scheme, financed by payments from workers, employers and the state. Lloyd George claimed that workers got 'nine pence for four pence'. There was also an unemployment insurance scheme, financed in the same way, for workers in certain industries such as building, shipbuilding and engineering (the industries where demand for labour fluctuated most).

Assessment

The problem is defining a welfare state. One answer is to call the outcome of the Liberal reforms a social service state.

Some historians claim that these measures laid the foundations of the welfare state. Undoubtedly they relieved the worst effects of poverty. Equally certainly they involved an increased role for the state. But they fell short of a comprehensive system of social security. This had to wait until after the Second World War.

Two important criticisms have to be made. Firstly, some of the Liberal reforms were limited in scope. The old age pensions were very small and paid to only the very poorest. Unemployment insurance covered only a small proportion of the workforce. Secondly, nothing was done about the Poor Law. Balfour had set up a Royal Commission on the Poor Law in 1905. Because of disagreements between its members, it did not report until 1909, and then it produced two reports. The Majority Report proposed reform of the Poor Law, the Minority Report abolition. Neither was acted upon and the Poor Law survived until 1929 alongside the pension and insurance schemes of the Liberals.

> These reforms were a great step forward in social welfare. The Liberals tried to make sure that the state provided minimum standards of social services and thus laid the foundations for the welfare state.
>
> **KEY POINT**

The 1909 budget and the struggle with the Lords

AQA	M2
EDEXCEL	M2
OCR	M1, M2

This is why the Lords were accused of being 'Mr Balfour's poodle'.

Apart from the law lords and the bishops, the House of Lords in the early twentieth century consisted entirely of hereditary peers, two-thirds of whom were Conservatives. The Lords rejected Gladstone's Second Home Rule Bill in 1893 but did not interfere with any bills during the Conservative ministries of 1895–1905. After the Liberal victory in 1906 Balfour used the built-in Conservative majority in the Lords to obstruct Liberal government policies. Several important bills were rejected between 1906 and 1908. The hereditary House was thus thwarting the will of the electorate. Matters came to a head with Lloyd George's 1909 budget.

Lloyd George had to raise revenue to pay for pensions and for building eight

The budget was 'redistributive' – taxing the rich to pay old age pensions to the poor.

Dreadnought-type battleships. As a New Liberal, he proposed to tax the wealthy by raising income tax and imposing a supertax on high incomes. He also proposed a tax on land values. This was particularly objectionable to the House of Lords, most of whose members were landowners. Some historians believe Lloyd George intended to provoke a quarrel with the Lords, but there is no clear evidence for this. The Lords rejected the budget. This was unprecedented, as it had always been accepted that they did not reject finance bills. Their action raised the question of the power of the hereditary house to overrule the elected house and thus caused a constitutional crisis.

After a general election in January 1910, which returned the Liberals to power with the support of the Labour and Irish MPs, the Lords accepted the budget. But the Liberals were now determined to limit the powers of the Lords. The problem was that, for a Bill to this effect to become law, the Lords themselves would have to pass it. Matters were further complicated by the death of King Edward VII in the middle of the crisis. A second general election was held in December 1910 on the specific issue of limiting the powers of the Lords; it produced an almost identical result to the first. The Lords then accepted the Parliament Act, though only because King George V promised to create up to five hundred new peers if necessary.

The Act had three main provisions:

- the Lords were no longer able to reject a money bill
- their power to reject other bills was reduced to a two-year delaying power
- the interval between general elections was reduced to five years.

> The Parliament Act was a triumph for democracy. It ensured that in the end the will of the elected House of Parliament would prevail over the hereditary House.
>
> **KEY POINT**

Ireland

AQA	M3
EDEXCEL	M2
OCR	M2

Gladstone's Home Rule Bill of 1893 had been rejected by the House of Lords. The Parliament Act removed that obstacle to home rule. The Irish Nationalists supported the Parliament Act in the expectation that home rule would be their reward. Moreover, the elections of 1910 gave them the balance of power between Liberals and Conservatives. A Home Rule Bill was introduced in 1912 and became law in 1914 under the Parliament Act despite the opposition of the Lords.

The Unionists believed that home rule would put Ulster Protestants under a Catholic government in Dublin.

Ireland, however, had changed since 1893. Its sense of nationhood had been enhanced by the Irish cultural revival. Linked with this was the foundation in 1905 of Sinn Fein, which aimed for an independent Irish republic rather than home rule. It was as yet relatively obscure but its existence made it more difficult for Redmond, the leader of the Irish Nationalists, to compromise. Of more immediate importance was the rise of a militant Ulster Unionist movement under the leadership of Carson. In 1912 he set up the Ulster Volunteers to prepare for armed resistance to home rule. The nationalists responded by forming the Irish Volunteers. The 'Curragh Mutiny' in March 1914 (actually a threat of mutiny) showed that the government could not rely on the army to enforce home rule. Both sides smuggled arms into Ireland in the spring and summer of 1914. Ireland seemed on the verge of civil war. The outbreak of the First World War enabled the government to escape from the problem for the time being by suspending the Act.

Assessment of the role of Asquith –

Many historians blame Asquith for mishandling the Irish problem. He adopted a policy of 'wait and see'. He should have been firmer in banning private armies and arms imports. He put forward a plan for partition in 1914; if he had proposed it earlier, it might have succeeded.

– and Bonar Law.

The Conservative leader, Bonar Law, must also be blamed for the situation in 1914. He openly encouraged Ulster Unionist preparations for armed resistance.

> By 1914, home rule could only be enforced at the cost of civil war in Ireland. Home rule might have solved the Irish problem in Gladstone's time; by 1914, the problem had changed.
>
> **KEY POINT**

You should be able to explain the significance of each of these dates.

1905	Resignation of Balfour; Campbell-Bannerman Prime Minister	
1906	General election; overwhelming Liberal victory	**KEY DATES**
1908	Asquith Prime Minister; Old Age Pensions Act	
1909	Lloyd George's 'People's Budget'	
1911	Parliament Act; National Insurance Act	
1912	Third Home Rule Bill – rejected by the Lords	
1914	Third Home Rule Bill becomes law; Curragh Mutiny	

Britain and the outbreak of war in 1914

AQA	M2
WJEC	M1

See also pages 118–121 for causes of the war

The Triple Entente.

This aroused strong anti-German feeling in Britain.

The Agadir crisis.

Perhaps a clearer indication of Britain's intentions would have deterred Germany.

Sir Edward Grey, the Foreign Secretary, built on the agreements made with Japan and France by the Conservatives. In 1905 the German Emperor tried to undermine the Anglo-French Entente by declaring an interest in the future of Morocco. In the ensuing conference on Morocco at Algeciras in 1906, Britain supported France. Germany's clumsy diplomacy strengthened the Anglo-French Entente. In 1907 an agreement was made with Russia to settle differences over Persia, Afghanistan and Tibet. This created the Triple Entente, which aligned Britain with France and Russia against the Triple Alliance, but it did not commit Britain to go to war as an ally of France and Russia.

Relations with Germany continued to deteriorate. The naval race intensified as both Britain and Germany built Dreadnought-type battleships. In 1909 public opinion in Britain demanded that eight should be built. Haldane's mission to Berlin in 1912 to propose a cut in the naval building programme was unsuccessful and Churchill's suggestion in 1913 of a 'naval holiday' was also rejected.

The second Morocco crisis (1911), when the German gunboat *Panther* was sent to Agadir, provoked Britain to threaten war (Lloyd George's Mansion House speech). Germany backed down, though with some 'compensation' in the Congo. The crisis strengthened the Anglo-French Entente and led to the Anglo-French Naval Agreement (1912). Britain was to concentrate its naval strength in the North Sea and France in the Mediterranean. At the same time, however, Grey continued to try to improve relations with Germany and had some success in co-operating over the Balkan Wars (1912–13).

In 1914 Britain was still not firmly committed to an alliance with France and Russia. As the crisis sparked off by the assassinations at Sarajevo developed, drawing in Russia and France, it still seemed possible that Britain would remain neutral. The German invasion of Belgium tipped the balance.

> 1 The official reason for Britain's entry into the war was to defend Belgium.
> 2 Some would argue Britain had a moral obligation to support France.
> 3 Perhaps the real reason was that a German victory would mean German domination of Europe, which would upset the balance of power and threaten Britain's trading interests.
>
> **KEY POINTS**

You should be able to explain the significance of each of these dates.

1906	Algeciras Conference; first 'Dreadnought' launched	
1907	Triple Entente	**KEY DATES**
1911	Second Morocco (Agadir) crisis	
1912	Anglo-French Naval Agreement	
1913	Churchill's 'naval holiday' proposal rejected by Germany.	
1914	German invasion of Belgium; war declared	

4.3 Votes for women

After studying this section you should be able to:

- *explain the development of the movement to improve the status of women*
- *assess the contribution of the suffragettes to gaining the vote for women*

The suffragettes

EDEXCEL	M1
AQA	M2
OCR	M1, M2
WJEC	M2

> The status of women was the underlying issue.

The status of women in the mid-nineteenth century was that of second-class citizens. Working-class women often worked long hours for low wages, e.g. in textile mills or domestic service, but middle-class women were not expected to have careers. Women were barred from the universities and the professions. When they married, their property passed to their husbands. They were not allowed to vote or to become MPs.

In the second half of the nineteenth century things began very slowly to improve. Girls' schools and women's colleges at Oxford and Cambridge were founded. The status of women was indicated by the fact that, although they could sit the examinations, they were not allowed to take degrees. Florence Nightingale's work established nursing as a recognised career. Increasing numbers of women went into teaching as a career. A few began to qualify as doctors. The Married Women's Property Act (1882) gave them the legal right to own their own property. In 1886 women were given the right to claim custody of the children if the marriage broke up.

The question of votes for women was raised during the debates on the 1867 Reform Act by John Stuart Mill, who also wrote a treatise *On the Subjection of Women*. During the 1860s a number of women's suffrage societies were formed in various parts of the country. In 1897 Millicent Fawcett formed the National Union of Women's Suffrage Societies (NUWSS) to co-ordinate their work. Its campaign won much support but failed to persuade the Conservative governments of Salisbury and Balfour to take action. The members of the NUWSS were known as suffragists.

> Note the differences between the suffragists and the suffragettes.

In 1903 Mrs Pankhurst, together with her daughters Christabel and Sylvia, founded the Women's Social and Political Union (WSPU; suffragettes). Mrs Pankhurst had long been associated with the suffrage movement in Manchester. She was also associated with the Independent Labour Party, which was sympathetic to the cause of votes for women. The Pankhursts, impatient with the failure of the suffragists to achieve results, advocated more militant tactics to draw attention to their demands.

> Male voting rights were also an issue – one which is often forgotten.

Both political parties were divided on the issue. Among the Liberals Lloyd George favoured women's suffrage but Asquith opposed it. The Liberals were, however, generally more sympathetic than the Conservatives. The question was complicated by the fact that only 60 per cent of men had the vote because they had to be householders living in the constituency for one year to qualify. If the vote were given to all women, they would outnumber men. The solution of giving the vote to all men and women was too radical for all except a minority of Liberal and Labour MPs. On the other hand, giving the vote only to women who owned property might benefit the Conservatives.

Several attempts were made between 1907 and 1912 to get a Bill through the House of Commons but without government backing none succeeded. The suffragettes became increasingly militant. They progressed from disrupting political meetings to breaking windows and chaining themselves to the railings of Buckingham Palace. In 1913 they began a campaign of arson and physical attacks on ministers. Emily Davidson threw herself under the king's horse at the Derby. When imprisoned, suffragettes went on hunger strike. The suffragettes' tactics had some success at first.

They gained much publicity and ensured that the issue had to be faced. By 1912 even Asquith accepted that women must be given the vote. The extremism of 1912–13, however, made the cabinet reluctant to proceed because they did not want to be seen to give in to violence. They countered the suffragettes' violence with the Cat and Mouse Act.

When war broke out the suffragettes called off their campaign. Mrs Pankhurst urged women to join in the war effort. Women worked in factories, farms, offices, and transport and as nurses. Their contribution to the war effort played a vital part in winning votes for women in 1918, though even then only for women aged 30 and over.

> At the same time the vote was given to men aged 21 and over.

> **KEY POINT**
>
> The suffragettes' campaign won valuable publicity for the issue of votes for women, but in the end their militancy was probably counterproductive.

4.4 The rise of the Labour Party

After studying this section you should be able to:

LEARNING SUMMARY

- explain how trade unions expanded their influence and power in the second half of the nineteenth century
- discuss the origins and development of the Labour Party (to 1918)

Trade unions

OCR ▶ M2

The 'New Model' unions

In 1851 the Amalgamated Society of Engineers was founded. This was the first successful attempt to form a large-scale national trade union and it was followed by a number of other unions of skilled workers. These 'New Model' unions had high subscriptions from which they provided unemployment and sickness benefits. They tried to avoid strikes. In 1868 a number of their leaders, known as the 'Junta', set up the Trades Union Congress (TUC).

> The legal status of trade unions and their activities was an issue throughout their history.

In 1867, however, the case of *Hornby v. Close* presented them with a problem: the courts did not recognise their right to protect their funds. The Trade Union Act (1871) gave them the legal status to protect their funds in the court, but Gladstone forfeited the support he gained from this by the Criminal Law Amendment Act of the same year. The Conspiracy and Protection of Property Act (1875) legalised peaceful picketing, reversing the Criminal Law Amendment Act.

'New Unionism'

> Note the differences between New Model unions and 'New' unions.

In the 1880s 'New Unionism' emerged – unions for unskilled workers. The success of the London dockers' strike (1889), showed that the lowest paid workers could organise a successful strike in support of reasonable demands. The 'New' unions had lower subscriptions and did not provide unemployment or sickness benefits. They tended to be more militant than the New Model unions and many of their leaders were socialists. But in the 1890s the 'New' unions had limited success, mainly because of the economic depression. By 1900 only about 10 per cent of all union members belonged to 'New' unions.

The Taff Vale Case

More legal issues.

At the turn of the century the trade union movement faced two new legal problems. In 1899 the *Lyons v. Wilkins* case cast doubt on the legality of peaceful picketing. Then in 1901 in the Taff Vale Case the Amalgamated Society of Railway Servants was ordered to pay £23,000 damages, plus costs, to the Taff Vale Railway Company for losses suffered as a result of a strike. This ruling meant that strike action became virtually impossible, since it would bankrupt the union.

> The Taff Vale Case highlighted the need for parliamentary representation.

KEY POINT

Formation of the Labour Party

AQA	M2
OCR	M1, M2
WJEC	M1

The origins of the Labour movement

The Labour Party has its origins in the social and economic changes of the nineteenth century. By the second half of the century Britain had a large and growing industrial working class. Skilled workers enjoyed a rising standard of living during the nineteenth century. But social surveys showed that around 30 per cent of the working class were living in severe poverty. Agricultural workers, too, often received starvation level wages. Awareness of these inequalities fuelled a demand among both the working classes and middle-class intellectuals for social reform. At the same time socialist ideas, such as those of Karl Marx, who spent half his life in London, had their impact.

But a socialist/working-class party was slow to emerge in Britain compared with continental Europe.

In 1884 two socialist societies, the Social Democratic Federation (SDF) and the Fabian Society, were founded. Their members were largely middle class. Another important organisation, the Independent Labour Party (ILP), was formed in 1893 by Keir Hardie with the aim of securing the election of MPs who would represent the interests of 'labour', i.e. the working classes. He aimed for a group of working-class MPs who were not tied to the Liberals and would press for social reform. Hardie was elected MP for West Ham in 1892 but lost his seat in 1895. The 1867 and 1884 Reform Acts enfranchised many working-class voters and a few working-class men had been elected as 'Liberal-Labour' MPs. The lack of social reform from both Gladstone's second ministry and Salisbury's ministries disappointed many working-class electors.

The formation of the Labour Representation Committee

The TUC was dominated by leaders of the New Model unions. They were slow to get involved in politics and their changing attitude was crucial.

In the 1890s trade union interest in political action began to develop. Many of the leaders of the 'New' unions were socialists and wanted political action to improve the condition of the poor. The failure of the engineers' strike in 1897–98 and the *Lyons v. Wilkins* case in 1899 convinced the TUC of the need for MPs to represent them in parliament. In 1900 the TUC called a meeting in London which was attended by the SDF, the Fabians and the ILP. They agreed to set up the Labour Representation Committee (LRC). Its secretary was Ramsay MacDonald. Keir Hardie was one of two LRC candidates elected to parliament in 1900.

At first many trade union leaders were unenthusiastic, but the Taff Vale Case changed their minds. MacDonald made an electoral pact with the Liberals in 1903 as a result of which 29 Labour MPs were elected in 1906. In that year the name Labour Party was adopted.

The development of the Labour Party, 1906–18

Labour supported the Liberal government which came into office in 1905 and succeeded in persuading it to reverse the Taff Vale judgement by the Trade Disputes Act of 1906. This enabled the party to win further support from the unions, including in 1909 the mineworkers.

Another legal obstacle.

The Osborne judgment (1909), which ruled that it was illegal for trade unions to charge a political levy, was a setback. Labour MPs depended on trade union support since MPs were not paid. In 1911, however, payment for MPs was introduced and by the Trade Union Act of 1913 unions were allowed to charge a political levy, though members were allowed to contract out.

Ramsay MacDonald, the Labour leader, opposed Britain's entry into the First World War and resigned the leadership. The new leader, Henderson, was a member of Asquith's coalition (1915–16) and Lloyd George's war cabinet (1916). He resigned in 1917 as a protest against Lloyd George's dictatorial methods. Up to this point many people saw Labour as a radical group on the left wing of the Liberals. To emphasise its distinctive nature Henderson gave Sidney Webb the task of producing a Labour Manifesto, which included a commitment to nationalisation (Clause 4).

You should be able to explain the significance of each of these dates.

1851	Amalgamated Society of Engineers founded	**K E Y**
1884	Foundation of Social Democratic Federation and Fabian Society	**D A T E S**
1889	London dockers' strike	
1893	Foundation of the Independent Labour Party	
1900	Labour Representation Committee	
1901	Taff Vale Case	
1906	29 Labour MPs; Trade Disputes Act	

4.5 The First World War and British politics

After studying this section you should be able to:

- *explain how and why the First World War changed the political parties and the role of the state in Britain*

LEARNING SUMMARY

The effects of the war on politics

AQA   M2
OCR   M1, M2

The political parties

The war was a major factor in the decline of the Liberals. In 1915 Asquith bowed to criticism of his conduct of the war by forming a coalition including some leading Conservatives and the Labour leader, Henderson. Lloyd George, as Minister of Munitions, was the outstanding member: his energy contrasted markedly with Asquith's detachment. In December 1916, with Conservative support, Lloyd George forced Asquith to resign and became Prime Minister. The Liberal Party remained split between supporters of Lloyd George and of Asquith until 1923, by which time Labour had overtaken it as the main opposition to the Conservatives. Meanwhile the Conservatives revived, entering the government in 1915, and Labour began to create a distinctive image after Henderson resigned from Lloyd George's war cabinet. An important development affecting all the parties was the Representation of the People Act (1918), by which voting rights were extended to all men over 21 and women over 30.

This caused much bitterness. Supporters of Asquith found it difficult to forgive Lloyd George.

> The split between Asquith and Lloyd George was a crucial moment in the decline of the Liberal Party – and therefore in the post-war rise of the Labour Party.
>
> **KEY POINT**

The government

The demands of modern war revolutionised the functions of government.

Lloyd George reorganised the government and gave it unprecedented powers:

- He set up a small war cabinet of five men.
- He set up the Cabinet Secretariat to co-ordinate the different departments.
- Government controls were set up over merchant shipping, farming and factories and the coal mines were put under direct government management.
- Food was rationed in 1918 and wages and prices were controlled.
- Conscription was introduced (while Asquith was still Prime Minister, but against his will).
- A Ministry of Propaganda was set up.

> Lloyd George's wartime government accustomed people to the idea of a bigger role for the state – one of the big changes between the nineteenth and twentieth centuries.
>
> **KEY POINT**

The social and economic consequences

 M2

The war had important social and economic effects:

- The status of women advanced; women of all classes took jobs.
- The living standards of the aristocracy and the middle classes declined while those of the working classes rose.
- The British economy suffered: export markets were lost and huge debts incurred, mainly to the USA.
- There was a loss of respect for authority.
- There was a decline in church attendance.

Sample question and model answer

The suffragettes

Study the following sources and then answer the questions which follow.

source 1

From a report of a speech by Mr S. Evans, MP, in a debate in the House of Commons on the enfranchisement of women, 25 April 1906

He thought the view of all really sensible men who had considered the subject was that they did not desire or require the assistance of women in the House of Commons and that they did not deem it fitting that women should come down into the arena of politics and engage generally in public affairs. They thought that women had their own honourable position in life, that the position had been accorded them by nature and that their proper sphere was the home, where they might exercise their good and noble influence in the sacred circle of the family.

source 2

From *The Emancipation of Women* by W.L. Blease, 1910

It is useless to declaim upon the equal or superior worth of women, so long as men exercise their power to exclude them from any sphere of activity which they may desire to enter. It is useless to declare that they are willing to admit women into everything except politics. The person who, being an adult, is not fit to take part in English politics, will inevitably encounter all the consequences of subjection in education, in professional and industrial employments, and in social relations.

source 3

From *The Clarion*, a Labour newspaper, 6 June 1913

The women are winning again. What they lost by window-smashing has been restored to them and multiplied a hundred fold by the Government's Cat and Mouse Act. That, by God, we can't stand. Consider what it means: this lady is sentenced to three years' imprisonment and is serving it in five-day instalments with four week intervals for recovery. Forcible, Feeble, Wait-and-See Asquith has tried obstinacy, promises, trickery, bullying and cowardly cruelty. The women have opposed with persistence, wit, indomitable pluck and endurance. The fact is undeniable that their combined skill and courage have beaten him.

source 4

From *My Own Story* by Mrs Emmeline Pankhurst, 1914

The contention of the old-fashioned suffragists has always been that an educated public opinion will ultimately give votes to women without any force being exerted. In the year 1906 there was an immensely large public opinion in favour of woman suffrage. But what good did that do the cause? We called upon the public for a great deal more than sympathy. We called upon it to give women votes. We have tried every means – processions and meetings – which were of no avail. We have tried demonstrations, and now at last we have to break windows. I wish I had broken more. I am not in the least repentant.

source 5

From *A Speaker's Commentaries* by Viscount Ullswater, 1925. Here he is writing about 1913, when he was Speaker of the House of Commons

The activities of the militant suffragettes had now reached the stage at which nothing was safe from their attacks. Churches were burnt, public buildings and private residences were destroyed, bombs were exploded, the police and individuals were assaulted, meetings broken up. When offenders were caught they were sent to prison; but as they generally resorted to a hunger strike which would have resulted in death, they were released and immediately repeated their former offences. The feeling in the House, caused by the extravagant and lawless action of the militants, hardened the opposition to their demands.

Sample question and model answer *(continued)*

(a) Study source 1. What can you learn from this source about the difficulties facing campaigners for votes for women? [3]

Amplify by quotation or paraphrase of points in source 1.

Many men believed that women should not interfere in politics: the home was their proper sphere and gave them an 'honourable position'. It was difficult to find enough common ground with such views even to open a dialogue.

(b) Study source 4. Use your own knowledge to explain what Mrs Pankhurst meant by 'the old-fashioned suffragists'. [4]

Refers to the National Union of Women's Suffrage Societies, founded by Mrs Fawcett in 1897. It campaigned for votes for women but the Pankhursts became impatient with its failure to achieve results and set up the WSPU as a breakaway movement.

(c) Study sources 1 and 2. How far does source 2 answer the arguments advanced against women's suffrage in source 1? [5]

This is a comparison question.

Conclude with a view on 'how far'.

Source 2 attacks the two claims made in source 1: that women should not take part in politics and that they have equal worth but in their own sphere. Source 2 argues that the consequence of exclusion from politics is discrimination against women in education, employment and social relations. Source 1 does not address that issue. The statement that 'their proper sphere was the home' indicates that Evans opposed women's emancipation in general.

(d) Study sources 3 and 5. Assess the usefulness to the historian of these sources as evidence for the effectiveness of the suffragettes' campaign. [6]

Assessing usefulness means 'What does it tell me?' and 'How reliable is it?'

Use quotations to illustrate the points about language.

Source 3 thinks the militant campaign is succeeding. It notes that window-smashing lost them support but claims that the Cat and Mouse Act has more than compensated for it. The language indicates strong support for the women; the extract may therefore exaggerate their success. It does less than justice to Asquith's difficulties. Source 5 is more measured and suggests that the campaign was counter-productive. Since it was written in 1925, the writer will have had time to reflect – in contrast to the passion of source 3. As Speaker, Ullswater is probably well informed about 'feeling in the House'. But his tone suggests some lack of sympathy for the suffragettes.

(e) Study sources 3, 4 and 5. Using these sources, and from your own knowledge, explain why the Liberal governments found the campaign of the suffragettes difficult to deal with. [12]

Amplify these points from the sources and from your own knowledge.

Sources 4 and 5 describe some of the militants' actions in 1913. Source 5 shows that when arrested they went on hunger strike and points out that they could not be allowed to starve to death. But if released they then re-offended, hence the Cat and Mouse Act (source 3). Source 3 also refers (indirectly) to forced feeding. The problem for the government was that forced feeding and the Cat and Mouse Act won public sympathy for the women. Another difficulty was that because of the suffragettes' campaign, the government could be seen as giving in to force if it gave women the vote. Arguably the suffragettes' tactics were unwise, but the government's response was insensitive.

Practice examination questions

1 (a) Why did the Conservatives lose the general election of 1906? [10]

   (b) 'The period from 1910 to 1914 was marked by serious unrest.' Assess the success of the Liberal government in dealing with **at least three** causes of unrest. [20]

2 (a) Why did the Liberals come into conflict with the House of Lords in 1909? [15]

   (b) Explain how the resulting constitutional crisis was resolved in the years 1909–11. [15]

3 Read the following source and then answer the questions which follow.

From *The Rise of the Labour Party, 1880–1945*, by Paul Adelman

… a small committee representing the trade unions and the socialist societies met together and arranged for the summoning of a conference to discuss the problems of organising increased labour representation. This met in London on 27 February 1900, at the Memorial Hall in Farringdon Street, and it is this meeting that has been looked upon as marking the foundation of the Labour Party.

   (a) Explain why 'this meeting has been looked upon as marking the foundation of the Labour Party'. [3]

   (b) Explain what had been the 'main problems of organising increased labour representation' in the years before 1900. [7]

   (c) How successful, both in influencing the policies of the two major parties and in gaining support for its own, was the new Party in the years from 1900 to 1914? [15]

(adapted from NEAB, 1995)

4 Read the following source and then answer the questions which follow.

From *Britain since 1789* by Martin Pugh, 1999

Until the end of the nineteenth century Britain managed to maintain her traditional policy of 'splendid isolation'. However, during the 1890s governments increasingly regarded diplomatic isolation as a dangerous liability.

   (a) What was meant by the traditional policy of 'splendid isolation'? [3]

   (b) Explain why Britain made the Entente Cordiale with France in 1904. [7]

   (c) Why did relations between Britain and Germany deteriorate between 1898 and 1911? [18]

The following topics are covered in this chapter:

- *The Lloyd George coalition 1918–22*
- *The General Strike, 1926*
- *The Labour Governments, 1924 and 1929–31*
- *Britain's inter-war economy*
- *Britain and the Second World War*

5.1 The Lloyd George coalition, 1918–22

After studying this section you should be able to:

LEARNING SUMMARY

- *explain why Lloyd George won an overwhelming victory in the 1918 election and why he was overthrown in 1922*
- *assess the achievements and failings of the coalition government*
- *discuss Lloyd George's handling of the Irish problem*

Politics, 1918–22

OCR ▷ M2

Think why this arrangement suited both Lloyd George and the Conservatives.

The Coupon Election, 1918

The election of 1918 was not fought on normal party lines. The coalition which Lloyd George had formed in 1916 fought the election as a coalition. Its supporters – the majority of the Conservative Party and the Lloyd George Liberals – were identified by a 'coupon' or letter from their party leader. Opponents of the coalition were the Asquith Liberals, the Labour Party and a few Conservatives. Since Lloyd George was popular as the man who had led Britain to victory, the coalition won an overwhelming victory. But Lloyd George as Prime Minister was dependent on the Conservatives, who formed two-thirds of the coalition MPs.

The economy and industrial relations

The coalition tried to honour the promise that post-war Britain would be 'a land fit for heroes to live in' by Addison's housing drive, the Unemployment Insurance Act of 1920 and an increase in old age pensions. Before long, however, the coalition faced serious economic difficulties. After a brief post-war boom, there was a slump in 1921. Unemployment rose to nearly 2 million and as a result, public expenditure rose. The government's response was to make expenditure cuts (the Geddes Axe). The cuts affected mainly the armed forces, education and housing (Addison's housing drive was abandoned).

The miners, railwaymen and transport workers had agreed to support each other. Remember 'Black Friday' when you come to study the General Strike.

There were also serious industrial troubles, especially in the coal industry. The issue was whether the mines, which had been put under government control during the war, should be nationalised or returned to private ownership. The Sankey Commission was appointed in 1919 to investigate the problem but failed to reach agreement. In 1921, because of the slump, the government decided to hand the mines back to the owners, who immediately proposed wage cuts. The miners went on strike, but were defeated after the collapse of the Triple Alliance (Black Friday).

The end of the coalition

In 1922 Lloyd George was overthrown when the Conservatives decided to withdraw from the coalition (Carlton Club meeting).

- They had become increasingly unhappy with Lloyd George as Prime Minister because he was a Liberal at the head of a mainly Conservative coalition.
- Lloyd George was criticised for selling honours to finance the Liberal party.
- The Conservatives disliked the Irish treaty, which broke up the Union.
- They thought Lloyd George had handled the Chanak crisis badly.

> **KEY POINT**
>
> Lloyd George held office after 1918 by courtesy of the Conservatives who used his popularity as the man who won the war and then cast him off when he no longer served their purpose.

Ireland, 1916–22

OCR ▶ M2

You need to understand what happened in Ireland in 1912–14 as background – see pages 55–56.

The most serious domestic problem facing Lloyd George was Ireland. The Easter Rising (1916) had strengthened support for Sinn Fein, which triumphed in Ireland in the 1918 general election and set up an (illegal) Irish parliament in Dublin. A rebellion broke out, which the government tried to suppress with the 'black and tans'. Finally, a 'treaty' was made with Sinn Fein in 1921, as a result of which most of Ireland was given dominion status, but the six counties of Northern Ireland remained part of the United Kingdom, with a parliament for local affairs. This solution came into effect with the establishment of the Irish Free State in 1922, although there was then a civil war in Ireland itself.

5.2 The General Strike, 1926

LEARNING SUMMARY

After studying this section you should be able to:

- *account for the calling of the General Strike*
- *explain its course and consequences*

Causes and significance of the General Strike

EDEXCEL ▶ M3
OCR ▶ M2
WJEC ▶ M2

The coal owners, the mine workers' union leaders, the TUC and the government were all partly responsible. Consider the aims and behaviour of each.

The General Strike had its origins in the problems of the coal industry, which was inefficient and in need of modernisation. The miners believed this could only be achieved by nationalisation, which the government rejected. The mines were put under government control during the war but in 1921 Lloyd George handed them back to the owners. The problems of the industry worsened in the 1920s. In 1925, following the return to the gold standard and the ending of the Ruhr crisis, coal exports dropped. The coal owners proposed a wage cut, which the mine workers rejected. The government averted a strike by providing a subsidy and appointing the Samuel Commission to investigate the problems of the industry. When the commission reported, both sides rejected its proposals. A miners' strike followed and the miners turned to the TUC for support. Mindful of the collapse of the Triple Alliance in 1921, the TUC ordered a general strike.

The government was well prepared and the TUC half-hearted. After ten days the strike was called off. The miners were eventually defeated.

The General Strike failed because of the following reasons:

- the government had prepared emergency plans to safeguard food supplies and transport, and to maintain order
- the TUC had embarked on the strike without proper preparations and without a clear idea of how far they were prepared to go
- moderate leaders in the TUC began to fear that the strike might lead to violence and that they would lose control of it

- they also realised that trade union funds were likely to run out before the government gave way.

As a result of the General Strike, trade union membership dropped because workers were disillusioned with industrial action. Instead they looked to parliament for improvements – hence the increase in Labour votes in the 1929 general election. The coal industry was not modernised and continued to decline. The government made general or sympathetic strikes illegal in the Trade Disputes Act (1927); this Act also hit Labour Party funding by making the political levy subject to contracting in.

> Be sure you understand the distinction between 'contracting out' and 'contracting in'. Contracting in hit Labour Party funds and Labour considered the Act vindictive and unfair.

> **KEY POINT**
>
> The government feared the revolutionary implications of a general strike and the TUC came to think it had been playing with fire. Both were probably wrong about the risks of revolution.

5.3 The Labour Governments, 1924 and 1929–31

LEARNING SUMMARY

After studying this section you should be able to:

- *assess the record of the two Labour ministries*

The two Labour ministries

OCR ▶ M2

> You need to think why the Liberal Party declined so rapidly.

The first Labour ministry, 1924

Labour's rise to power was very rapid – partly because of the split in the Liberal Party. In the 1922 election Labour gained more seats than the Liberals and became the official opposition. A year later, in the 1923 election, it made further gains. The Conservatives, who had called the election to seek the voters' approval for tariff reform, lost their overall majority. MacDonald, as leader of the next largest party, was asked to form a minority government.

The main domestic achievements of the first Labour ministry were the Wheatley Housing Act and increases in unemployment benefits and old age pensions. In foreign affairs MacDonald restored diplomatic relations with the USSR and played an important role in negotiating the Dawes Plan and the Geneva Protocol. However, the ministry depended on Liberal support, which it lost over the Campbell case. The subsequent general election was heavily influenced by the Zinoviev Letter. It was probably a forgery but it caused great alarm. The Conservatives won a big majority.

> The Zinoviev Letter was important, but Labour would probably have lost anyway.

The second Labour ministry, 1929–31

In the general election of 1929 Labour emerged for the first time as the biggest party, though still without an overall majority and therefore dependent on the Liberals. It had achieved little apart from a new Housing Act before it was overtaken by a financial crisis resulting from the Great Depression. By 1931 unemployment had risen to 2.75 million. As a result, expenditure on benefits went up, while the tax yield went down. The May Committee, appointed to find ways of balancing the budget, produced an alarming report in July 1931, which led to a run on the pound. The Chancellor of the Exchequer, Snowden, wanted to cut unemployment benefit to save the pound, as proposed by the May Committee, but the Cabinet could not agree on this and the Labour government resigned.

> This would hit the poor hardest and went against Labour principles.

You need to consider the case for and against MacDonald. A lot depends on assessment of his personality.

To the surprise of his colleagues, MacDonald then accepted office as Prime Minister of a National Government to deal with the crisis. He was supported by the Conservatives and most of the Liberals, but only a handful of Labour MPs followed him. In the 1931 general election the National Government won an overwhelming victory; Labour was reduced to 52 seats. The majority of the Labour Party condemned MacDonald. They claimed that he had betrayed the party in the pursuit of personal ambition.

> 1 The Labour government was overwhelmed by the economic crisis.
> 2 MacDonald's critics accuse him of betraying the Labour Party.
>
> **KEY POINTS**

Compare what happened in the Labour Party with the extremist responses explained on page 70.

Labour swung to the left after the disaster of 1931. The new leader, Lansbury, was an idealistic socialist. There was much debate in the party, in which young left-wing intellectuals played a prominent part. Many of them looked to Stalin's Russia as an example of socialist planning in action. Some, such as Cripps, wanted Labour to join with the Communists in a common front. There was also much debate about defence and rearmament and it was over this that Lansbury, who was a pacifist, resigned the leadership in 1935. He was succeeded by Attlee.

In the 1935 election Labour won 154 seats – back to the position of 1924, but still a long way from gaining office.

You should be able to explain the significance of each of these dates.

1924	First Labour ministry	**KEY DATES**
1926	General Strike	
1929–31	Second Labour ministry	
1929	Wall Street crash	
1931	Resignation of Labour ministry; National Government	

5.4 Britain's inter-war economy

After studying this section you should be able to:

- *account for Britain's economic problems between the war, especially the high level of unemployment*
- *explain the impact of the Great Depression on the economy and society*
- *discuss the National Government's economic policies*
- *explain government responses to unemployment between the wars*
- *assess the importance of the responses of the extreme right and left in Britain to the Depression*

LEARNING SUMMARY

Britain's economic problems

AQA	M2
EDEXCEL	M3
OCR	M2
WJEC	M2, M3

Causes of unemployment – long term.

Unemployment never fell below one million between 1921 and 1939 and reached over three million in 1932–33. The underlying cause of this was Britain's long-term economic decline, dating back to the 1870s, which was exacerbated by the First World War. The older export industries – coal, textiles, shipbuilding, iron and steel – faced increasing competition from foreign countries where more modern machinery resulted in greater efficiency. In the areas where these industries were concentrated – the north of England, South Wales and Scotland – there was high unemployment throughout the period.

– short term.

The Great Depression, which began in the USA with the Wall Street crash in 1929, made the problem much worse. As world trade shrank, demand for British goods dropped. Exports in 1932 were one-third less than in 1928. In that year 23 per cent of the insured workforce was unemployed. In shipbuilding the figure was 59.5 per cent.

The Keynesian remedy.

Governments of the period took the view that there was little they could do about Britain's economic problems and generally adopted a policy of deflation. Some alternatives were suggested but not adopted. J.M. Keynes argued that, instead of cutting expenditure and wages, the government should spend its way out of depression through a programme of public works. This would create jobs. The workers would then spend what they earned and this would stimulate economic activity. In 1935 a group of young Conservative MPs led by Harold Macmillan suggested a programme of public works. Sir Oswald Mosley, a minister in the 1929–31 Labour government, proposed cutting unemployment by raising the school leaving age to 16 and reducing the pension age to 60. The Labour cabinet was, however, too cautious to adopt his ideas.

> **KEY POINTS**
>
> 1 Britain's long-term economic decline was made worse in the inter-war period by the economic effects of the First World War and the Great Depression.
>
> 2 The most serious effects were felt in the old staple industries in which Britain had led the world in the nineteenth century.

The National Governments' economic policies

AQA	M2
EDEXCEL	M3
OCR	M2
WJEC	M2, M3

This was equivalent to devaluation and made Britain's exports cheaper for foreigners to buy.

The National Governments of 1931–39 did take some steps to counter the Depression. The immediate financial crisis was tackled by orthodox deflationary methods: 10 per cent cuts in public sector pay and unemployment benefit. The government was nevertheless forced to abandon the gold standard in 1931. Although great efforts had been made to avoid this, it actually benefited British exports. In 1932 free trade was abandoned and protective tariffs were introduced. This increased the domestic market for British goods and brought in increased revenue to the government. However, an attempt to set up a scheme of imperial preference at the Ottawa Conference of 1932 met with only limited success. The Bank Rate was cut to 2 per cent. An attempt was made to tackle the problem of the decline of the older industrial areas by the Special Areas Act (1934). Marketing boards were set up for agricultural products such as milk.

You need to be able to make a balanced assessment of the success of the National Government's policies.

By 1933 economic recovery was under way. This was more due to a housing boom, stimulated by the reduction in bank rate, and the revival of world trade than to government policies. By 1937 unemployment had fallen to just over one million, though much of this was concentrated in the older industrial areas, where it remained a serious problem and a source of much bitterness. In the south and the midlands, by contrast, the second half of the 1930s was a time of growing prosperity. New industries such as car manufacturing were expanding. Sales of consumer goods such as radios, electric cookers and vacuum cleaners, were increasing rapidly. The number of private cars doubled in ten years. Annual holidays at the seaside were becoming usual.

The depressed areas were another world. In Jarrow in 1934, 68 per cent of the workforce was unemployed compared with 3 per cent in High Wycombe. Why did the unemployed not migrate from the depressed areas to the prosperous ones? Many did, but others, especially men with families, could not afford to move long distances to low-paid jobs in areas where housing was expensive.

> **KEY POINT**
>
> There was a great contrast between the relatively prosperous south and midlands and the depressed areas of the north, Wales and Scotland. The National Government failed to reduce unemployment below 1.4 million.

The treatment of the unemployed

AQA	M2
EDEXCEL	M3
OCR	M2
WJEC	M2, M3

The Means Test took into account all family income, so unemployed men could be dependent on the wages of their wives or unmarried children.

The main efforts of governments were concentrated on helping the unemployed, though their preoccupation with keeping public expenditure to the minimum often made their efforts seem inadequate. In 1920 the original 1911 National Insurance scheme was extended to most workers with incomes below £250 a year and benefits were increased to 15 shillings a week for 15 weeks in any one year. In 1921, as a result of the slump of that year, an additional 16 week period of 'uncovenanted' benefit (i.e. benefit not covered by the worker's insurance contributions) was instituted. This became known as the dole. In 1927 the dole was made available for an indefinite period if the unemployed person was genuinely seeking work.

In 1931, because of the financial crisis, benefits were cut by 10 per cent and means testing was imposed for all those unemployed for more than six months. The 10 per cent cut was restored in 1934 when the Unemployment Assistance Board was set up to take over administration of the dole. These measures, together with the abolition of the Poor Law in 1929, meant that the State had taken responsibility for supporting the unemployed. But the benefits left the long-term unemployed living in poverty.

> 1 The most bitterly resented aspect of the benefit system was the Means Test. It became a symbol of the plight of the unemployed.
> 2 Memories of the plight of the unemployed in the 1930s played a large part in the Labour victory in 1945.

KEY POINTS

Extremist responses to the Depression

AQA	M2
WJEC	M3

Communists.

Fascists.

Extremist parties of the right and the left gained support as a result of the Great Depression but they were never a real threat to British democracy.

On the left, the Communist Party won sympathy among left-wing intellectuals. The National Unemployed Workers' Movement, led by the Communist Wal Hannington, made some impact by organising hunger marches which aroused the conscience of the middle classes.

On the right, Sir Oswald Mosley, a former Labour minister, founded the British Union of Fascists (BUF) in 1932. It was based on Mosley's admiration for Mussolini. Like the Italian fascists, its members wore a blackshirt uniform and relied on marches and violence. It was anti-Semitic. The BUF gained some 20 000 members at its peak, with particular strength in the East End of London, but never gained any seats in parliament.

5.5 Britain and the Second World War

After studying this section you should be able to:

- *explain why Britain went to war against Germany in 1939*
- *assess the effect of the war on British politics*
- *assess how the war affected Britain's role in the world*

LEARNING SUMMARY

Appeasement

AQA   M2

> Public opinion was behind the government. No one wanted another war.

> Appeasement of Hitler was explained by the belief that Germany had genuine grievances.

> Did appeasement cause the war by encouraging Hitler's aggression?

The 1930s were overshadowed by the growing threat of war. The National Governments responded to the aggressive nationalism of Japan, Italy and Germany by pursuing a policy of appeasement. Unfortunately each successive act of appeasement was taken as a sign of weakness and led to further aggression. Failure to take action against Japan over Manchuria encouraged Mussolini and Hitler. The ineffective response of Britain and France to Mussolini's invasion of Ethiopia had several unfortunate consequences. Italy got away with her aggression but felt aggrieved that sanctions had been imposed at all. Mussolini responded by realigning himself with Hitler. Meanwhile Hitler was able to reoccupy the Rhineland unopposed.

Appeasement of Hitler reached its climax in 1938. In March Britain accepted the *Anschluss* on the grounds that Austria was German in nationality. When Hitler demanded the Sudetenland, Chamberlain flew to Germany three times to negotiate with him, and finally gave way to all of his demands at Munich (September). Chamberlain was unwilling to risk war on behalf of a 'far away' country and believed Hitler's statement that this was his last territorial claim in Europe.

In March 1939 he was proved wrong when Hitler took over the rest of Czechoslovakia. Chamberlain changed his policy and offered guarantees to Poland, which seemed likely to be Hitler's next victim. When Hitler invaded Poland in September 1939, Britain declared war.

Historians debate whether Britain's policy of appeasement caused the war. Some argue that an earlier stand against Hitler would have deterred him. They claim that appeasement led him to think that Britain would offer only token resistance to his invasion of Poland. Others think that Hitler was determined on a policy of aggressive expansion into Eastern Europe. If so, Britain went to war because of the failure of the policy of appeasement – a policy based on a misunderstanding of Hitler. On the other hand, it can be argued that appeasement allowed Britain time to press on with rearmament.

> Appeasement failed, and Chamberlain was blamed for pursuing a mistaken policy. Whether any other policy would have contained Hitler is more debatable.
>
> KEY POINT

Britain and the Second World War: Churchill's wartime coalition

In May 1940 Chamberlain lost the support of a substantial number of Conservative MPs and resigned. Churchill became Prime Minister and formed a wartime coalition government. Attlee, the leader of the Labour Party, was a member of the Cabinet and later Deputy Prime Minister. Other Labour leaders who were ministers during the war included Cripps, Morrison and Dalton. Bevin, the Secretary of the Transport and General Workers' Union, was a highly successful Minister of Labour. When Labour came to power in 1945, all these men had experience in government, unlike the members of the first Labour ministry in 1924. Churchill also brought in the newspaper proprietor, Lord Beaverbrook, as Minister of Aircraft Production. The coalition was a genuinely national government.

Churchill as a war leader.

Churchill's impact on the war effort was considerable. He contributed enormously to lifting the morale of the British people in the dark days of 1940–41. He communicated the will to win through his speeches, especially his effective use of the radio. It is true that he made mistakes in the conduct of the war (e.g. underestimating the Japanese) and that some of his ideas were wildly impractical. Nevertheless his relationship with the military leaders was fruitful if sometimes stormy.

Britain's relationship with the USA

| AQA | M2 |
| OCR | M2 |

Lend-Lease.

In 1940–41 Britain stood alone against Germany. The Battle of Britain (August–September 1940) saved Britain from invasion. The USA was intent on remaining neutral but Britain's war effort depended heavily on buying goods from America. In 1941 America approved the Lend-Lease scheme: American goods would be supplied on credit, though the long-term cost to British overseas trade was considerable. In the same year Churchill met Roosevelt and agreed the 'Atlantic Charter', the basis of the later United Nations.

It was an uneasy alliance between two capitalist states and a communist one. They were united only by a common enemy.

In 1941 Hitler invaded Russia and at the end of the year, following the outbreak of war between the USA and Japan, he declared war on the USA. Thus from 1942 Hitler faced the Grand Alliance, of which Britain was a member. A number of meetings took place between the wartime leaders. The most important were:

- Moscow (August 1942): Churchill persuaded Stalin that Britain and America should mount an attack on North Africa. This meant postponing an invasion of north west Europe. The timing of this was the main bone of contention between the three leaders in 1942–43.
- Casablanca (January 1943): Churchill and Roosevelt agreed on the invasion of Italy, which again meant postponing the invasion of France.
- Teheran (November 1943): The three leaders agreed on the invasion of France in 1944.

With hindsight the origins of the Cold War can be seen here.

- Yalta (February 1945): The three leaders agreed on the division of Germany into zones of occupation and the organisation of a conference to set up the United Nations. Poland was effectively to be left to the mercy of the USSR. By this time Churchill was suspicious of Stalin's intentions in Eastern Europe but Roosevelt did not share his doubts.
- Potsdam (July–August 1945): Stalin met with Truman (replacing Roosevelt, who had died) and Churchill (replaced half way through the conference by Attlee as a result of the 1945 general election). Truman shared Churchill's suspicions about Stalin. Some further details of the post-war treatment of Germany were agreed but otherwise there was deadlock.

Churchill's personal relationship with Roosevelt and Stalin was important for the co-ordination of the war effort. As a member of the Grand Alliance, Britain appeared to have an equal role with the USA and the USSR. The reality was that it was the least powerful of the three.

> 1 Britain's war effort depended heavily on the USA. The post-war relationship between the two reflected this: Britain was to be clearly the junior partner.
> 2 Britain's economy was severely stretched by the war. It emerged from the war greatly weakened.

KEY POINTS

Sample question and model answer

Source

The National Governments and unemployment

Study the source and then answer the questions which follow.

A table showing unemployed as a percentage of insured workers in selected regions of Great Britain

	1929	1932	1937
London and SE England	5.6	13.7	6.4
Midlands	9.3	20.1	7.2
Northern England	13.5	27.1	13.8
Scotland	12.1	27.7	15.9

(a) What conclusions can be drawn from the source about recovery from the Depression by 1937? [5]

Amplify this answer by referring in detail to the figures.

In all regions unemployment had fallen, but to varying degrees. It had more than doubled everywhere between 1929 and 1932. By 1937 it was below the 1929 level in the Midlands and not much above it in London and the South East. Scotland suffered most – unemployment was still well above that of 1929. In the North it was back to the 1929 level – but that was about the level which London and the South East had experienced at the height of the Depression.

(b) How did the National Governments between 1931 and 1939 attempt to deal with unemployment? [7]

This is largely a factual question. Add detail from your own knowledge.

They tried to cut unemployment by reviving the economy and to help the unemployed through benefits and the Special Areas Act. In 1931 at the height of the crisis, unemployment benefits were cut by 10 per cent and a stringent Means Test imposed, but by 1934 economic recovery allowed the benefit level to be restored. The benefit system was reformed in 1934 through the establishment of the Unemployment Assistance Board. The Special Areas Act (1934) provided money to create new jobs in the worst affected areas.

(c) What impact did the social and economic policies of the National Governments have on the lives of the British people? [18]

The key issue is 'impact on lives'.

- Going off the gold standard and the introduction of protection helped recovery. Cheap money, the housing boom and growth of 'new' industries also helped. By 1937 unemployment was down to 1.4 million. In the south and midlands it was back to 1929 levels. These areas enjoyed prosperity. Much of this was, however, due to the cyclical revival of trade after the depression rather than the policies of the National Government.

- The older industrial areas – the north of England, Wales and Scotland – did not share in the prosperity and unemployment remained high. The Special Areas Act had only marginal effects – the sums of money provided were small. So National Government's economic policies benefited these areas little. Its social policies left the unemployed living in relative poverty and bitterly resentful of the Means Test.

Practice examination questions

1   Study the following sources and then answer the questions which follow.

source 1

From the Diary of Malcolm MacDonald, the son of Ramsay MacDonald, 24 August 1931

The Cabinet meeting last night lasted until after midnight. The P.M. got a majority in the Cabinet to agree with his proposals, but Henderson, Graham and Alexander led a strong opposition. Despite the P.M.'s majority, a decision to go ahead with his plan would have involved seven or eight resignations, so that it was obviously impossible for the government to carry on. The King has implored J.R.M. to form a National Government. Baldwin and Samuel are both willing to serve under him. This Government would last about five weeks, to tide over the crisis. It would be the end, in his own opinion, of his political career.

source 2

From *The Times*, 25 August 1931

The Prime Minister and the colleagues of his own party who have followed him deserve in particular unqualified credit. No Conservative or Liberal – it may be earnestly hoped – will deny his share in an arrangement to carry out that part of a national task which all are agreed must come first and cannot be delayed.

source 3

From the *Autobiography* of Philip Snowden, Chancellor of the Exchequer in the Labour Government (1929–31) and in the National Government (August –October 1931)

Mr MacDonald at the Palace meeting on the Monday morning agreed to the formation of a National Government, with himself as Prime Minister, without a word of previous consultation with any of his Labour colleagues. When the Labour cabinet as a whole refused to agree to a reduction of unemployment pay, Mr MacDonald assumed too readily that this involved the resignation of his government. He neither showed nor expressed any grief at this regrettable development. On the contrary, he went about the formation of the National Government with an enthusiasm which showed that the adventure was highly agreeable to him.

source 4

From an article by P. Williamson in *Modern History Review*, November 1993

MacDonald, it was said, must have been seduced into 'betraying' his party by royal flattery. That the king took an unusually active part during the August crisis is now beyond doubt. Once it became clear that the Labour cabinet would probably resign, in separate audiences with the party leaders and then at a Buckingham Palace conference with all three, the king did not so much seek advice as press for agreement with his own preference for a National government.

(a) Study source 3. Using your own knowledge, explain what was meant by 'a reduction of unemployment pay' in the context of the crisis of 1931.   [3]

(b) Study source 1. How useful is this source as evidence concerning Ramsay MacDonald's behaviour during the crisis of August 1931?   [7]

(c) Study all the sources and use your own knowledge. Do you agree or disagree with the view that Ramsay MacDonald betrayed the Labour Party out of personal ambition in August 1931?   [15]

2 (a) Explain the achievements of the first Labour ministry (1924).   [10]

  (b) Why were the Labour governments of 1924 and 1929–31 so
      short-lived?   (20)

3 Read the following source and answer the questions which follow.

  **From the *Daily Mail* editorial, 3 May 1926 (the newspaper workers refused
  to print this article)**

  The general strike is not an industrial dispute; it is a revolutionary movement,
  intended to inflict suffering upon the great mass of innocent persons in the
  community and thereby put forcible constraint upon the government. It is a
  movement that can only succeed by destroying Government and subverting
  the rights and liberties of the people. This being the case, it cannot be
  tolerated by any civilised government and it must be dealt with by every
  resource at the disposal of the community.

  (a) What, according to the source, was the nature of the threat posed by the
      General Strike?   [5]

  (b) Why did a dispute over miners' wages lead to a General Strike?   [7]

  (c) What factors explain the failure of the General Strike?   [18]

Post-war Britain 1945–64

The following topics are covered in this chapter

- *The Labour Governments, 1945–51*
- *The Conservatives, 1951–64*

6.1 The Labour Governments, 1945–51

After studying this section you should be able to:

- *explain why Labour won a decisive victory in 1945 but was defeated in 1951*
- *discuss the significance of the Labour government's welfare reforms*
- *evaluate Labour's economic policies*

LEARNING SUMMARY

The 1945 election

AQA   M2
OCR   M2

Most people, including Churchill, were surprised. The result was a verdict on the National Governments of the 1930s rather than Churchill.

Labour won an overall majority of 146 – the first time it had won an outright majority in an election. This was in spite of the popularity of Churchill as the man who had won the war. Labour won because the electors blamed the Conservatives for inadequate social policies and failures in foreign policy in the 1930s. Labour caught the mood of the time with its manifesto 'Let Us Face the Future'. After the sacrifices of the war, there was a general desire for a government committed to building a better future. Labour offered a more wholehearted commitment to social reform, promising full employment, a housing drive and a national health service. The role of the Labour leaders in the wartime coalition ensured that they could not be accused of inexperience.

The welfare state

AQA   M2, M3
OCR   M2

This was the great achievement of Bevan.

Labour's social reforms, which set up the welfare state, were based on the Beveridge Report (1942). Beveridge had identified five evils to be overcome: want, disease, ignorance, squalor and idleness. The main reforms were:

- The National Health Service Act (1946) provided free medical care for the whole population. It was to be financed partly from National Insurance contributions but mainly from taxation. All hospitals, including voluntary ones, were taken into the National Health Service. Opposition from doctors was overcome by paying them fees based on the number of patients on their lists rather than a salary. The NHS was inaugurated in 1948.
- The National Insurance Act (1946) covered all adults and provided increased sickness and unemployment benefit, old age pensions, widows' and orphans' pensions, maternity allowances and death grants.
- The National Assistance Act (1948) provided benefits for those not covered by National Insurance, e.g. old people receiving pensions under the scheme set up in 1908. It also required local authorities to provide welfare services for the elderly and handicapped.
- The National Insurance Industrial Injuries Act provided compensation for injuries and pensions for the disabled.
- In education the Butler Act of 1944 was carried out. Secondary education was provided for all children and the school leaving age was raised to 15 from 1947.
- Over a million houses were built (though because of demographic changes there was still a serious shortage in 1951). Many were prefabricated and were at first intended to be temporary.

- The New Towns Act aimed to create towns which were healthy and pleasant. By 1951 fourteen New Town Corporations had been set up.
- The Town and Country Planning Act (1946) made county councils responsible for planning.
- The Trade Disputes Act (1946), though not strictly a welfare measure, may also be mentioned. This reversed the Act of 1927, which Labour supporters had always regarded as a vindictive measure designed to cripple Labour Party funds. Trade unions were now able to levy a contribution for political purposes provided members were allowed to contract out of it.

> **KEY POINT**
> Labour's greatest achievement was to set up the welfare state it had promised.

The economy

AQA ▶ M2
OCR ▶ M2

At the end of the war Britain had lost two-thirds of its export trade, faced a huge balance of payments deficit and had incurred massive debts, mainly to the USA. Moreover, the need to modernise industry was even greater than in the 1930s. Labour attempted to solve these problems by a planned economy.

Nationalisation.

A key part of this was nationalisation. Labour believed that the most important industries should be owned by the state and run in the public interest, with the profits going to the Treasury. Between 1945 and 1951 Labour nationalised the Bank of England, air transport, Cable and Wireless, the coal mines, the railways, docks, canals, road haulage, electricity and gas. It also nationalised iron and steel, but only after a struggle with the House of Lords, which rejected the proposal. The government reduced the delaying powers of the Lords to one year by the Parliament Act of 1949. It then completed the nationalisation of iron and steel, but the Conservatives denationalised the industry in 1953.

Economic controls.

Government controls were another key feature of Labour's economic policy. Food rationing continued – indeed, some allowances were even lower than during the war. In the harsh winter of 1946–47 there were power cuts and fuel rationing. Rents, profits, interest rates and foreign exchange were all controlled. There were strict building restrictions. Britain was helped through its immediate post-war difficulties by an American loan in 1946. This was given on condition that the pound sterling was made convertible, but when this was put into effect in 1947 it led to a balance of payments crisis.

Cripps and austerity.

Immediately after this, Cripps became Chancellor of the Exchequer. He believed that austerity was the solution to Britain's economic problems. Import controls were imposed to direct economic activity towards exports and there was a wage freeze between 1948 and 1950, even though prices were rising. Together with Marshall Aid, Cripps's measures achieved some success. By 1950 exports were 75 per cent above the 1938 level. Even so, the balance of payments continued to be a problem and it was necessary in 1949 to devalue the pound. This made imports dearer and exports cheaper, which helped the balance of payments.

Devaluation.

> **KEY POINTS**
> 1 Labour carried out its promises on nationalisation, maintained full employment and led Britain to recovery after the war.
> 2 The performance of the economy remained a long-term problem. In the short term, continuing austerity produced growing disillusionment.

Britain's position in the world

| AQA | M2 |
| OCR | M2 |

You need to think why it was hard for the British to accept their changed role in the world.

At the end of the war Britain still had its empire and a worldwide military presence with troops in Germany, the Middle East, India, Malaya and Singapore. As one of the 'big three' in the wartime Grand Alliance, it still aspired to a position as one of the world's leading powers. In reality the post-war world was dominated by the two superpowers, the USA and the USSR. Britain's resources had been stretched to the limit by the war and it faced the problem of adjusting to a reduced role to match its relative economic decline. Under the Labour government this took two forms: the beginning of the retreat from empire and the American alliance.

The retreat from empire

In 1947 the British left **India**. The 1919 and 1935 Government of India Acts had given India a measure of self-government. Before the war the Labour Party had produced plans for Britain to withdraw from India and Indian nationalists expected independence to follow soon after the Labour election victory in 1945. Britain could no longer afford to rule India and, since British exports to India had declined since the First World War, had little economic interest in continuing to do so.

The problem which faced Labour was the religious division of India between Hindus and Muslims. The Hindu Congress Party, led by Gandhi and Nehru, wished to preserve the unity of India. The Muslims, led by Jinnah, wanted partition and an independent state of Pakistan. Faced by a serious risk of civil war, Mountbatten, who was sent to India as Viceroy in 1947, decided that partition was the only answer and that the inevitable bloodshed would be lessened if Britain withdrew as quickly as possible. In August 1947 the independent states of India and Pakistan came into being. There was widespread violence and huge numbers of both Hindus and Muslims became refugees as they moved across the new borders. This was probably inevitable.

> Attlee and Mountbatten are generally credited with doing the best possible in the circumstances.
>
> **KEY POINT**

Palestine became a British mandate in 1919. Between 1919 and 1939 large numbers of Jews settled there. At the end of the war there was a further influx of Jewish refugees. The Jews aimed to set up a 'national home' in Palestine and began a terrorist campaign. The problem for Britain was to reconcile this with the presence of the Arab population. The two sides refused to compromise. Britain was unable to maintain law and order, despite the presence of 100,000 troops. Bevin, the Foreign Secretary, handed the problem over to the United Nations and withdrew British troops in 1948.

Compare the handling of the Palestine problem with the withdrawal from India.

Britain and the Cold War

Origins of the Cold War. There is an explanation of this from the Russian point of view on page 159.

In 1944–45 Britain and the USA became increasingly suspicious of Russian intentions in Eastern Europe. At the end of the war Russian troops occupied Poland, Romania, Bulgaria and Hungary. It had been agreed at the Yalta conference that the peoples of states occupied by Germany during the war should be able to decide their own future in free elections. Nevertheless, the Communists soon took control in all these states and established one-party regimes. Yugoslavia and Albania also had Communist governments established by partisans who had fought against the German occupying forces. East Germany was the Russian zone of occupation. Thus by 1946 Churchill was able to speak of an Iron Curtain across Europe. In 1948 Czechoslovakia was the last state in Eastern Europe to come under an entirely Communist government.

Bevin was as alarmed as Churchill by this development. He thought the best way to deal with it was by Anglo-American co-operation. He was, however, worried that the Americans would retreat into isolationism at the end of the war, as they had in 1919. He played a key role in the steps by which the USA became increasingly involved in the defence of Western Europe.

- The Truman Doctrine. Bevin feared that, without American help, Greece would fall under Russian control. In 1947 he told the Americans that Britain could no longer afford to defend the Greek monarchist government against the Communists. President Truman's response was the Truman Doctrine, promising American support for free peoples resisting attempts by armed minorities or outside powers to take them over. Its significance was that it committed the USA to defending non-communist Europe against Russia.

- The Marshall Plan. In 1947 the United States Secretary of State offered American aid towards the economic recovery of Europe. Bevin took the lead in establishing the Organisation for European Economic Co-operation in 1948 to administer the scheme, under which Britain received substantial sums. He also played a key role in setting up the Brussels Treaty of 1948, a mutual defence pact between Britain, France and the Benelux countries.

- The Berlin Airlift. The first big crisis of the Cold War occurred in June 1948, when Stalin cut off the western sectors of Berlin from the west, hoping to force the western powers to abandon it. The immediate causes of this were the integration of the three western zones of Germany into a single economic unit and the introduction of the new West German currency into West Berlin. Britain and the USA worked closely together to overcome the blockade by the Air Lift (June 1948–May 1949). They then set up the Federal Republic in Western Germany in 1949.

- NATO. As a result of the Berlin blockade, and building upon the foundations of the Brussels Treaty, NATO was set up in 1949. Bevin regarded this as his crowning achievement.

The next major crisis of the Cold War occurred in the Far East, when North Korea attacked South Korea in 1950. Although the United Nations force which was sent to defend South Korea was overwhelmingly American, Britain sent a contingent and embarked on a rearmament programme which posed considerable financial problems for the Labour ministry in its last year.

> Labour began the slow process of adjusting Britain to a world dominated by two superpowers. Bevin played a major role in engaging the USA in the defence of Western Europe as the Cold War developed. He regarded the setting up of NATO as his crowning achievement.
>
> **KEY POINT**

Bevin and Truman feared that, if Greece fell to the Communists, Turkey and the Middle East would follow.

Why did Labour lose the 1951 election?

- Despite what had been achieved in the setting up of the welfare state and the revival of the economy, people were tired of rationing, austerity, controls and the continuing housing shortage. The Conservative manifesto offered to end all of these.

- Despite the success of the export drive, the balance of payments deficit worsened in 1950–51 because the Korean War caused a sharp rise in the price of imported raw materials.

- The Korean War also made it necessary to increase the period of national service to two years, which was unpopular.

- The government faced financial problems resulting from the unexpectedly high cost of the National Health Service and the cost of the Korean War. The Chancellor, Gaitskell, tackled them by making expenditure cuts, and introducing charges for spectacles and dental treatment.

- This in turn led to the resignation of Bevan and Wilson from the government and a split in the party.
- The Conservative Party had overhauled its organisation and its election campaign was much more effective.
- The Liberal Party had very little money for a second election in less than two years and put up very few candidates. This benefited the Conservatives.

Despite all this, Labour only lost by a narrow margin (295 seats to the Conservatives' 321).

Labour had won by an even narrower margin in 1950 but during 1950–51 ministers seemed tired.

You should be able to explain the significance of each of these dates.

1945–51	Labour government; Attlee Prime Minister	
1947	British withdrawal from India; India and Pakistan set up	
1948	National Health Service inaugurated; Organisation for European Economic Cooperation set up; Brussels Treaty; Berlin Air Lift	**KEY DATES**
1949	Devaluation of the pound; NATO set up	
1950	General election; narrow Labour victory	
1950–53	Korean War	
1951	Labour defeated in general election	

6.2 The Conservatives, 1951–64

After studying this section you should be able to:

- discuss the record of Macmillan as Prime Minister
- assess the economic policies of the Conservatives
- give reasons for the defeat of the Conservatives in 1964

LEARNING SUMMARY

Eden and Macmillan

OCR ▶ M2

Macmillan talked of a 'wind of change' blowing through Africa. Many of Britain's African colonies gained independence during his ministry.

Of the four Conservative Prime Ministers in this period, Macmillan requires most attention. Churchill was 77 in 1951 and left much of the work to the Deputy Prime Minister, Eden, who succeeded him in 1955. Eden's ministry was cut short by illness and notable chiefly for the disastrous Suez campaign (1956). Macmillan (1957–63) was a 'one nation Tory', believing in social reform in the tradition of Disraeli. Something of a showman and a natural leader, he restored the Conservatives' confidence after Suez and led them to a third successive election victory in 1959. His ministry was marked by prosperity and rising standards of living but the underlying economic problems remained unsolved. It was also a period when Britain began to come to terms with its reduced influence in a world dominated by the superpowers, the USA and the USSR, and with the need to dismantle its empire.

Economic and social changes

 OCR ▶ M2

Note the contrast with the austerity of the Labour government.

Living standards improved markedly in the 1950s. This was the period of the 'affluent society'. Food rationing and building restrictions were ended and controls swept away. Wages rose faster than prices and people were able to afford more consumer goods such as cars, refrigerators and TVs. A vigorous 'national housing crusade' by Macmillan as Minister of Housing produced a 50 per cent increase in the number of new houses. Further subsidies to agriculture led to higher productivity. Income tax was lowered. Unemployment was low. National service was ended.

How much this prosperity was due to government policies is a matter of debate. Some historians argue that it was primarily caused by the growth in world trade and that the government's policies actually prevented Britain's economy from developing as rapidly as it should have done. Economic policy in the period came to be called 'stop–go'. The Conservatives inherited a balance of payments deficit and inflation in 1951. They tackled the situation by credit restrictions and import controls. When the balance of payments moved into surplus, the government cut interest rates and taxes, which led to a period of boom. This in turn caused rising wages and prices and increasing imports, and thus the balance of payments moved into deficit again. The boom had to be curbed by credit restrictions and tax increases.

> Stop–go.

> The link between the political and economic cycles was no accident.

The timing of the 'go' phases helped the Conservatives to win the elections of 1955 and 1959 but by the early 1960s it was becoming clear that the underlying growth of the economy was lagging behind Britain's European competitors. Ominously, unemployment was rising towards the million mark by 1963. One reason for this was that 'stop–go' discouraged long-term investment in industry. Some would argue that the Conservatives' failure to join the European Economic Community (EEC) when it was set up in 1957 was a crucial mistake.

> **KEY POINT**
>
> Economic policy in the period 1951–64 produced the 'affluent society' but no solution to Britain's long-term economic problems. This is why it has been described as 'thirteen wasted years'.

The election of 1964

> OCR   M2

As well as the economic problems, the Conservatives were losing popularity in the early 1960s for other reasons.

- An application to join the EEC was vetoed by France in 1963.
- The government was damaged by the Profumo scandal.
- Some Conservatives opposed Macmillan's policy of granting independence to African colonies.
- Home, Macmillan's successor as Prime Minister in 1963, was an electoral liability because of his aristocratic background and lack of experience in the Commons, and the way he was chosen was seen as undemocratic.

> Conservative unpopularity.

> Labour's revival.

Meanwhile, Labour's fortunes were reviving. In the 1950s Labour was torn by divisions, firstly about health service charges and then, more seriously, about nuclear disarmament. Under the leadership of Wilson, elected in 1963 on the death of Gaitskell, Labour presented a more dynamic image, offering modernisation and planning of the economy and encouragement for technological change. In the 1964 election Labour won a small overall majority and Wilson became Prime Minister.

> You should be able to explain the significance of each of these dates.

		KEY DATES
1951	Conservative election victory; Churchill Prime Minister.	
1955	Eden Prime Minister; Conservative election victory	
1956	Suez campaign	
1957	Macmillan Prime Minister	
1959	Conservative election victory	
1963	Retirement of Macmillan; Home Prime Minister	
1964	Labour victory in general election; Wilson Prime Minister	

Sample question and model answer

The Labour government's economic policies

Read the following source and then answer the questions that follow.

Source

From *Modern Britain 1885–1955*, by Henry Pelling, 1960.

[Labour's] election manifesto, *Let Us Face the Future*, was a model of simple and clear explanation of a limited programme of nationalisation and a planned transition to a peacetime economy with the retention of government controls as a safeguard 'against the chaos which would follow the end of all public control'.

(a) How did Labour carry out its 'limited programme of nationalisation'? [10]

Give full details and comment on 'limited'.

Labour nationalised the Bank of England, electricity, gas, air transport, railways, docks, canals, coal mines, road haulage, iron and steel. This still left most of manufacturing industry privately owned – hence 'limited'.

(b) How successful were the Labour governments of 1945–51 in tackling Britain's post-war economic problems? [20]

Explain the problems first.

- The main problems were war damage, the pre-war decline of old industries, loss of overseas investments, indebtedness to the USA, the need to export in order to pay for food and raw materials. There were continuing balance of payments problems.

The key issue is 'success'.

- The American loan of 1946 helped with the immediate post-war difficulties. This was given on condition that the pound sterling was made convertible but when this was put into effect in 1947 it led to a balance of payments crisis.

Another comment on 'success'.

- Marshall Aid and the appointment of Cripps as Chancellor in 1947 aided recovery. Cripps directed economic activity towards exports and there was a wage freeze between 1948 and 1950, even though prices were rising. He believed that austerity was the solution to Britain's economic problems. Import controls were imposed. These measures achieved some success. By 1950 exports were 75% above the 1938 level.

And another.

- Even so, the balance of payments continued to be a problem and it was necessary in 1949 to devalue the pound. This made imports dearer and exports cheaper, which helped the balance of payments.
Overall by 1951 much economic progress had been made but at the price of continuing austerity. The underlying problems of the economy remained.

Practice examination questions

1 (a) Explain the reasons for the Labour victory in the general election of 1945. [10]

(b) Assess the success of the Labour governments of 1945–51 in tackling Britain's social and economic problems. [20]

2 (a) Why did Labour lose the general election of 1951? [10]

(b) Explain why the Conservatives held office continuously from 1951 to 1964. [20]

Chapter 7

France, 1814–75

The following topics are covered in this chapter:

- *The restored Bourbons and the July Monarchy*
- *Napoleon III*

7.1 The restored Bourbons and the July Monarchy

After studying this section you should be able to:

- *assess the success of Louis XVIII*
- *account for the overthrow of Charles X in 1830*
- *assess the rule of Louis Philippe*

LEARNING SUMMARY

Louis XVIII

OCR ▶ M3

Louis XVIII was restored in 1814 by the victorious allies after the abdication of Napoleon I. He was, therefore, to many Frenchmen the symbol of defeat in the Napoleonic Wars. The enthusiastic reception given to Napoleon when he returned to France from Elba underlined this. Louis had to flee and was then restored again by the allies after Waterloo. To make matters worse for the restored monarchy, the allies then imposed on France a harsher treaty, including an indemnity and an army of occupation.

Political divisions in France

> Make sure you understand these. They are fundamental for nineteenth-century French politics.

The revolutionary period left France politically divided between republicans, Bonapartists and royalists. Republicans saw the monarchy as a symbol of a hated social and political system. They believed that only a republic would guarantee political liberty. They were also largely anti-clerical. Bonapartism was relatively weak after Waterloo, but it became a powerful element in French politics later in the century, when many Frenchmen began to look back to the Napoleonic era as a period when France had dominated Europe and had had a strong, centralised, progressive government. Royalists saw the return of the monarchy as offering stability against the possibility of revolution and as the best way to restore normal relations with the rest of Europe.

The Charter

Louis XVIII had the good sense to realise that the monarchy must win the loyalty of the French nation. He began by issuing the Charter in 1814. He promised to rule as a constitutional monarch in co-operation with an Assembly elected on a narrow middle-class franchise. He guaranteed freedom of speech and of the press, religious toleration and equality before the law. Thus he made it clear that there was to be no return to the *ancien régime*. He also won the support of the middle classes by a prudent financial policy and kept the Napoleonic legal and administrative systems.

Louis and the 'Ultras'

Nevertheless, Louis was subject to much pressure to restore at least some features of pre-Revolutionary France. The restored monarchy brought with it a host of émigré nobles who wanted to recover their land and their social and political power. In 1815 the 'Ultras', who favoured these policies, won a majority in the Assembly and proceeded to carry out a purge of the Bonapartists (the 'White Terror'). Louis realised that this was a mistake and checked it by appointing new ministers. In 1820, however, after the murder of the Duc de Berry, the Ultras were able to persuade him to reduce some of the freedoms granted in the Charter, especially freedom of the press.

Charles X

Compare the attitudes and personality of Charles X with Louis XVIII. Remember that Louis died in his bed, while Charles was overthrown in a revolution.

The 1830 Revolution.

The triumph of the Ultras came when Charles X succeeded Louis in 1824. Almost at once he ordered compensation to be paid to émigré nobles who had lost their estates during the Revolution. The religious ceremonies he insisted on at his coronation alarmed anti-clericals, who were further upset when the Church was given control over education. Press censorship was tightened.

Finally, in 1829, Charles appointed one of the most extreme of the Ultras, Polignac, as his chief minister. The result was a clash with the Chamber of Deputies. A general election produced an even more hostile Chamber. Polignac then issued the Ordinances of St Cloud, dissolving the new chamber before it met and reducing the already tiny electorate by three-quarters. This virtually destroyed the Charter of 1814. Economic hardship gave the liberals the support of the working classes in Paris. In July 1830 revolution erupted and Charles was overthrown.

> 1 Louis XVIII ruled as a constitutional monarch and tried to heal the divisions in post-Napoleonic France.
> 2 Charles X pursued right-wing policies which appeared to be an attempt to restore the pre-revolutionary monarchy.
>
> **KEY POINT**

Louis Philippe

The restored Bourbons had ruled by divine right, so this was an important change.

Consider why Louis Philippe was called the 'Citizen King'.

The revolution of 1830 had been a spontaneous uprising against Charles X. The rebels had no plans for replacing him. In this confused situation a liberal journalist, Adolphe Thiers, took the lead and the outcome was that the crown was offered to Louis Philippe, head of the House of Orléans, a junior branch of the Bourbon family. The offer was made by the Chamber of Deputies, so in effect Louis Philippe was elected king.

Despite his aristocratic origins, Louis was a typical bourgeois in his habits. He seemed the ideal choice. As a member of the royal family he was acceptable to royalists, yet moderate republicans also approved of him because he was willing to accept the role of a constitutional monarch and because his father, Philippe Egalité, had been a supporter of the revolution of 1789. The constitution was based on the Charter of 1814. The widening of the franchise to include those who paid 200 francs a year in taxes placed electoral power in the hands of the middle classes. Press censorship was abolished and the power of the church was again restricted.

In domestic affairs the Orléans monarchy had some reforms to its credit: a Factory Act, elected district councils and an Education Act which planned state-aided primary schools in every commune. There was rapid industrial development in some areas. Nevertheless, the benefits of economic prosperity were not felt by the working classes. The government was unwilling to interfere in the economy by introducing legislation which would have protected the working classes. The combination of social unrest and the French revolutionary tradition caused sporadic outbreaks of violence. The worst of these were risings in Paris and Lyons in 1834, which were brutally suppressed.

Louis Philippe avoided an adventurous foreign policy because of the expense of war and because he was uncertain whether his regime enjoyed sufficient support in

France to take the risk. His critics accused him and Guizot, his Foreign Minister from 1840 to 1847, of subservience to Britain. He co-operated with Palmerston over Belgium, withdrawing his original idea of establishing a French king there and accepting Leopold of Saxe-Coburg instead. He was outwitted by Palmerston in his Middle Eastern policy but scored a diplomatic victory over him in the affair of the Spanish marriages in 1846. Unfortunately, this deprived him of British sympathy when he most needed it in 1848.

Causes of the 1848 revolution

In the 1840s Louis Philippe faced increasing opposition.

- The economic hardship of the 'hungry forties' aroused working-class discontent.
- A new revolutionary movement grew up in the early socialists, led by Louis Blanc. Blanc preached the 'right to work' and advocated state-supported 'social workshops' in which workers would be fairly treated. Since this was a period of industrial growth in some areas of France, particularly Paris, an urban proletariat developed which provided Blanc with considerable support.
- The failure of Louis Philippe's government to tackle social problems added to working-class discontent.
- The king's advisers, such as Guizot, were anti-liberal and the regime became corrupt and inefficient.
- Bonapartism experienced a revival. Napoleon I's nephew, Louis Napoleon, exploited the mood of disillusion with Louis Philippe's foreign policy (it was claimed that 'France was bored' with it) to build up support.

> These ideas were put into practice in 1848.

> He had written two books in which he built up the Napoleonic Legend and portrayed Napoleon as the champion of progress.

> You should be able to explain the significance of each of these dates.

KEY DATES	
1814	Restoration of Louis XVIII; Charter issued
1815	Return and defeat of Napoleon; Louis restored again
1824	Accession of Charles X
1830	Ordinances of St Cloud; revolution; abdication of Charles X
1830–48	Louis Philippe
1848	Revolution; abdication of Louis Philippe

7.2 Napoleon III

After studying this section you should be able to:

- *explain the course and outcome of the 1848 Revolution in France*
- *account for the establishment of the Second Empire*
- *assess the domestic and foreign policies of Napoleon III*
- *evaluate the social and economic development of France in the Second Empire*
- *explain why the Second Empire was overthrown in 1870*

LEARNING SUMMARY

The 1848 Revolution in France

 OCR ▶ M3

By 1848 Louis Philippe faced opposition from republicans, socialists (with growing working-class support) and Bonapartists. Discontent focused on the demand for extension of the franchise. In February revolution broke out when Guizot banned a 'reform banquet' in Paris. On 24 February Louis Philippe was forced to abdicate.

The rebels then set up a provisional government which included liberals, radicals and the socialist Louis Blanc. At his suggestion 'National Workshops' for the unemployed were set up in Paris. Arrangements were made for elections to a

The division between republican Paris and conservative rural France was a key feature of French politics. It culminated in the Commune in 1871.

National Constituent Assembly on the basis of universal male suffrage in April. Most of the members of the Assembly were royalists, liberals or moderate republicans. The radicals and socialists, who were powerful in Paris, were heavily outnumbered.

In May the provisional government was replaced by a new government, from which the radicals and socialists were excluded. An attempt by the socialists and the Paris mob to overthrow this government (which had an overwhelming majority in an assembly elected by the largest electorate in French history) was frustrated by the National Guard. Louis Blanc fled and other socialist leaders were arrested.

A final desperate attempt by the Paris mob to overthrow the government was provoked by the decision to close the National Workshops. Without leaders or organisation, the working classes of Paris seized control of the city. The army under General Cavaignac turned the guns on the rebels and hundreds were massacred. Afterwards 11 000 prisoners were punished by imprisonment or exile. These 'June Days' turned the mass of Frenchmen outside Paris – especially the middle classes – against socialism and even liberalism.

The National Constituent Assembly finished drawing up the constitution by November. In December elections were held for a President. Five and a half million out of seven and a half million votes went to Louis Napoleon.

> **KEY POINTS**
>
> Napoleon triumphed because:
> - the name of Napoleon was a symbol of France's past glories
> - he offered stability against the 'red peril'
> - his schemes for social reform won working-class support

The Second Republic

OCR ▸ M3

Under the constitution Napoleon was President for four years only and not allowed to seek re-election. He was not prepared to accept this, so he set out to make himself popular:

- he opposed demands by republicans in the Assembly to reduce the electorate;
- he won support from the Catholics by sending troops to Rome to overthrow the Roman Republic set up by Mazzini and restore the Pope.

Note the symbolism.

By December 1851 Napoleon felt confident enough to take the first step towards making his power permanent. In a well-organised *coup d'état*, many of his leading opponents were arrested during the night. The next day, the anniversary of the coronation of Napoleon I as Emperor, he declared himself President for ten years. A year later he abolished the Second Republic and made himself the Emperor Napoleon III. Both these steps were approved by plebiscite.

The Constitution of the Second Empire

OCR ▸ M3

He was in effect a dictator – but with popular approval.

The constitution of the Second Empire gave Napoleon III autocratic powers. His power was based on popular approval through plebiscites. He appointed ministers, was commander-in-chief of the armed forces, and had the right to declare war, make treaties and institute legislation. The Legislative Assembly, elected by universal male suffrage, met for only three months a year and had very little power. In any case the elections were managed. There was strict press censorship. Many political opponents were exiled to Algeria. Political associations were suppressed. Provincial administration was in the hands of prefects appointed by the Minister of the Interior.

The 'Liberal Empire'.

In 1859 Napoleon granted an amnesty to political opponents exiled in 1851. From 1860 he began to liberalise the system of government. The Legislative Assembly was given the right to debate its reply to the address from the throne and the press was allowed to report parliamentary debates. During the 1860s there were further concessions. Press censorship was relaxed and opposition journals and newspapers sprang up. Trade unions were legalised. It became increasingly accepted for ministers to be questioned in parliament. A liberal and republican opposition developed, which won 35 seats in the elections of 1863 and 93 in 1869.

In 1869–70 a new constitution gave the Legislative Assembly the power to propose laws and vote on the budget. A ministry representing the majority in the Legislative Assembly was formed in January 1870. These reforms received overwhelming support in a plebiscite. But the emperor still retained considerable powers, including the power to change the constitution, subject to a plebiscite.

> Historians debate whether these changes sprang from a genuine desire to liberalise the constitution or were concessions forced on Napoleon by a succession of failures in foreign policy.
>
> **KEY POINT**

Social and economic developments

OCR ▶ M3

This helps to explain why many Frenchmen approved of the Second Empire.

The Second Empire saw considerable economic growth. New banks were founded to raise capital for commercial and industrial development. Low interest rates encouraged investment. The railway network was vastly increased and mining and heavy industry were expanded. A great deal of slum clearance was undertaken in Paris and new boulevards and squares were created under the guidance of Baron Haussmann. In his early days Napoleon had written a pamphlet on *The Ending of Poverty* and as Emperor he made a genuine attempt to improve social conditions. 'Conciliation Boards' were set up which negotiated improvements in wages and working conditions. Public works helped to create full employment.

Foreign policy

OCR ▶ M3

Napoleon wanted – and was expected – to restore to France the glory it had had in his uncle's day. He therefore pursued a more active foreign policy than Louis Philippe. At first he had some success. France and its allies were victorious in the Crimean War of 1854–56, though the French army did not earn the glory Napoleon had hoped. The fact that the peace conference was held in Paris gave the Second Empire prestige.

Napoleon managed to offend Frenchmen at opposite ends of the political spectrum.

Then in 1859 Napoleon went to war against Austria in alliance with Piedmont, winning victories at Magenta and Solferino. The French did, however, suffer heavy losses and the intervention in Italy aroused opposition from both Catholics and liberals. The Catholics feared that the unification of Italy would endanger the papacy, while the liberals felt that Napoleon had let the Italians down by making the Truce of Villafranca. But he did acquire Savoy and Nice as his reward.

In the 1860s Napoleon's foreign policy was largely a catalogue of failures.

- He lost prestige by the ill-considered Mexican adventure of 1861–67. He sent French troops to overthrow the anti-religious republic in Mexico and set up a Catholic empire under Maximilian, brother of the Austrian emperor. He hoped to win the approval of Catholic opinion as well as prestige. Under pressure from the USA he had to withdraw his troops, leaving Maximilian to be executed.

Napoleon miscalculated. He expected a long war, not a quick Prussian victory.

- In 1866 Napoleon was persuaded by Bismarck to remain neutral while Prussia defeated Austria. Prussia's victory left France facing a much more powerful Prussia. It was a long-standing principle of French foreign policy to prevent the emergence of a powerful state in Germany.

- Napoleon's unsuccessful attempt to restore the balance of power by trying to annex Luxemburg as compensation discredited him further. By revealing that Napoleon aimed to do this, Bismarck humiliated France.

The Franco-Prussian War

Another miscalculation.

In view of these failures it is doubtful how much longer the Second Empire would have survived after 1870, but what destroyed it was the catastrophic failure of its armies at the beginning of the Franco-Prussian War. Napoleon tried to use the issue of the Hohenzollern candidature for the Spanish throne to score a diplomatic victory over Prussia and thus restore his prestige. He demanded that William I of Prussia should guarantee that the candidature would not be renewed. This provided Bismarck with the opportunity to provoke a war by editing and publishing the Ems Telegram. Napoleon gave way to French public opinion and declared war.

The French armies were unprepared for war. One army was driven into Metz, where it was besieged and eventually surrendered in October 1870. The other suffered a disastrous defeat at Sedan in August and Napoleon himself was taken prisoner. The Legislative Assembly proclaimed the overthrow of the Second Empire and the establishment of a republic and a provisional government.

The Paris Commune and the constitution of 1875

The first task facing the provisional government was to rally resistance against the Prussians. Despite heroic efforts, Paris fell after a four-month siege in January 1871. By the Treaty of Frankfurt, France was forced to surrender Alsace and Lorraine, to accept an army of occupation and to pay an indemnity.

The Commune was a separate government for Paris, independent of the National Assembly.

The rising of the Paris Commune (March–May 1871) followed almost immediately after the end of the siege of Paris. On the orders of Thiers, head of the government, the army suppressed the Commune. There was great brutality on both sides and the episode left deep divisions in French society.

The Comte de Chambord ruined his cause by insisting on restoring the Bourbon flag.

After the suppression of the Commune, the way was clear for the National Assembly to draw up a new constitution. Royalists had a majority in the Assembly but were divided between the supporters of the Comte de Chambord (Bourbon) and the Comte de Paris (Orléanist). Since they were unable to agree who should be king, the Assembly in 1875 accepted a republican constitution, with a President as head of state, a Chamber of Deputies elected by universal male suffrage and an indirectly elected Senate.

Sample question and model answer

Napoleon III

(a) Explain why the Second Republic was so short-lived. [10]

Begin by explaining underlying problems.

- Origins of the Second Republic: overthrow of Louis Philippe by liberals and socialists who had different aims. Liberals in the National Assembly closed down the National Workshops established by the Socialist Louis Blanc, leading to the 'June Days'.

Then go on to role of Napoleon, which is the key issue.

- Election of Louis Napoleon as President. He offered stability against the 'red peril' to the middle classes and peasants, social reform to the working class. His name was a symbol of France's past glories.

- Napoleon bolstered his position by sending troops to Rome, which gained Catholic support, and by opposing republican plans to reduce the electorate. By 1851 he was in a position to carry out a coup, extending his period of office to ten years. But he also used force, arranging for the arrest of many of his leading opponents during the night.

- Plebiscites gave overwhelming support to this and to the establishment of the Second Empire a year later.

(b) Assess the success of Napoleon III's conduct of foreign policy. [20]

The key issue is 'success'.

- At first he was successful in making France the centre of European diplomacy. The Crimean War ended with a peace conference in Paris, gaining prestige for France and Napoleon.

You should expand the factual material – but be sure to comment on 'success'.

- His next venture had more mixed results. In alliance with Piedmont, France defeated Austria and thus opened the way to the unification of Italy. But after the battles of Magenta and Solferino, he backed out (Truce of Villafranca). The episode aroused opposition from both Catholics, who feared for the papacy, and liberals, who felt that he let the Italians down. He also forfeited the gratitude of the Italians, especially since French troops remained in Rome to defend the Pope.

Assessing success involves commenting on failures

- The Mexican adventure (1861–67) was a disaster. He eventually had to abandon Maximilian to his fate, losing prestige and alienating Austria (Maximilian was a Habsburg).

- He was consistently outwitted by Bismarck. When they met at Biarritz in 1865, he was taken in by vague promises of future compensation. Thus he stood aside during the Seven Weeks' War, with the result that Prussia emerged victorious and France had a much more powerful eastern neighbour. His failure to get compensation was regarded by many Frenchmen as a national humiliation. Bismarck's revelation of his secret ambition to annex Luxemburg helped to ensure that France was isolated in 1870.

You need to add a conclusion – probably critical.

- The Franco–Prussian War brought about his downfall. His handling of the Hohenzollern candidature for the Spanish throne enabled Bismarck to provoke a war for which France was ill-prepared and which was a disaster.

Practice examination questions

1 (a) Explain why Charles X was overthrown in 1830. [10]

(b) How important as a reason for the growing unpopularity of Louis Philippe was his foreign policy? [20]

2 (a) Explain the extent to which Napoleon III liberalised the Second Empire between 1859 and 1870. [10]

(b) Explain why the overthrow of the Second Empire in 1870 resulted in the establishment of the Third Republic in 1875. [20]

Chapter 8

Russia, 1825–1917

The following topics are covered in this chapter

- *Tsarist Russia, 1825–94*
- *Nicholas II, 1894–1917*
- *The 1917 Revolutions*

8.1 Tsarist Russia, 1825–94

After studying this section you should be able to:

- *explain Russia's political and social system*
- *account for the policy of repression pursued by Nicholas I*
- *assess the significance of the reforms of Alexander II*
- *assess the importance of the reign of Alexander III*

LEARNING SUMMARY

Nicholas I, 1825–55

| OCR | M3 |

These were the fundamental, distinctive features of Russian society.

Early nineteenth-century Russia was perhaps the most reactionary state in Europe. The system of government by a Tsar with absolute authority is generally termed **autocracy**. Russia's social structure was distinguished by the survival of **serfdom**, which had disappeared everywhere else in Europe. The majority of Russians were serfs, owned either by the crown or by the landed aristocracy. The middle class was tiny, reflecting the lack of industry and the relative unimportance of trade in Russia's backward economy. The **Orthodox Church** had a central role in society in the state and acted as a brake on change.

Even in Russia, however, the liberal ideas of the French Revolution had penetrated among some of the educated nobles. In the last years of the reign of Alexander I (1801–25) secret societies favouring reform grew up. The result was the Decembrist movement. When Alexander died in December 1825, the secret societies rose up and demanded a national assembly. The new Tsar, Nicholas I, suppressed the revolt with great severity.

Nicholas then followed a policy of repression based on the army and the police – particularly the 'Third Section' or secret police. There were no further revolts in Russia. In Poland, however, there was a revolt in 1830, inspired by the revolutions elsewhere in Europe. For a short time the rebels were able to set up a provisional government but in 1831 the Tsar's armies crushed them. Poland was placed under military rule and Polish nationalism was suppressed.

If Russia was backward in 1825, it was even more so in 1855.

The backwardness of Russia was highlighted by defeat in the Crimean War (1854–56). Nicholas died in the middle of the war, leaving Russia in need of reform.

Alexander II, 1855–81

AQA	M1
OCR	M3
WJEC	M2

This section sets out the case for regarding Alexander as the 'Tsar Liberator'.

Reforms

Alexander II recognised the need for reform and the first half of his reign was in marked contrast to that of Nicholas I. The most important reform was the **emancipation of the serfs** in 1861. The peasants were freed from all their obligations to the landlords, whether money payments or labour services. The government compensated the landlords and reclaimed the money from the peasants by redemption payments over a period of 49 years. The land was not transferred to individuals but to the 'mir' or village commune, which was responsible for the redemption payments.

> The emancipation of the serfs was a fundamental change in Russian society and the economy. It involved over 40 million people and it was inevitable that other reforms would follow.
>
> **KEY POINT**

In 1864 'zemstva' were set up. These were elected district councils which were made responsible for roads, hospitals, schools, sanitation and poor relief. They were particularly active in setting up elementary schools. They were elected on a system which favoured the nobility and gentry, but they were nevertheless a step towards democracy. In 1870 town councils were also set up.

Alexander introduced important legal reforms, including trials in public, trial by jury and salaries for judges (to reduce bribery). The army was reformed: the general staff was reorganised and all classes became liable for conscription. Conscription played an important part in reducing illiteracy, since conscripts were taught to read and write.

There was also some economic development. Some 20 000 km of railways were built. A State Bank was set up and there was some industrial development.

How effective were these reforms?

This section and the next set out the case against.

Although the emancipation of the serfs was a huge step, the way it was carried out had serious weaknesses. Generally the peasants got the poorer land and their farms were small. Because the 'mir' was collectively responsible for the redemption payments, it was very difficult for peasants to leave the village. Since the land was communally owned and regularly redistributed, there was no incentive to improve it. Russian agriculture therefore remained backward and inefficient. As the population grew, famines became more frequent. Since the peasants were tied to the 'mir', there was little migration either to the underpopulated territories of Siberia or to the towns. Industrial progress was therefore slow.

Although serfdom had been abolished, the other key features of nineteenth-century Russia, the autocracy and the Orthodox Church, remained untouched.

Repression again

After 1866 Alexander's regime became more repressive. The powers of the 'zemstva' were reduced. Press censorship was strict, the secret police were active and political cases were tried without a jury. Over 150 000 people were sent to penal servitude in Siberia.

This was the beginning of the revolutionary tradition which culminated in the revolutions of 1917. Can Alexander be accused of stimulating it?

The reasons for this change were the Polish Revolt (1863) and the growth of revolutionary movements among the intellectuals. Many intellectuals were desperately aware of Russia's backwardness. Their disappointment at Alexander II's reforms led to the formation of reformist movements. Repression turned some of them into revolutionary movements. The two most important were the 'Narodniki', who wanted to educate the peasants to demand reforms, and the anarchists, led by Bakunin, who called for armed rebellion. Anarchists made several unsuccessful attempts on the life of Alexander II. They succeeded in 1881.

> Alexander's reforms gave hope of modernising Russia but they failed to make the Tsarist system popular.
>
> **KEY POINT**

Alexander III, 1881-94

AQA ▶ M1

The keynote of the reign of Alexander III was repression. His chief minister, Pobedonostsev, firmly believed in autocracy. The Okhrana (secret police) were active hunting down revolutionaries, many of whom were executed or exiled to Siberia. There was strict press censorship and education was strictly controlled. The 'zemstva' were put under the supervision of Land Captains – gentry appointed by the Tsar. Anti-semitism was encouraged by the government and by the Orthodox Church, which was also controlled by Pobedonostsev as Procurator of the Holy Synod. Pogroms (armed attacks on Jews) were common.

The combination of economic advance and political repression was likely to lead to trouble in the end

There were important developments in the economy. Industrialisation increased. Alexander authorised the beginning of work on the Trans-Siberian Railway. In 1892 he appointed Witte as Minister of Finance. There was also an important change in foreign relations in 1893 when Russia allied with France.

You should be able to explain the significance of each of these dates.

1825–55	Reign of Nicholas I	**KEY DATES**
1854–56	Crimean War	
1855–81	Reign of Alexander II	
1861	Emancipation of the serfs	
1881–94	Reign of Alexander III	

8.2 Nicholas II, 1894–1917

After studying this section you should be able to:

LEARNING SUMMARY

- *explain the main political and economic developments between 1894 and 1905*
- *account for the outbreak of the Revolution of 1905 and its failure*
- *assess the strengths and weaknesses of Tsarist Russia in 1914*
- *evaluate the consequences for Russia of involvement in the First World War*

Economic advance and political repression, 1894–1905

AQA ▶ M1
OCR ▶ M3

Economic development gained momentum. The state played a key role with Witte the driving force. He was particularly successful in encouraging foreign investment, especially from France. The rail network more than doubled in extent between 1890 and 1914, the outstanding achievement being the Trans-Siberian Railway. The rate of growth of industrial production was the highest in the world, particularly in coal, iron, oil and cotton. The urban population grew with corresponding speed, especially in Moscow and St Petersburg, where housing and working conditions were appalling. The growth of an industrial proletariat played a major part in the development of a more western type of socialist movement.

Politically, Nicholas II continued the policies of Alexander III. Repression continued unabated. Nevertheless, reformist and revolutionary movements continued to develop.

These differences were important. The Bolsheviks – the majority at the conference – were actually the smaller group.

- In 1898 the **Social Democratic Party** was founded by Plekhanov. Its ideas were Marxist and it sought support from Russia's newly emerging industrial working class. At its 1903 Congress, held in exile in Brussels and London, it divided into two wings. The **Bolsheviks**, led by Lenin, wanted membership restricted to a small number of dedicated activists who would bring about a socialist revolution and the dictatorship of the proletariat. The **Mensheviks** wanted a mass party of the working class which would aim to overthrow the Tsar, set up a democratic republic and then introduce an eight-hour working day and other social reforms.

- In 1902 the **Social Revolutionary Party** was formed. This aimed to unite the intellectuals, workers and peasants and to bring about revolution by propaganda and terror.
- In 1904 at a meeting of 'zemstva' leaders the **Liberals** set up the Union of Liberation which demanded political reform.

The 1905 Revolution

AQA   M1
OCR   M3

At the beginning of the twentieth century Russia was seething with unrest. The peasants and the urban working class were equally discontented, as shown by the frequency of peasant uprisings and strikes. Political repression was as fierce as ever. Discontent boiled over into revolution as a result of the **Russo-Japanese War** (1904–05). The cause of this was the conflicting ambitions of Russia and Japan in Manchuria and Korea. The Russian government expected 'a short victorious war that would stem the tide of revolution'. In fact the Japanese won handsomely: in Manchuria they won the great battle of Mukden, while the Russian fleet, after sailing half-way round the world, was virtually wiped out in the battle of Tsushima.

News of defeat in the Far East brought discontent to a head on 22 January 1905, when government troops opened fire on a procession of peaceful, unarmed demonstrators carrying a petition to present to the Tsar at the Winter Palace in St Petersburg. Several hundred were killed and the incident, known as **Bloody Sunday**, marked a turning point. This atrocity provoked a wave of strikes and peasant uprisings. In June there was a mutiny on the battleship *Potemkin* and in September a general strike. In St Petersburg a **Soviet** (committee of workers' representatives) was set up with Trotsky as co-chairman.

The first appearance of a Soviet.

The Tsar was forced to make concessions.

- In August he promised to set up a **Duma** (assembly), though with a narrow franchise which would exclude industrial workers.
- In October, on the advice of Witte, he issued a manifesto promising a wider franchise and legislative powers for the Duma. This satisfied the Liberals and divided them from the workers in the Soviet.

The government was then able to suppress the revolution. The leaders of the Soviet were arrested and a rising in Moscow was brutally suppressed. By April 1906 the Tsarist government was back in control and some 15 000 people had been killed.

> Tsarist Russia was shaken by the 1905 Revolution but recovered. But it never fully regained the loyalty it lost on Bloody Sunday.
>
> **KEY POINT**

Why did the Revolution of 1905 fail?

AQA   M1
OCR   M3

- The revolutionaries were not united, so eventually the Tsar was able to split the liberals from the socialists.
- There was no central leadership: the strikes and peasant uprisings were spontaneous and not organised.
- Lenin and other revolutionary leaders were in exile abroad and arrived too late to influence events.
- At the critical moment the Tsar made concessions in the October Manifesto (though only under pressure from Witte).

This was crucial.

- The army and navy for the most part remained loyal (mutinies such as that on the *Potemkin* were the exception). This enabled the Tsar to revert to repression once he had regained the upper hand.

The Dumas and Stolypin, 1905–14

AQA   M1
OCR   M3

Nicholas II believed in the autocracy and saw political concessions as weakness. He had no intention of observing the spirit of the October Manifesto. He showed this in May 1906 by dismissing Witte, whom he blamed for having forced him to issue the Manifesto. Stolypin replaced him.

The First Duma met in May 1906. The electoral system was rigged to favour the landowners and middle classes over the peasants and workers. The biggest political grouping in the Duma was the Cadets (liberals). The Duma demanded sweeping reforms, including a democratic electoral system. Nicholas dissolved it after ten weeks.

> But perhaps, given time, Russia might have developed a form of constitutional monarchy. The main obstacle was Nicholas himself.

> You need to revise the terms of the emancipation – see page 91.

The Second Duma (1907) was also soon dissolved because its demands were unacceptable to Nicholas. The Third Duma (1907–12) and the Fourth Duma (1912–17) were elected on a revised franchise, which increased still further the power of the gentry and middle classes. They were dominated by Octobrists (moderate liberals) and achieved some modest reforms, e.g. factory legislation. They had little power and the regime remained fundamentally autocratic.

Stolypin introduced important agrarian reforms which were intended to win the support of the peasants. Redemption payments were ended. Peasants were given complete freedom to leave the 'mir' and they were allowed to turn their holdings into their own individual properties. Stolypin hoped that this would create a class of prosperous peasant farmers and would make agriculture more efficient.

> **KEY POINTS**
>
> 1 The Dumas could have been the foundation for the gradual development of democracy in Russia, but the attitude of Nicholas II and the onset of the war prevented this.
> 2 Stolypin's reforms might have transformed Russian agriculture eventually, but only over a lengthy period.

Russia in 1914

AQA   M1
EDEXCEL   M1
OCR   M3
NICCEA   M3

At the outbreak of the First World War there were indications that Tsarist Russia might survive.

- The Third and Fourth Dumas co-operated with the government.
- A class of prosperous peasants was slowly beginning to emerge.
- There were some signs of improvement in the conditions of industrial workers.
- Industrial output was growing, especially in coal and iron; other industries were slower to grow.

But Russia's problems were enormous.

- The regime was still autocratic and repressive.
- The reputation of the monarchy never fully recovered from Bloody Sunday.
- Industry was still small in scale and inefficient by Western European standards.
- Agricultural productivity was still poor despite Stolypin's reforms, which in any case needed many years to have a real effect.

> Don't exaggerate the importance of Rasputin as a factor in the downfall of the Tsar.

- Nicholas II lacked the intelligence to deal with his problems. He failed to acknowledge the need for change and did not realise how much prestige the monarchy had lost in 1905. The growing influence of Rasputin further discredited the court.
- His advisers were mediocre. Only two had real ability – Witte, who was dismissed in 1906, and Stolypin, who was assassinated in 1911.

The First World War

AQA   M1, M3
EDEXCEL   M1
OCR   M3
NICCEA   M3

The war exposed Russia's inefficiency. Losses were enormous. Millions of men were drafted into the armed forces but the Russian state was unable to provide them with adequate clothing, training or equipment. Against the highly efficient German army defeat was inevitable. In 1914 the Germans inflicted crushing defeats at the battles of Tannenberg and the Masurian Lakes. In 1915 the Russians were driven out of Poland. In 1916 an offensive against Austria met with some success – but then equipment began to run short.

Since the Tsar had unwisely decided to take personal command of the army, the defeats were blamed on him.

The strain of war also brought great hardship to the civilian population. Germany and Turkey closed Russia's Baltic and Black Sea ports and thus virtually cut Russia off from its allies. The internal transport system was in chaos. Food became increasingly difficult to obtain in the towns and prices rose.

To make matters worse, the government itself became increasingly unstable. In the first two years of the war there were four prime ministers, three foreign ministers and three war ministers. In the absence of the Tsar at army headquarters continuity was provided only by the Tsarina Alexandra and her favourite Rasputin, whose corrupt influence further discredited the monarchy.

> The war exposed the weaknesses of Tsarist Russia and brought about its downfall.
>
> **KEY POINT**

You should be able to explain the significance of each of these dates.

		KEY DATES
1894	Accession of Nicholas II	
1898	Foundation of the Social Democratic Party	
1903	Split between Bolsheviks and Mensheviks	
1904–05	Russo-Japanese War	
1905	Bloody Sunday; Revolution of 1905	
1906	First Duma; Witte dismissed and replaced by Stolypin	
1914	Outbreak of First World War	
1917	February Revolution: abdication of Nicholas II	

8.3 The 1917 Revolutions

After studying this section you should be able to:

* account for the establishment of the Provisional Government in February 1917 and its overthrow eight months later

LEARNING SUMMARY

Why were there two revolutions in 1917?

AQA   M1, M3
EDEXCEL   M1
OCR   M3
NICCEA   M3

At this stage it seemed possible that Russia would develop into a democratic republic.

The February Revolution

On 23 February 1917 (Russian calendar) a great wave of strikes and food riots broke out, particularly in Petrograd (formerly St Petersburg). Troops sent to quell the rioters joined them. The authority of the government had collapsed. Six days later the Fourth Duma established a Provisional Government under Prince Lvov. Most of its members were Liberals, but there was one socialist, Kerensky. The next day the Tsar abdicated.

The Provisional Government

This proved to be a crucial mistake – but was any other decision possible?

The Provisional Government never enjoyed widespread support. In July Prince Lvov was replaced as Prime Minster by Kerensky. The Provisional Government decided to continue the war, which led to further military disasters and continuing food shortages. When rumours began to spread that land was to be redistributed, the peasants in the army deserted and went home to claim their land; the Russian armies disintegrated. By the autumn the Provisional Government was discredited. A disastrous offensive in Galicia in July provoked a rising in Petrograd, which the Bolsheviks tried unsuccessfully to turn into a coup.

Lenin

In April Lenin returned to Russia. In the 'April Theses' he set out his aim, 'all power to the soviets', which meant overthrowing the Provisional Government. Soviets had been set up all over the country. The most important was the Petrograd Soviet of Workers' and Soldiers' Deputies, set up three days before the Provisional Government. The soviets claimed that, as their members were elected by the workers, they represented the will of the people more faithfully than the Provisional Government. They certainly enjoyed more popular support. When Lenin returned to Russia, the soviets were dominated by Social Revolutionaries and Mensheviks. The Bolsheviks, despite being a minority, had one advantage: they were a highly disciplined body of determined revolutionaries. After the failure of Lenin's first attempt to seize power in July, he fled to Finland and many of his followers were arrested.

The October Revolution

Make a list of reasons why the Bolsheviks succeeded in overthrowing the Provisional Government.

An attempted right-wing coup by General Kornilov in September restored the Bolsheviks' fortunes. They played a big part in defeating Kornilov and this enabled them to gain majorities in the Petrograd and Moscow Soviets. The Bolshevik Party's Central Committee decided on an armed insurrection. Lenin, Trotsky and Stalin were part of the majority which made this decision; only Kamenev and Zinoviev opposed it. The revolution took place on the night of 6–7 November (24–25 October by Russian dating), the day before a meeting of the All-Russian Congress of Soviets. The Congress immediately confirmed the Bolsheviks in power.

> **KEY POINT**
>
> In the October Revolution a determined minority seized power from a weak Provisional Government which had failed to address the problems which led to the downfall of the Tsar.

You should be able to explain the significance of each of these dates.

> **KEY DATES**
>
> | February | Abdication of Nicholas II; Provisional Government Soviet set up in Petrograd |
> | April | Return of Lenin to Russia; April Theses |
> | July | Kerensky Prime Minister; unsuccessful Bolshevik attempt to seize power in Petrograd |
> | September | Kornilov's attempted coup |
> | October | Bolshevik revolution |
>
> (Dates are given according to the Russian calendar)

Sample question and model answer

source

Russia 1881–1905

Read the following source and then answer the questions which follow.

From *Reaction and Revolutions: Russia 1881–1924* by M. Lynch

The reign of Alexander III could hardly have begun in worse circumstances. The new Tsar came to the throne prematurely.

(a) What is meant by saying that Alexander III 'came to the throne prematurely'? [3]

Link this to the rise of revolutionary movements.

Alexander II had been assassinated. The word 'prematurely' draws attention to the violent circumstances of his accession.

(b) Explain Tsar Alexander III's response to the 'circumstances' of his premature accession to the throne. [7]

The question requires explanation of Alexander's repressive policies.

He clamped down on opposition. The Okhrana (secret police) sought out revolutionaries. Many were executed or exiled to Siberia. There was strict press censorship and education was strictly controlled. The power of the zemstva – the only representative institutions in Russia – was restricted by appointment of Land Captains. Minority nationalities were subjected to Russification. Jews were attacked in pogroms.

(c) How successful were Alexander III and Nicholas II in tackling the domestic problems facing the Tsarist regime before 1905? [15]

(NEAB, 1999)

The key issue is 'success'.

• There was a retreat to a more autocratic and repressive regime – with a corresponding rise in disaffection. Despite the measures just mentioned, opposition was never totally suppressed. In the early twentieth century illegal parties were formed: the SDs, SRs, Liberals. In 1905 opposition broke out into revolution.

• Little progress in tackling social problems. Peasants remained tied to the commune, with a low standard of living. Little attempt to combat the problems of urbanisation. Little advance in education: universities restricted, low level of literacy among the masses.

Success and failure are balanced here.

• Economic policies more successful. Witte achieved rapid expansion of railways and industry. This was financed by foreign investment and tariffs (which also protected industry). The main problem was that failure to tackle the problem of the communes meant that the peasants were heavily taxed and yet unable to increase production sufficiently to provide the exports needed to finance industrialisation and the grain to feed the growing urban proletariat.

Practice examination questions

1 Read the following source and then answer the questions which follow.

From *The Making of Modern Russia* by L. Kochan, 1962

The emancipation was not only epoch-making in itself in its effects on rural Russia; it also opened the way to further reforms, which became indispensable now that the most solid bulwark of the old regime had gone down in semi-ruin.

(a) What is meant by 'the most solid bulwark of the old regime'?　　　[3]

(b) What were the effects of the emancipation on rural Russia?　　　[7]

(c) How far did Alexander II's reforms fulfil the high hopes with which his reign had opened?　　　[15]

2 (a) Identify and explain **any two** reasons why the Revolution of 1905 in Russia failed.　　　[10]

(b) Compare the importance of **at least three** reasons for the downfall of the Tsarist regime in 1917.　　　[20]

3 Study the following sources and then answer the questions which follow.

The February Revolution

From a memorandum from Durnovo, Minister of the Interior, to the Tsar, February 1914. He considers the likely effects of a war against Germany

source 1

The trouble will start with the blaming of the Government for all disasters. In the legislative institutions a bitter campaign against the government will begin, followed by revolutionary agitations throughout the country, with Socialist slogans, capable of arousing and rallying the masses, beginning with the division of the land and succeeded by a division of all valuables and property. The defeated army, having lost its most dependable men, and carried away by the tide of the primitive peasant desire for land, will find itself too demoralised to serve as a bulwark of law and order.

From the diary of Florence Farmborough, an Englishwoman living in Russia. In January 1917 she was serving as a nurse with the Russian army in Galicia

source 2

Discontent among the masses in Russia is daily becoming more marked. Rancour is turning towards the military chiefs. Why are the soldiers allowed to rot in the snow-filled trenches? 'Bring the men home.' 'Conclude peace.' Cries such as these penetrate to the cold and hungry soldiers in their bleak earthworks and begin to echo there among them. Now that food has grown scarce in Petrograd and Moscow, disorder takes the shape of riots and insurrections. We are told that mobs of the lower classes parade the streets shouting 'Peace and Bread'. They are aware that the war is at the root of their hardships. We devour the newspapers and are amazed to find that some of them openly describe the turmoil in the cities.

Rodzyanko, President of the State Duma, recalls February 1917

source 3

Unexpectedly for all, there erupted a soldier mutiny such as I have never seen. These of course were not soldiers but *muzhiki* [peasants] taken directly from the plough. In the crowd all one could hear was 'Land and Freedom', 'Down with the Dynasty', 'Down with the Romanovs'.

Practice examination questions (continued)

A report to the Duma, based on information from its provincial agents, June 1917

A widespread myth that the Russian peasant is devoted to the Tsar and that he 'cannot live' without him has been destroyed by the universal joy and the relief of the peasants upon discovering that in reality they can live without the Tsar. Now the peasants say: 'The Tsar brought himself down and brought us to ruin'.

source 5

From *Modern Europe 1789–1989* by A. Briggs and P. Clavin, 1997

The war alone was not responsible for the ruin of the Russian Empire. It took the sufferings, deprivations and defeats of the war, however, to fuse the discontents of the Russian peasants, workers and middle classes, and it was because Nicholas lost the support of his armed forces that the Russian dynasty perished.

(a) Study sources 3 and 4. Compare these sources as evidence for the attitude of Russian peasants towards the Tsar in 1917.   [5]

(b) Study source 2. How useful is this source as evidence of the causes of the revolution of February 1917?   [5]

(c) Use sources 1 and 5 and your own knowledge. How far do you agree that it was the war which destroyed Tsardom in Russia?   [15]

Chapter 9

The unification of Italy

The following topics are covered in this chapter:

- The Risorgimento
- The Creation of a United Italy

9.1 The Risorgimento

After studying this section you should be able to:

- *explain the development of Italian nationalism in the first half of the nineteenth century and the obstacles that it faced*
- *account for the failure of the revolutions of 1848*

LEARNING SUMMARY

The unification of Italy, 1859–70

Kingdom of Sardinia, 1859
Added to Sardinia by conquest, 1859
Added to Sardinia by plebiscite, March 1860
Added to Sardinia by plebiscite, Oct–Dec 1860
--- Territories claimed by Italy, but still under Austrian rule
— Boundary of Kingdom of Italy, 1870

Italy before 1848

EDEXCEL M2
OCR M3
WJEC M1

In 1815 Italy was divided up into a number of states, as it had been before the Napoleonic wars. It was dominated by the influence of Austria and its Chancellor, Metternich. Lombardy and Venetia were part of the Austrian Empire. Parma, Modena and Tuscany were ruled by relatives of the Austrian Emperor. The Kingdom of the Two Sicilies (Naples and Sicily) and the Papal States looked to Austria as their protector. Only Piedmont-Sardinia was independent of Austrian influence. In all the Italian states the system of government was autocratic.

These were the legacy of the French Revolution, exported by Napoleon's armies.

The Napoleonic period stimulated liberal and nationalist ideas in Italy. Secret societies, the most famous of which was the Carbonari, spread these ideas. There were liberal revolts in Naples (1820), Piedmont (1821) and the Papal States, Parma and Modena (1830–31). All were suppressed with Austrian help.

Three possible national leaders emerged.

- **Mazzini** founded the Young Italy movement in 1831 with the aim of making Italy 'united, independent and free'. He believed the Italians could do this themselves in a popular uprising which would establish a democratic republic.
- **Charles Albert**, who became King of Piedmont-Sardinia in 1831, aimed to create a kingdom of north Italy rather than to unite the whole peninsula. To bring this about, he embarked on economic reforms to strengthen Piedmont. But he was not a liberal and his rule was repressive.
- **Pius IX**, who became Pope in 1846, had the reputation of being a liberal. He began his papacy by releasing political prisoners, an act which played a part in touching off the revolutions of 1848. For many Italians the papacy was the natural focus of leadership. Some, e.g. **Gioberti**, aimed not for unification but for a confederation of Italian states under the papacy.

> Obstacles to unification were:
> 1 The domination of Italy by Austria.
> 2 Differences among Italian nationalists as to what sort of united Italy they aimed for.
> 3 Catholic fears that the papacy might lose the Papal States.
>
> **KEY POINTS**

The 1848 revolutions

EDEXCEL ▸ M2
OCR ▸ M1, M3
WJEC ▸ M1

Revolts in Sicily and Naples in January 1848 forced King Ferdinand to set up a constitutional government and touched off a series of uprisings. Charles Albert and Pius IX granted constitutions in Piedmont and Rome. Revolts in Milan and Venice expelled the Austrians. Charles Albert then declared war on Austria but was defeated at the battles of Custozza (1848) and Novara (1849). In 1849 he abdicated in favour of Victor Emmanuel II. The Austrian general, Radetzky, regained control of Milan.

Meanwhile in Rome Pius IX, whose reputation for liberalism had been greatly exaggerated, fled when faced by further demands. Mazzini set up the Roman Republic, but France then intervened. Louis Napoleon, President of the newly created Second Republic, sent troops to restore the Pope. His motive was to win support from French Catholics. In Naples King Ferdinand dismissed his liberal government and restored his autocracy by bombarding Sicily into submission. Finally, in August 1849, Austria regained control of Venice.

The 1848 revolutions in Italy failed for two main reasons.

- The Italians could not defeat Austrian military power unaided.
- The Italian revolutionaries were divided over their aims. Mazzini aimed for a republic, Charles Albert for a monarchy (of northern Italy only). Many Italians gave higher priority to setting up constitutional government in the separate states than to a unified Italy.

> 1848 marked an important step towards unification.
> 1 Piedmont had emerged as the only Italian state capable of challenging Austria.
> 2 It was clear that it would need allies to do so effectively – a lesson learnt by Cavour.
> 3 Mazzini's Roman Republic, and especially the heroic resistance led by Garibaldi during the siege of Rome by the French, provided inspiration to Italian nationalists.
>
> **KEY POINTS**

9.2 The creation of a united Italy

After studying this section you should be able to:

- explain the roles of Cavour and Garibaldi in the unification of Italy by 1861
- assess the importance of foreign help in the process of unification
- compare the reasons for the success of the movement for unification in 1859–60 and failure in 1848–49
- show how Venice and Rome were incorporated into the Kingdom of Italy
- discuss the main features of the constitution and economy of the unified Italy

LEARNING SUMMARY

Cavour and Piedmont

EDEXCEL ▶ M2
OCR ▶ M1, M3
WJEC ▶ M1, M3

By 1849 only Piedmont under its new king, Victor Emmanuel II, still had a constitutional government. It was now the focus of nationalist hopes. Cavour, who was appointed Prime Minister in 1852, aimed to build up Piedmont's strength. His reforms improved communications, expanded trade and strengthened finance. By 1859 Piedmont was a model to the rest of Italy for efficient government and thriving trade.

Cavour also realised that Piedmont would need a powerful ally against Austria. He sought the friendship of Napoleon III of France. Piedmont's participation in the Crimean War as an ally of France and Britain helped. In 1858 Cavour reached an agreement with Napoleon, the Pact of Plombières, by which France promised to help to expel Austrian troops from Lombardy and Venetia.

> Compare this with the Austrian victories in 1848. Even so, French and Piedmontese losses were heavy.

The war which resulted was the first crucial stage in unification. The Franco-Piedmontese armies occupied Lombardy, defeating the Austrians at Magenta and Solferino. At this point, however, Napoleon made peace (the Truce of Villafranca), leaving Venetia in Austrian hands.

The war inspired rebellions in other parts of northern Italy and this enabled Cavour to use plebiscites to join Parma, Modena, Tuscany and the Romagna to Piedmont and Lombardy in a new kingdom in northern Italy in 1860.

> In 1859–60 Piedmont took over northern Italy, as Cavour had planned. The crucial factors in this were:
>
> 1 the modernisation of Piedmont by Cavour
> 2 the French alliance.
>
> **KEY POINTS**

Garibaldi and Sicily

EDEXCEL ▶ M2
OCR ▶ M1, M3
WJEC ▶ M1, M3

Inspired by Cavour's success, Garibaldi collected a force of a thousand volunteers and later in 1860 sailed from Genoa to Sicily. Landing in the west, he quickly gained control over the whole island. In August he crossed to the mainland and in September captured Naples. He then intended to march on Rome.

> Public opinion made it impossible for Cavour to stop Garibaldi, so he aimed to control him.

At this point Cavour became alarmed, for he realised that if Garibaldi attacked Rome, the Catholic powers of Europe might intervene. He therefore sent troops into the Papal States from the north to forestall Garibaldi. The Italian army occupied the Marches and Umbria (the eastern part of the Papal States) but kept well clear of Rome itself. They then linked up with Garibaldi, who handed over his conquests to Victor Emmanuel. Thus by the end of 1860 the whole of Italy except Venetia and the area around Rome had been annexed by Piedmont. In January 1861 the first all-Italian parliament met in Turin. Less than six months later Cavour died.

Garibaldi's expedition forced Cavour to change his plans and accept the southern states as part of a unified Italy.

Venice and Rome

EDEXCEL M2
OCR M1, M3
WJEC M1, M3

Italian nationalists could not rest content until Rome and Venetia had been 'liberated'. Venetia became part of Italy in 1866 as a by-product of the Seven Weeks' War, in which Italy fought against Austria as the ally of Prussia.

Rome presented more of a problem as the Pope had had the protection of French troops since 1848. Napoleon III, in deference to French Catholic opinion, could not withdraw them; and Italy could not contemplate a war against France. Consequently two attempts by Garibaldi in 1862 and 1867 to occupy Rome were unsuccessful and it was not until the Franco-Prussian War of 1870–71 that Rome was acquired. Because of the war, French troops were withdrawn from Rome, which was then occupied by Italian troops and became the capital. The Pope refused to recognise the loss of Rome and became a virtual prisoner in the Vatican until an agreement was made with Mussolini in 1929.

KEY POINT

By 1871 the ambitions of Italian nationalists had been almost completely realised. Only South Tyrol, Trentino, Trieste and Istria remained 'unredeemed' – 'Italia Irredenta'.

The Kingdom of Italy

OCR M3

The system of government of Italy after unification was based on that of Piedmont. The republican ideas of Mazzini and Garibaldi were rejected. Victor Emmanuel II of Piedmont, the first King of Italy, was the head of a constitutional monarchy rather like that of Britain, which Cavour admired. The ministers were responsible to a parliament elected on a rather narrow middle-class franchise. This system survived for over half a century, but eventually it failed to give effective government and gave way to the dictatorship of Mussolini.

Because of the number of parties the system depended on bribery and corruption to make it work.

The division between north and south also worked against the development of national political parties.

United Italy, unlike Germany, did not enjoy rapid economic development. This was partly because it lacked coal and iron, which were essential for industrial development in this period. Industry did develop in the north, but Italy remained comparatively poor and was, therefore, unable to play as effective a part in European affairs as many Italians had hoped. In the south, industrial development made no progress at all and the extreme poverty and ignorance of this region remained one of Italy's most serious social problems.

You should be able to explain the significance of each of these dates.

	KEY DATES
1831	Foundation of 'Young Italy' by Mazzini
1846	Pius IX elected Pope
1848	Revolutions throughout Italy; all ultimately unsuccessful; Roman Republic set up by Mazzini; heroic but unsuccessful defence by Garibaldi
1852	Cavour Prime Minister of Piedmont
1859	War: Piedmont and France v. Austria; victories at Magenta and Solferino; Lombardy annexed by Piedmont
1860	Kingdom of North Italy set up after plebiscites in Parma, Modena, Tuscany and the Romagna; Garibaldi's invasion of Sicily; Sicily, Naples, the Marches and Umbria taken over
1861	Kingdom of Italy set up
1866	Venetia added to Kingdom of Italy
1870	Rome occupied by Italian troops and incorporated into Italy.

Sample question and model answer

The unification of Italy

(a) In what ways did Cavour seek to strengthen Piedmont in the period from 1852 to 1859? [15]

This descriptive question requires clear organisation:
– the economy

- Politically and economically Piedmont was modernised and became a model to the rest of Italy for efficient government and thriving trade. Cavour admired British economic achievements and aimed to imitate them through the expansion of trade by free trade treaties. Railways were built and financial institutions developed. Piedmont's trade trebled.

– political change

- He also admired Britain's parliamentary system of government. The liberal constitution granted in 1848 was retained and Piedmont's administration modernised. The privileged position of the Catholic Church was reduced. All this won for Piedmont admiration from European liberal opinion.

– foreign affairs.

- Cavour recognised the need for powerful allies. By sending Piedmontese troops to join with those of Britain and France in the Crimean War he gained European recognition for Piedmont and won the sympathy of Napoleon. In 1858 Napoleon made the Pact of Plombières with Piedmont.

(b) Explain why, in the course of 1859–61, Italy was unified under King Victor Emmanuel. [15]

The question requires explanation of cause and effect.

- The strengthening of Piedmont laid the foundation. The forces of patriotism, which had been stimulated by Mazzini in 1848, were harnessed by Cavour to his aim of expanding Piedmont into a kingdom of Northern Italy.

- The alliance with Napoleon III made possible victory over Austria, which was the principal obstacle to this. Even though Napoleon backed out at the Truce of Villafranca, the defeat of Austria gave Lombardy to Piedmont.

- Plebiscites in the Central Italian duchies led to annexation by Piedmont. This development was brought about by Cavour, backed by Britain. This was probably as far as Cavour wanted to go.

- Garibaldi's expedition to Sicily and Naples forced Cavour to change his plans. Cavour feared that Garibaldi would go on to attack Rome, which could endanger all that had been achieved. So he sent troops into the Papal States, which linked up with Garibaldi. Naples and Sicily were handed over to Victor Emmanuel, who thus became King of a united Italy (except Venice and Rome).

Practice examination questions

1 Study the following sources and then answer the questions which follow.

source 1

A proclamation issued by Garibaldi in April 1860

Italians! – The Sicilians are fighting against the enemies of Italy and for Italy. To help them with money, arms, and especially men, is the duty of every Italian.

The chief cause of the misfortunes of Italy used to be disunion and the indifference one province showed for the fate of another. The salvation of Italy dates from the day when the sons of the same soil hastened to support their brothers in danger. If we abandon the brave sons of Sicily to themselves, they will have to fight the mercenaries of the Bourbon, as well as those of Austria and of the priest who rules Rome. Let the people of the free provinces raise their voices in favour of their brethren who are fighting – let them send their generous youth to where men are fighting for their country.

A handful of brave men, who have followed me in battles for our country, are advancing with me to the rescue.

To arms, then! Let us by one blow put an end to our chronic misfortune.

source 2

A *Punch* cartoon of 1860 entitled 'Right Leg in the Boot at Last'. Garibaldi advises the King – 'If it won't go on, sire, try a little more powder'.

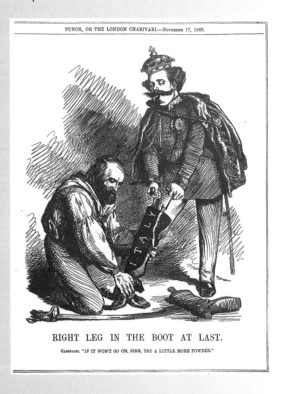

PUNCH, OR THE LONDON CHARIVARI.—November 17, 1860.

RIGHT LEG IN THE BOOT AT LAST.

Garibaldi. "IF IT WON'T GO ON, SIRE, TRY A LITTLE MORE POWDER."

source 3

A letter from Cavour to the Piedmontese envoy in Paris, 1860

Garibaldi has become intoxicated by success and by the praise showered on him from all over Europe. He is planning the wildest, not to say absurdest, schemes. As he remains devoted to King Victor Emmanuel, he will not help Mazzini or republicanism. But he feels it is his vocation to liberate all Italy before turning it over to the King. He wants to keep the dictatorial powers which will enable him to raise an army to conquer first Naples, then Rome and in the end Venice. The Government here has no influence over him.

We must prevent Garibaldi from conquering Naples. Were Garibaldi to become master of all the Neapolitan provinces we would not be able to stop him from compromising us with France and Europe.

source 4

Alberto Mario, one of Garibaldi's followers, describes the meeting of the King and Garibaldi in Naples in October 1861.

Garibaldi was at his wit's end to direct their attention from himself to the King. Keeping his horse a few paces behind, he cried, 'This is Vittorio Emmanuele, your King, the King of Italy'. The peasants stared and listened and then not understanding, again shouted, 'Viva Galibardo!'.

1 (a) Study source 3. From this source and from your own knowledge, explain what is meant by 'compromising us with France and Europe'. [3]

   (b) Study source 1. How useful is this source as evidence about obstacles to the unification of Italy? [5]

   (c) Study sources 2 and 4. Compare and explain these sources as evidence for Garibaldi's aims in his campaign in Sicily and Naples. [5]

   (d) Study all the sources. Using your own knowledge, and these sources, assess the importance of Garibaldi's contribution to the unification of Italy. [12]

2 (a) Identify and explain **any two** problems faced by Italian nationalists in 1848. [10]

   (b) Compare the importance of **at least three** factors in the unification of Italy between 1859 and 1861. [20]

The following topics are covered in this chapter:

- Germany, 1815–62
- Bismarck

- The German Empire, 1871–90
- William II

10.1 Germany, 1815–62

After studying this section you should be able to:

- *explain the working of the German Confederation*
- *account for the failure of the Frankfurt Parliament to unite Germany*
- *analyse the growth of Prussian power before the rise of Bismarck*

The German Confederation

EDEXCEL   M3
WJEC   M1

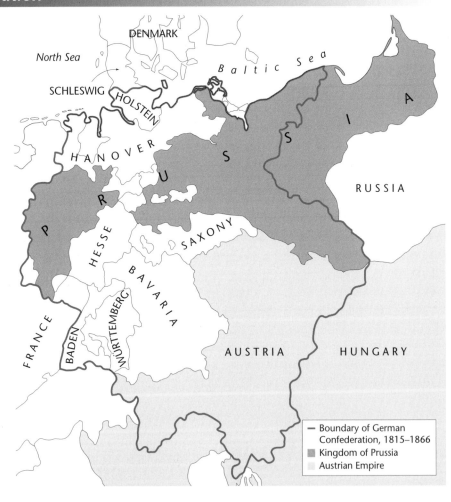

Germany in 1815

— Boundary of German
  Confederation, 1815–1866
■ Kingdom of Prussia
□ Austrian Empire

In 1815 Germany was divided into 39 separate states, which formed the German Confederation. The Bundestag (Federal Assembly) consisted of representatives of the governments of the states and was no more than a co-ordinating body. It was presided over by Austria and from 1815 to 1848 was effectively run by the Austrian Chancellor, Metternich, who used it to repress liberals. The two biggest states by far were Austria and Prussia, both of which also ruled territories outside the borders of the Confederation. It is important to note, however, that Austria's non-German territories were much more extensive and more racially diverse than Prussia's.

> Prussia included part of modern Poland. Austria ruled Czechoslovakia, Hungary, Slovenia and parts of Italy, Romania and Poland.

The 1848 Revolution and the Frankfurt Parliament

Think about the arguments for and against each point of view.

In 1848 there were revolutions throughout Germany. These led to the election of a parliament for the whole of Germany, the Frankfurt Parliament of 1848–49. Its members were largely middle-class liberals who aimed to draw up a constitution for a united Germany. But they faced a problem: what was 'Germany'? Some argued for a Little Germany (Kleindeutschland), which would exclude Austria, while others wanted a Great Germany (Grossdeutschland) which would include the Austrian lands except Hungary. The latter would mean including many Slav peoples and offering the federal crown to the Austrian Emperor.

Neither was prepared to accept the crown from a parliament.

While the members of the Frankfurt Parliament were debating, the German princes were regaining control of their states. The Parliament offered the crown of a federal Germany in turn to the Austrian Emperor and the King of Prussia, but they both declined. The Parliament broke up in 1849, having failed to unite Germany. In 1850 in the Submission of Olmütz, Frederick William IV of Prussia acknowledged Austria's revival of the Confederation.

> 1848 left many Germans disillusioned with liberalism: the attempt to set up a united Germany by constitutional means had failed. Nationalist feeling had been roused and then disappointed. **KEY POINT**

Despite the failure of 1848, nationalist sentiment remained strong in Germany. It derived much of its force from the ideas of Hegel, who believed, in essence, that the development of the nation was the motive force in the unfolding logic of history. If liberalism had failed to create a German nation-state, other means must be found.

Although Austria's predominance in Germany had been restored after 1848, by 1860 its position had weakened. The Crimean War isolated it from Russia. Its defeat by France and Piedmont in Italy in 1859 lowered its military prestige. Prussia, with troops in the Rhineland, began to seem a better defence against the growing power of Napoleon III's France.

The Zollverein and the growth of the Prussian economy

Economic development also played an important part in the growth of Prussian power. Free trade was established in Prussia in 1821 and this led to the creation of the Zollverein (customs union) in 1834, which established free trade throughout most of Germany with the exception of Austria. This, along with its natural resources, the growth of heavy industry and the development of the railway network, gave Prussia economic predominance in Germany by the middle of the nineteenth century. The development of industry and the railways also assisted the expansion and reorganisation of Prussia's military strength by Roon and William I, who came to the throne in 1861.

> The foundation for the unification of Germany under Prussia was laid by the Zollverein and the economic strength of Prussia.

10.2 Bismarck

After studying this section you should be able to:

- *explain the successive stages in the unification of Germany by Bismarck*
- *evaluate Bismarck's diplomacy in the period 1863 to 1871*
- *account for his success in bringing about unification*

Bismarck 1862–67

AQA	M1
EDEXCEL	M3
OCR	M3
WJEC	M1

He claimed there was a 'gap in the constitution' which allowed the king to collect taxes if he could not reach agreement with the parliament.

The cost of Roon's plans to expand the army led to a crisis between the King and the Prussian Parliament. This was the situation in which William I appointed Bismarck as Prime Minister in 1862. Bismarck came from a family of Junkers – Prussian landowning gentry. He was a successful diplomat with a reputation for strong anti-liberal views, which was why William called on him in his battle with the liberals in the Prussian Parliament. Bismarck simply carried on collecting the taxes needed to enlarge the army, even though the parliament refused to approve them. Between 1864 and 1871 Bismarck engaged in three wars which brought about the unification of Germany.

The Danish War, 1864

Note that Bismarck did not plan a war against Denmark – he simply took advantage of a situation that arose.

The King of Denmark was also Duke of Schleswig-Holstein. Christian IX, who succeeded to the throne in 1863, wanted to make Schleswig part of Denmark. The majority of the people of Schleswig were German and there was an outcry in Germany. Bismarck took the opportunity to present himself as the champion of German interests. In co-operation with Austria, which would not let Prussia act alone, he made war on Denmark, which was quickly defeated. By the Convention of Gastein (1865), Prussia took Schleswig and Austria Holstein. This gave Bismarck the chance to pick a quarrel with Austria whenever he liked.

The Austrian War (The Seven Weeks' War), 1866

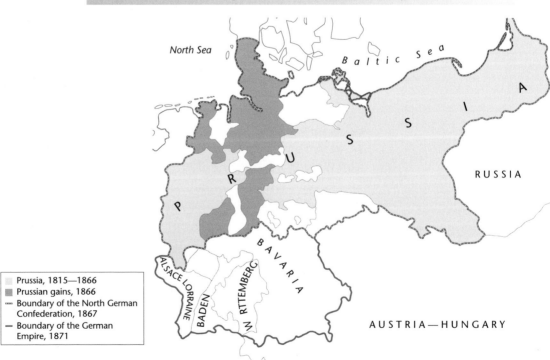

- ▢ Prussia, 1815—1866
- ◾ Prussian gains, 1866
- ┅ Boundary of the North German Confederation, 1867
- ── Boundary of the German Empire, 1871

The German Empire, 1871

Compare this with the Danish war. This time Bismarck created the situation himself.

Bismarck's second war was against Austria. He had made his mark as a diplomat by his opposition to Austrian power within Germany. This war was one he seems to have planned.

- He made an alliance with Italy, which wanted Venetia.
- At a meeting with Napoleon III at Biarritz he made vague promises of future compensation for France.

This won Bismarck the support of some of the Liberals with whom he had quarrelled over the army in 1862. Those who supported him formed the National Liberal Party.

In 1866 he provoked war by proposing that the German Confederation should be dissolved and a new confederation set up excluding Austria. The war, which only lasted seven weeks, proved the efficiency of the Prussian army with its new breech-loading rifle. The main Austrian army was overwhelmingly defeated at Sadowa in Bohemia. By the Treaty of Prague the German Confederation was abolished and a new North German Confederation was set up. The south German states were to be independent. Schleswig-Holstein was handed over to Prussia and soon afterwards Prussia annexed Hanover and several other north German states. Venetia was duly handed to Italy, even though Austria had defeated the Italian army.

Venetia and Holstein were the only territories Austria lost. Bismarck did not want territory, but to deprive Austria of its predominant position in Germany.

The Franco-Prussian War, 1870–71

AQA	M1
EDEXCEL	M3
OCR	M3
WJEC	M1

Historians debate whether a war against France was part of Bismarck's long-term plans, but after 1866 it became increasingly difficult to avoid one. Public opinion in France regarded the defeat of Austria by Prussia and the establishment of the North German Confederation as in effect a defeat for France. It had long been an aim of French foreign policy to prevent the emergence of a strong power in western Germany. Prussia's gains in the war were greatly resented and between 1866 and 1870 relations between France and Prussia were tense. Bismarck's disclosure that Napoleon had asked for compensation in the Rhineland or Luxemburg inflamed relations further.

The explosion came in 1870 over the issue of the succession to the Spanish throne. One of the candidates, Prince Leopold, was a member of the Hohenzollern family, of which William I was the head. Napoleon III, fearing the encirclement of France if a Hohenzollern became King of Spain, demanded that Leopold should withdraw. This was agreed, but Napoleon then demanded guarantees that the candidature would not be renewed. It was clear that he was seeking a diplomatic victory at Prussia's expense in order to boost his prestige. Bismarck altered the telegram in which William announced his rejection of the latest French demands (the Ems Telegram) so that the French government could only take it as a rebuff. Public opinion in Paris was outraged and demanded war.

Public opinion in France exaggerated the seriousness of this. It was really a pretext for war and could easily have been solved without it.

> Did Bismarck provoke the war? There is some evidence that he encouraged Leopold's candidature, perhaps with the aim of provoking a crisis. He certainly altered the Ems telegram with that aim. He appears to have thought war was inevitable in the end.
>
> **KEY ISSUE**

The war was a triumph for Prussia. One French army was surrounded at Metz and another which was sent to relieve it was itself surrounded and forced to surrender at Sedan. Napoleon was taken prisoner and a republic was set up in Paris. Paris was besieged from September 1870 to January 1871. The French were unable to find allies as Bismarck's diplomacy had kept Napoleon isolated. In January an armistice was signed and in May 1871 peace was made at Frankfurt. Alsace and Lorraine became part of Germany and France was to pay an indemnity and accept the occupation of its northern provinces. The war enabled Bismarck to complete the unification of Germany. It aroused nationalist enthusiasm throughout Germany and the southern states of Bavaria, Baden and Württemberg, which had remained outside the North German Confederation of 1867, were swept into a unified Germany. On 18 January 1871 William I was proclaimed Emperor of Germany. The new Empire excluded Austria.

Why was Bismarck successful in uniting Germany?

AQA ▶ M1
EDEXCEL ▶ M3
OCR ▶ M3
WJEC ▶ M1

Three factors were of great importance.

You can relate this to Bismarck's remark (made much later) that Prussia's aims would be achieved not by speeches but by 'blood and iron'.

This is known as Realpolitik.

- The first was Prussian military power. Only military strength could overcome the hostility of Austria, in whose interest it was to keep Germany divided. Similarly it was likely that sooner or later France would try to prevent the emergence of a greater power to its east. Thus the roles of Roon, the Prussian Minister of War, and Moltke, the Chief of the General Staff, in building up the Prussian army, were crucial to Bismarck's success.
- The economic development of Prussia underlay its military power. Prussia was already the most industrialised state in Germany before Bismarck came to power and through the Zollverein it had gained economic supremacy over the other German states. It was the economic and military strength of Prussia which allowed Bismarck to achieve political unification.
- Bismarck's own contribution through his cynical and unscrupulous diplomacy was vital. He believed that 'reasons of state' justified any action. He could only have been thwarted if those powers threatened by the unification of Germany (or the growth of Prussian power) had worked together, but his diplomacy prevented this. The two powers which certainly should have worked together were France and Austria, but Bismarck's deception of Napoleon III at Biarritz kept Austria isolated in 1866, while his lenient treatment of Austria after the Seven Weeks' War ensured Austria's neutrality in the Franco-Prussian War. He ensured Britain's neutrality in 1870 by revealing that Napoleon III had had his eye on Belgium in 1866 as 'compensation' for Prussia's gains in the Seven Weeks' War. He encouraged Russia to take advantage of France's involvement in war to repudiate the Black Sea clauses of the Treaty of Paris of 1856.

The Black Sea clauses forbade Russia from keeping warships there. The Treaty of Paris had been imposed on Russia by Britain and France after the Crimean War.

KEY POINT

Did Bismarck plan the three wars against Denmark, Austria and France with unification as his long-term goal? Historians debate this issue. Most historians believe that he aimed simply to extend Prussian power and weaken Austria and that he was an opportunist who took advantage of events as they happened.

You should be able to explain the significance of each of these dates.

KEY DATES

1815	Establishment of the German Confederation
1834	Zollverein set up
1848–49	Frankfurt Parliament
1862	Bismarck Prime Minister of Prussia
1864	War against Denmark over Schleswig-Holstein
1866	Seven Weeks' War (Prussia v. Austria)
1867	Establishment of the North German Confederation
1870–71	Franco-Prussian War
1871	German Empire set up

10.3 The German Empire, 1871–90

After studying this section you should be able to:

- *explain the nature of the 'Bismarckian' political system*
- *assess how successful Bismarck was in dealing with the liberals, the socialists and the Roman Catholic Church*
- *discuss the success of Bismarck's foreign policy between 1871 and 1890*

LEARNING SUMMARY

The constitution of the Empire

AQA ▶ M1
OCR ▶ M3
WJEC ▶ M2

The new German Empire (the Second Reich) was a federal state. William I of Prussia was the Emperor (Kaiser) and Bismarck the Chancellor. The Emperor was head of the executive and the army. He had the right to declare war or martial law in an emergency. The Chancellor was appointed by and responsible to the Emperor.

There were two houses of parliament. The upper house (**Bundesrat**) consisted of representatives of the German states. Prussia, as the biggest state, had the most representatives in the Bundesrat. Prussia's government was controlled by the Junkers, who were thus able to block constitutional change through their representatives in the Bundesrat. While Bismarck was Chancellor he was able to control the Bundesrat through his position as Minister President of Prussia. The lower house (**Reichstag**) was elected by universal male suffrage and this made the constitution appear unusually democratic for its time.

> Make sure you understand the arguments for describing it as autocratic.

In reality, however, the constitution was autocratic, since the Reichstag had little power. It had no control over the Chancellor and could not secure his dismissal. Its powers were limited to a veto over legislation and control over the federal budget. This meant that it was desirable but not essential for the Chancellor to secure its co-operation; he could not be overthrown if he was unable to do so. Ultimately power lay with the Emperor.

Domestic affairs

AQA ▶ M1
OCR ▶ M3
WJEC ▶ M2

The Liberals

At first Bismarck relied on the Liberals for a majority in the Reichstag, partly because he needed their support in his quarrel with the Catholics (see below). From 1874, however, his relationship with the Liberals cooled. The first dispute was over the size of the army, which accounted for 90 per cent of the federal budget. In 1874 Bismarck forced through a proposal that its size should be fixed for seven years, thus greatly reducing what little power the Reichstag had. The second issue was protection. After a brief economic boom prompted by the euphoria of unification, a prolonged period of economic depression began in 1873. Bismarck decided to abandon free trade in favour of protection. This not only won him support from both industrialists and landowners but had the further advantage of making the imperial government's finances less dependent on contributions from the states. Strong opposition from the Liberals, who supported free trade, led to a decisive break with them in 1879 when tariffs were introduced. Henceforth Bismarck relied on the Conservatives and the Catholic Centre Party in the Reichstag.

> Tariffs would be part of the federal budget. The contributions paid by the states were often a source of dispute.

The Kulturkampf

Ultramontanism placed great emphasis on the absolute authority of the Pope over Catholics.

The May Laws.

The North German Confederation was predominantly Protestant but southern Germany was Roman Catholic. When the German Empire was set up in 1871, it therefore had a substantial minority of Catholics. Bismarck feared that their loyalty to Rome would conflict with their loyalty to the Empire. The growth of ultramontanism in the Roman Catholic Church, highlighted by the proclamation of the doctrine of Papal Infallibility in 1870, strengthened his suspicions. In the 1870s he conducted a struggle with the Catholics, known as the Kulturkampf. By the May Laws of 1873–75 education was brought under state control and state approval was required for the licensing of priests. The campaign backfired. Catholics rallied round and the Catholic Centre Party made gains in the Reichstag elections of 1877. Since Bismarck needed their support against the Liberals over tariffs, he toned down the Kulturkampf and withdrew some of the May Laws.

> Little was achieved by the Kulturkampf and it is generally thought that it was a mistake. **KEY POINT**

The Socialists

Another reason why Bismarck relaxed the Kulturkampf was the growth of socialism. There were socialist groups in Germany as early as the 1840s but the establishment of the Empire with a Reichstag elected by universal suffrage provided the spur to bring them together. In 1875 the Social Democratic Party was founded on the basis of the Gotha Programme. In 1877 the party won half a million votes in the Reichstag election. Bismarck was alarmed and in 1878 introduced the anti-Socialist laws which banned socialist organisations, meetings and newspapers. The socialists were not, however, banned from membership of the Reichstag. Although it was handicapped, the Socialist Party continued to grow in strength. The anti-Socialist law was renewed every three years until the fall of Bismarck but was then allowed to lapse.

> 1878–79 was a turning point for Bismarck. He broke with the Liberals, introduced the anti-Socialist law, ended the Kulturkampf and began to rely on the Conservative and Catholic Centre parties **KEY POINT**

State socialism.

Bismarck also introduced '**state socialism**'. In 1883–84 he instituted sickness and accident insurance and in 1889 old age pensions. One reason for the introduction of these welfare measures was to undermine support for the socialists, but they were also a response to concerns about the growing gap between rich and poor.

Foreign affairs

AQA M1
OCR M3

There is a fuller account of this crisis on page 45.

The main aim of Bismarck's foreign policy after 1871 was to keep peace. This meant keeping France isolated and thus preventing a war of revenge. This in turn meant cultivating good relations with both Austria-Hungary and Russia.

The Balkan crisis of 1875–78 presented a major threat to peace. Bismarck feared that it could lead to a war between Russia and Austria-Hungary. He therefore called the Congress of Berlin and, acting as 'honest broker', worked out a settlement which reduced the size of the Russian-dominated Bulgaria which had been created at the end of the Russo-Turkish War of 1877–78 and thus reassured Austria.

The crisis showed how difficult it was to maintain good relations with both Russia and Austria when their interests were in conflict in the Balkans. In the Congress of Berlin Bismarck had backed Austria, but this created the risk of driving Russia into an alliance with France. Over the next years he created a complex web of agreements to deal with this problem.

These agreements show how Bismarck put into practice the principles outlined at the beginning of this section.

- 1879 The Dual Alliance with Austria – a secret defensive alliance which was the cornerstone of German diplomacy until 1918.
- 1881 The Dreikaiserbund (League of Three Emperors) – a looser agreement with Austria and Russia in which all three promised not to help a fourth power (presumably France) in a war against one of the others. The agreement was renewed in 1884 but lapsed in 1887.
- 1882 The Triple Alliance – a defensive alliance with Austria and Italy.
- 1887 The Reinsurance Treaty with Russia. Germany and Russia promised to remain neutral in a war involving the other unless Germany attacked France or Russia attacked Austria-Hungary. This agreement was made because of the Balkan Crisis of 1885–87.

> **KEY POINT**
>
> Bismarck's diplomacy was extremely skilful but the system was so complex that it was bound to break down. The conflict of interest between Austria and Russia in the Balkans made an alliance system involving both unsustainable.

KEY DATES

1871–90	Bismarck Chancellor of the German Empire
1873–75	May Laws
1878	Anti-Socialist Law
1879	Introduction of tariffs; break with the Liberals; Dual Alliance – Germany and Austria
1881	Dreikaiserbund – Germany, Austria and Russia
1882	Triple Alliance – Germany, Austria and Italy
1887	Reinsurance Treaty – Germany and Russia
1888	Death of William I; accession of William II

You should be able to explain the significance of each of these dates.

10.4 William II

After studying this section you should be able to:

LEARNING SUMMARY

- *assess the impact of economic change on German life and politics*
- *explain the political structures and the role of the Kaiser in Wilhelmine Germany*
- *evaluate the political influence of the agrarian and industrial élites and the army*
- *give an account of the development of the Weltpolitik and its effect on Germany's foreign relations*
- *explain the relationship between foreign policy and domestic politics*
- *analyse the causes of the First World War from c.1890*

The economy

AQA ▸ M1

Germany's economic growth was an important reason for fears that it was a threat to the balance of power, especially after 1890.

In the period after 1870 Germany's economy developed very rapidly, so that by 1914 its industrial strength rivalled and in some spheres overtook Britain's. By 1914 coal production, which had quadrupled since 1870, almost equalled that of Britain, while iron and steel production was higher. The rail network trebled in extent between 1870 and 1910. Newer industries, such as electrical engineering and chemicals, expanded rapidly. By 1914 Germany's merchant navy was the second largest in the world after Britain's. Behind this growth was an equally impressive expansion of the financial sector.

Industrialisation was accompanied by urbanisation. Germany's population increased by 65 per cent between 1870 and 1914, from 41 million to 68 million. At the same time there was considerable internal migration from the countryside to the towns, many of which doubled or trebled in size. Migrants to the towns were attracted by the hope of employment and higher wages and undoubtedly wages did rise, reflecting the growth of the economy. Nevertheless, many of the new town-dwellers found themselves living in slums, working long hours in poor conditions and liable to periodic unemployment.

Economic change had political consequences. The rise of the Socialist Party, which had caused Bismarck so much concern, was closely linked to the growth of an urban proletariat.

> Industrialisation created unresolved social and political tensions in Wilhelmine Germany.
>
> **KEY POINT**

The structure of politics

AQA ▶ M1

It would be a good idea to revise the description of the imperial constitution on page 113.

The Reichstag and the political parties

The imperial constitution of 1871 made the Chancellor responsible to the Kaiser and not to the Reichstag. German Chancellors, unlike British Prime Ministers, did not owe their position to their ability to command a majority in parliament (the Reichstag). The Reichstag did not have the power to remove the Chancellor, nor did the defeat of a government measure in the Reichstag force him to resign. It did, however, have the power to veto legislation and it controlled the non-military part of the imperial budget. The Chancellor therefore needed to try to gain the support of enough parties or groups to approve his policies.

The divisions in German society, reflected in the Reichstag, made this difficult. The most notable development in the Reichstag in the reign of William II was the steady

The Socialists.

rise of the Socialist Party. In the 1890 election – after the lapse of Bismarck's anti-Socialist law – it gained 20 per cent of the votes; by 1912 this had risen to 35 per cent. In that year it gained 110 seats, even though the electoral system was weighted against urban voters. It was therefore the biggest party. Other groups with a significant presence in the Reichstag were the Catholic Centre Party, the

The Conservatives.

Liberals (divided into National Liberals and Progressives) and the Conservatives. Because of social changes in the 1890s support for the Conservatives declined. At the same time small right-wing, anti-Semitic fringe parties gained seats in the Reichstag. The Conservatives responded by adopting anti-Semitic policies themselves after 1900, along with strong support for protection of agriculture.

Pressure groups and the political élites

Because of the relative powerlessness of the Reichstag, much of the political activity of Wilhelmine Germany took place outside the parliamentary system. Pressure groups played an important part.

The Weltpolitik is explained on page 118

- The Pan-German League (founded 1891) built up support for William II's Weltpolitik.

The naval expansion programme is explained on page 119

- The Navy League (1891) helped to drum up enthusiasm for Tirpitz's programme of naval expansion.
- The Army League (1912) put pressure on the Reichstag to pass the army bills of 1912–13.

- The Agrarian League (1893), campaigned for protection for agriculture. Its success in mobilising peasant discontent played an important part in the radicalisation of the Conservative Party.

Much political influence was wielded by three powerful interest groups.

Examples are Krupp and Stumm.

- Agrarian interests. The Prussian Junkers (landed gentry) had a disproportionate political influence. The Prussian parliament was elected on a system which favoured them and allowed them to control the government of Prussia. Since Prussia was the largest state in the Empire, the Junkers controlled the Bundesrat (Federal Council), which consisted of representatives of the states. They used their power to block political reform and to protect the interests of agriculture.

Socialism and protection were two of the main issues in Wilhelmine politics.

- Industrialists. Industrialisation led to the emergence of a powerful and wealthy group of big industrialists. They supported William II's Weltpolitik as a means of securing markets for Germany's manufactures and sources of raw materials and provided the finance for the Pan-German League and the Navy League. They supported Tirpitz's plans for expansion of the navy because it would underpin the Weltpolitik and at the same time the appeal to German nationalism would divert support from the Socialists. Opposition to socialism united the industrialists and the landowners and this combination was one of the cornerstones of politics in the period. But there were also tensions between them over the issue of protection.
- The army. Members of the army swore loyalty exclusively to the Kaiser. William took his role as head of the army very seriously. The court was full of generals. Many historians argue that the army leaders, and especially Moltke, the Chief of the General Staff, had more influence than the Chancellor in 1914.

> **KEY POINT**
>
> The political structures of the German Empire were not democratic. Power lay with the agrarian and industrial elites, the army and the bureaucracy.

William II and his ministers

AQA ▸ M1

The Kaiser

In 1888 William I died. After the brief reign of Frederick III, William II succeeded as Kaiser at the age of 29. He was vain, neurotic and unpredictable. He was convinced of Germany's world-historic mission. Despite his relationship with Queen Victoria, he was anti-British, although at the same time he admired Britain.

It was because the system was autocratic that the Kaiser's character mattered so much.

William was an autocrat at the head of an autocratic system. Under the 1871 constitution the Kaiser appointed the Chancellor and thus was in ultimate control. William I had allowed Bismarck to carry on the government with relatively little interference. William II was determined to use his powers personally and exercised a much more direct control over government than his grandfather. As he was also head of the army his personal power was very considerable.

Note how many of William's Chancellors were forced to resign by the Kaiser.

A famous Punch cartoon described this as 'dropping the pilot'.

The significance of this quickly became apparent. William disagreed with Bismarck about the anti-Socialist policies, colonial expansion and relations with Russia. In 1890 Bismarck retired 'because of his health'.

Chancellors

There were four Chancellors between 1890 and 1914.

- Caprivi (1890–94) shared William II's views on the anti-Socialist laws and the alliance with Russia, both of which were allowed to lapse. But William became alarmed by the growth of the Socialist Party and after a series of intrigues, Caprivi was forced to resign.

> Hohenlohe was backed by industrial interests.

- Prince Hohenlohe (1894–1900) was an elderly and rather weak Chancellor. The real power lay with the Kaiser, whose direct interventions in government were increasingly frequent. From 1897 he often by-passed Hohenlohe and gave his confidence to Bülow (Foreign Secretary) and Tirpitz (Secretary for the Navy).

> This meant distracting the German people from social issues by using foreign policy to display Germany's power.

- Bülow (1900–09) pursued a policy of 'social imperialism', appealing to nationalistic fervour and enthusiasm for the naval building programme. He hoped by this to win the electorate from support for the Socialist and Liberal parties. In this he had some success but at the cost of growing budget deficits. His parliamentary support, the 'Bülow bloc', broke up over his tax proposals in 1908. At the same time William II's *Daily Telegraph* interview led to an open rift between the Kaiser and the Chancellor, who resigned in 1909.

> Another Chancellor forced out by the Kaiser!

- Bethmann-Hollweg (1909–17) faced continued financial crisis, though he was able to secure the passing of the army bills in 1912–13. When the Socialists emerged as the largest party in the Reichstag in 1912, it became increasingly difficult to achieve stable parliamentary majorities. The Chancellor was therefore dependent on the emperor and the army.

> Chancellors had to manoeuvre between the Kaiser, the political parties in the Reichstag, the élites and the army. In 1914 the crucial decisions were made by the Kaiser and the army leaders
>
> **KEY POINT**

Foreign policy

AQA M1

William quickly abandoned Bismarck's policy of keeping on good terms with both Austria and Russia. The Reinsurance Treaty with Russia was not renewed in 1890 and by 1893 Russia and France had formed an alliance. Thus the isolation of France, which Bismarck had seen as vital to Germany's security, ended.

Weltpolitik

At the heart of William's foreign policy was his 'Weltpolitik' (world policy), a term first used in 1896. Germany demanded a place 'in the sun' and that nothing should be settled 'without the intervention of Germany'. In practice this meant (a) colonial expansion; (b) building up the navy; and (c) the extension of German influence in the Balkans.

Colonies and Anglo-German relations

William's colonial ambitions were focused mainly on China and Africa. In China there was tension with Britain when Germany occupied Kiaochow. However, Germany co-operated with Britain and other western powers in suppressing the Boxer Rebellion (1900) and opening up China to trade.

Perhaps more important in the short term, especially for relations with Britain, was German interest in Africa. William's telegram to President Kruger of the Transvaal on the defeat of the Jameson Raid in 1896 caused friction with Britain and began the process by which Britain joined the Triple Entente. At this stage Britain was not aligned with any of the great powers and it seemed likely that, if she did seek an ally, it would be Germany. A number of approaches by Britain were, however, rebuffed, the last one in 1901. William appears to have been over-confident that Britain would ultimately join the Triple Alliance on his terms. The anti-British attitude of the German press during the Boer War did not improve relations. Britain, therefore, sought an alternative route out of its diplomatic isolation. In 1902 it made an alliance with Japan and in 1904 an entente with France.

> You should also note the effects of the Navy Laws on Anglo-German relations at this time.

> Germany did have a legitimate interest in Morocco but William undermined his case by exaggeration.

William next tried to undermine the Anglo-French Entente by visiting Tangier to uphold German interests in Morocco. William and Bülow demanded a conference on the future of Morocco. When it met at Algeciras in 1906, only Austria supported Germany. Morocco was left under French influence. Germany's clumsy diplomacy had strengthened the Anglo-French Entente. The Anglo-Russian Entente of 1907 completed the alliance system.

German diplomacy failed to repair relations with Britain in the period 1907–14:

- In 1908 William II's *Daily Telegraph* interview antagonised British public opinion.
- The second Morocco crisis (1911), when the German gunboat *Panther* was sent to Agadir, provoked Lloyd George to threaten war. Germany backed down, though with some 'compensation' in the Congo. The crisis strengthened the Anglo-French Entente and led to the Anglo-French Naval Agreement of 1912.

The naval race

> Public opinion in Britain could only view it as a threat to its naval supremacy, on which its security depended.

The German Naval Laws (1898 and 1900) began the naval race between Germany and Britain. Tirpitz argued that Germany needed an expanded navy to make it a world power and to compete with Britain. With the backing of the Navy League he succeeded in whipping up great enthusiasm for his programme. But it was also a major cause of friction with Britain. The race accelerated after 1906, when the *Dreadnought* was launched, and continued unabated up to the outbreak of war. Haldane's mission to Berlin in 1912 to propose a cut in the naval building programme was unsuccessful and Churchill's suggestion of a 'naval holiday' in 1913 was also rejected. Germany was only willing to limit naval building if Britain agreed unconditionally to remain neutral in a continental war, which was unacceptable to Britain. It was in these circumstances that Britain made the 1912 Anglo-French Naval Agreement: Britain was to concentrate its naval strength in the North Sea and France in the Mediterranean.

> This brought Britain and France close to being allies who would be obliged to help each other in a war.

> **KEY POINT**
>
> William's diplomacy drove Britain into the Triple Entente and did little to mend Anglo-German relations. Nevertheless, it was still possible for Germany and Britain to cooperate, as they did over the Balkan Wars in 1912–13.

The Balkans

The Balkans, 1913

Bismarck had no great ambition to expand German influence in the Balkans but he was concerned about the danger of war between Austria and Russia. This led to the formation in 1879 of the Dual Alliance with Austria, which was the cornerstone of German foreign policy from 1879 to 1914.

In William II's reign a new complication arose. Germany was developing its own interests in the Balkans through economic penetration. Thus the expansion of German influence in the Balkans became part of William's Weltpolitik. This produced a conflict of interest between Germany and Russia. The Berlin–Baghdad railway project, which William promoted by visiting Constantinople and winning concessions from the Sultan, was a symbol of this conflict.

In 1908 Balkan tensions boiled over when Austria annexed Bosnia, which was technically still part of the Ottoman Empire, though Austria had ruled it since 1878. This outraged Serbia, since there was a substantial Serbian population in Bosnia, and it looked to Russia for help. Russia, however, was unable to do anything since William made it clear that Germany would back Austria in the event of war. Russia was snubbed and Serbia became a bitter enemy of Austria.

In 1912 the First Balkan War broke out. The Balkan League, consisting of Serbia, Greece, Montenegro and Bulgaria, captured most of Turkey's remaining territory in Europe. Austria was alarmed that Serbia would become too powerful and especially that it would gain an outlet to the sea in Albania. There was a real danger that Austria and Russia would be drawn into the conflict and that a general war would result. The great powers called a peace conference in London, in which Germany, supported by Britain, insisted that Albania should be independent. The remaining territory conquered from Turkey was carved up between the victors. Disappointed in its hopes for Albania, Serbia occupied part of Macedonia, which was claimed by Bulgaria. This resulted in the Second Balkan War in 1913, in which Bulgaria went to war with her former allies. Bulgaria lost some of her gains, but once again Britain and Germany co-operated to prevent the war escalating.

The Bosnian Crisis.

Work out carefully the role of Serbia from 1908 to 1914.

The Balkan Wars.

> The outcome of the Balkan Wars was to strengthen Serbia. Austria feared an eventual attack on Bosnia by a militant Serbia. This might herald the break-up of the multi-national Austrian Empire. Austria was therefore determined to weaken Serbia.
>
> **KEY POINT**

War between Austria and Serbia was almost inevitable. What was not inevitable was that such a war should lead to a general European war. The assassination of Franz Ferdinand at Sarajevo provided Austria with the excuse to crush Serbia. Austria consulted Germany before issuing an ultimatum. It is unlikely that it would have taken such a strong line but for the fact that William gave the Austrian Chancellor a 'blank cheque' – a promise of German help without conditions.

Think about this when considering Germany's responsibility for the war.

Events then unfolded with dramatic speed

23 July	Austrian ultimatum to Serbia.
25 July	Serbia replied, accepting most but not all of the terms.
28 July	Austria declared war on Serbia. Russia could not allow herself to be humiliated again by failing to back Serbia, as in 1908.
30 July	Russian mobilisation was ordered.
31 July	Germany issued an ultimatum to Russia to stop mobilisation.
1 August	Germany declared war on Russia and activated the Schlieffen Plan.
2 August	Germany issued an ultimatum to Belgium.
3 August	Germany declared war on France.
4 August	German troops invaded Belgium. Britain declared war on Germany.

It was very difficult for Russia to do this in a short period of time.

You should be able to explain the significance of each of these dates.

1888	Accession of William II
1890	Retirement of Bismarck
1890–94	Caprivi Chancellor
1894–1900	Hohenlohe Chancellor
1898	First German Naval Law
1900-9	Bülow Chancellor
1904–05	First Moroccan Crisis, ending in the Algeciras Conference
1908	Bosnian Crisis
1909–17	Bethmann-Hollweg Chancellor
1911	Second Moroccan Crisis (Agadir Crisis)
1912–13	Balkan Wars
1914	Assassination at Sarajevo; outbreak of First World War

KEY DATES

Sample question and model answer

The unification of Germany

Study the following source and then answer the questions which follow.

From a report of an interview given by Bismarck to Karl Schurz, an American politician, on 28 January 1868 and published in 1908

We shall have that war with France. Do not believe that I love war. I know enough about war to detest it. But this war with France will surely come. It will be forced on us by the French Emperor. I do not think he is personally eager for war but the precariousness of his situation will drive him to it. By my reckoning the crisis will come in about two years. Of course we have to be ready for it – and we are. We shall win and the result will be just the contrary of what Napoleon aims at – the total unification of Germany except Austria and probably also Napoleon's downfall.

(a) What, according to the source, was Bismarck's attitude towards the possibility of war with France? [5]

Quote from the source and explain why he expected it.

He did not want it but was sure it would happen. He was prepared for it and confident of victory.

(b) Why did relations between Prussia and France deteriorate between 1866 and 1870? [7]

Focus on cause and effect.

• Public opinion in France regarded Prussia's victory over Austria in 1866 as a defeat for France. French foreign policy aimed to prevent the emergence of a major power in Germany: in 1866–67 Prussia emerged as such a power. Napoleon had miscalculated – he had expected a long war between Prussia and Austria which would weaken both.

• He had also been taken in by Bismarck when he met him at Biarritz. When he sought the compensation he thought Bismarck had agreed to, Bismarck revealed his designs to the world. Napoleon was forced to back down – a further humiliation.

• Consequently Napoleon was looking to restore French prestige and tried to use the Hohenzollern candidature for the Spanish throne to achieve this. Bismarck, sensing that war was inevitable eventually, used the Ems telegram to provoke it.

(c) What was the impact of the Franco-Prussian War on the political arrangements Bismarck had imposed on Germany after the Seven Weeks' War in 1866? [18]

Explain the changes of 1866–67 in detail.

After the Seven Weeks' War, the North German Confederation was set up. Austria was excluded and the south German states (Bavaria, Baden and Württemberg) were linked to Prussia by military alliances and a customs union. The Franco–Prussian War aroused nationalist enthusiasm throughout Germany and the South German states joined Prussia in the war. As a result there was irresistible pressure for them to join with the North German Confederation to form the German Empire.

Explain cause and effect.

Explain in detail.

The new Empire was basically an enlarged version of the North German Confederation. Its constitution was very similar. William I was Emperor, Bismarck Chancellor. It was federal: the member states retained their kings and governments. Prussia dominated the Empire. Through the Bundesrat, which represented the states, Prussia could block any unwelcome proposals.

Practice examination questions

1 Read the following source and then answer the questions which follow.

From *The Cambridge Illustrated History of Germany* by M. Kitchen, 1996

Persecution of the Church only served to strengthen the Centre Party and was opposed by most Conservatives. By 1875 Bismarck had begun to realise that the Kulturkampf had been a serious mistake.

(a) Explain what you understand by the term 'Kulturkampf' in relation to Bismarck's domestic policy as Chancellor of the German Empire. [3]

(b) Explain why Bismarck embarked on the Kulturkampf from 1871. [7]

(c) How successful were Bismarck's policies towards opposition in the German Empire from 1871 to 1890? [18]

2 (a) Explain the foreign policy aims of Bismarck from 1871 to 1890. [10]

(b) Compare the success of Bismarck's policies towards France, Russia and Austria in the period from 1871 to 1890. [20]

3 Read the following statement and then answer the questions which follow.

In 1906–07 two significant developments occurred. With the launch of the *Dreadnought* in 1906 the naval race entered a new phase. The formation of the Triple Entente in 1907 produced in Germany a 'fear of encirclement'.

(a) With reference to international relations in the early twentieth century, explain 'the Triple Entente'. [3]

(b) Why did Germany pursue a programme of naval expansion between 1898 and 1914? [7]

(c) Do you agree or disagree with the view that Germany's policies in North Africa and the Balkans between 1905 and 1913 were unwise and provocative? Explain your answer. [15]

Chapter 11

Italy, 1919–45

The following topics are covered in this chapter:

- The rise of Fascism
- The Fascist Dictatorship

- Mussolini's Italy
- Foreign affairs

11.1 The rise of Fascism

After studying this section you should be able to:

- analyse the problems faced by Italy at the end of the First World War
- explain Mussolini's rise to power

LEARNING SUMMARY

Italy at the end of the First World War

AQA	M1, M3
EDEXCEL	M2
OCR	M3
WJEC	M1
NICCEA	M2

See the map on page 101.

Italy was in poor shape at the end of the First World War. Its military record had been mixed. After entering on the Allied side in 1915, its armies were heavily defeated at Caporetto (1917) by the Austrians and Germans, who then advanced almost as far as Venice. This disaster, however, produced a spirit of national resistance and in 1918 the Italians defeated the Austrians at Vittorio Veneto. Austria was forced to seek an armistice. In view of this, the Italians were bitterly disappointed by the peace settlement. They gained South Tyrol, Trentino, Trieste and part of Istria but their claims to the remainder of Istria, part of Dalmatia and a protectorate over Albania were rejected. All of these had been promised by the Allies in the Treaty of London when Italy entered the war. Particularly galling was the failure to get Fiume, the population of which was largely Italian. Italy was also disappointed that it gained none of the former German colonies. It seemed small reward for the loss of nearly 700 000 men.

The economy

The Italian economy was weak even before the war. Because of the lack of coal and minerals, industrial development was slow. Agriculture was backward and peasants' standards of living were low, especially in the south. The war made matters worse: the total cost was as much as Italian government expenditure in the previous 50 years. Italy had to borrow heavily from the USA. Inflation became a serious problem, affecting the middle classes particularly badly as their savings were virtually wiped out. The end of wartime production led to widespread unemployment, which was added to by the demobilisation of 2.5 million soldiers. Many unemployed ex-servicemen joined the various para-military organisations which sprang up. Others resorted to banditry. Lawlessness was rife.

These were the sources of Mussolini's fascist fighting groups.

The political system

Thus the results of unification had been profoundly disappointing.

Italy's parliamentary democracy was discredited and failed to cope with Italy's post-war problems. In the half-century from the unification of Italy in 1859–60 to the First World War, governments had managed parliament by a system of bribery and corruption. This was known as 'transformism'. Regional differences, particularly between the north and the south, were strong and worked against the growth of truly national parties. Disagreements about whether Italy should enter the war added a further source of political division. There were many small parties in parliament and the introduction of proportional representation in 1919 made matters worse. The two largest parties, the Socialists and the Catholic Popular Party, were unable to co-operate and it was therefore impossible to form stable ministries. Between 1918 and 1922 there were five different governments.

> Many Italians thought that what Italy most needed was strong government rather than democracy.

Gabriele d'Annunzio

The weakness of the government was dramatically illustrated in 1919–20 when the poet Gabriele d'Annunzio with a band of nationalists and ex-soldiers in a uniform of black shirts captured Fiume and held it for eighteen months. The government could not support this venture, as d'Annunzio was acting in defiance of the peace settlement; neither could it oppose him since public opinion regarded him as a national hero. Eventually it had to send troops to remove d'Annunzio and his followers and Fiume became an international free city. The episode was a lesson to Mussolini in the use of force to achieve nationalistic ends.

Mussolini's rise to power

AQA	M1, M3
EDEXCEL	M2
OCR	M3
WJEC	M1
NICCEA	M2

By these tactics the Fascists helped to create disorder and then claimed that Fascism stood for the restoration of law and order by strong government.

The combination of weak government, anger at the peace settlement and social unrest made the period 1918–22 chaotic. Strikes, riots and lawlessness became widespread. The appearance of factory councils and leagues of farm workers aroused fears of a communist revolution. The anti-communists responded by forming armed bands, of which the most important were the *Fasci di combattimento* (fighting groups) formed in Milan in 1919 by Mussolini. Mussolini's message was that Italy needed strong government. Fascist groups were formed throughout Italy and began attacking socialists and communists. In 1921 Mussolini founded the National Fascist Party. He won the support of landowners and industrialists, who began to finance the party. In the general election of 1921 the Fascists won 35 seats.

A general strike in 1922 provided Mussolini with the chance to gain power. The Fascists helped to defeat the strike by taking control of public buildings and organising street battles with the socialists. Meanwhile the government stood by, apparently helpless, and failed to take on the socialists. In October 1922 Mussolini organised a 'march on Rome' (by train!) by 30 000 fascists. The Prime Minister, Facta, wanted to use the army and police to disperse them but King Victor Emmanuel III refused and instead invited Mussolini to form a government.

> Mussolini was invited to take office merely by threatening the use of force. At the time his party had only 35 MPs.

11.2 The Fascist Dictatorship

After studying this section you should be able to:

- *explain how Mussolini established himself as a dictator*
- *account for his success in doing so*
- *analyse the basic ideas of Fascism*

LEARNING SUMMARY

The consolidation of Mussolini's power, 1922–25

EDEXCEL	M2
OCR	M3
WJEC	M2
NICCEA	M2

When Mussolini became Prime Minister, he formed a coalition with only four Fascists in the government. But he also persuaded parliament to grant him dictatorial powers for a year. This enabled him to place Fascists in key positions in local government and the police. In 1923 a new electoral law (the Acerbo Law) provided that the party that gained most votes in a general election should have two-thirds of the seats in the Chamber of Deputies. The other parties agreed to this because they wanted to end the political paralysis that had afflicted the parliamentary system since 1918. In the election of 1924, the Fascists and their allies easily achieved the necessary number of votes. The election was marked by a good deal of violence, with the Fascist blackshirts destroying the printing presses of opposition newspapers and beating up socialists in the streets. Even so, 2.5 million votes were cast against the Fascists.

This is another example of the Fascists promoting disorder while claiming to be the party that would restore law and order.

The murder of Matteotti.

Shortly afterwards Matteotti, who had publicly blamed Mussolini for the violence in the election campaign, was murdered. Public opinion was outraged and there were demands for Mussolini's dismissal. When the king refused to dismiss him, opposition members left parliament, leaving Mussolini in control. This was known as the Aventine Secession. It was a mistake as it left Mussolini in complete control of parliament.

In 1925 he took advantage of the situation to establish himself as dictator. All other parties were banned, non-fascists removed from the government and opposition newspapers taken over. In December 1925 Mussolini became responsible to the king and not to parliament, and at the same time the king's right to appoint or dismiss ministers was taken away. In January 1926 Mussolini gained the power to make laws by decree.

> These changes made parliament a consultative body and Mussolini a dictator.
>
> KEY POINT

Why was Mussolini able to establish a Fascist dictatorship?

EDEXCEL	M2
OCR	M3
WJEC	M2
NICCEA	M2

Probably the most important reason was the virtual breakdown of parliamentary government between 1918 and 1922. For this the leaders of the existing parliamentary parties bear much of the responsibility. The Prime Ministers of the period 1918–22, unable to provide effective government, came to rely on the Fascist paramilitary bands as a counterweight to the left-wing paramilitaries who seemed to threaten Italy with revolution. Giolitti, the Liberal Prime Minister in 1921–22, actually encouraged the Fascists by including them in his list of government candidates in the 1921 election, with the result that 35 Fascists were elected.

The socialists, the biggest party after the 1919 election, refused to co-operate with other parties and this was a major reason why no stable government could be formed. Furthermore, the socialists split in 1921 when the Communist Party was formed. This made the parliamentary situation even more complicated and the street battles between the various paramilitary bands even more frequent.

Support for the Fascists

In these circumstances Mussolini won the backing of important groups who were afraid of a communist revolution, including:

The formation of the Communist Party, which had an openly revolutionary programme, alarmed the landowners, industrialists and middle classes.

- landowners, who welcomed Fascist attacks on leagues of farm workers
- industrialists, who similarly welcomed their attacks on the trade unions
- the middle classes, who had lost their savings in the wartime inflation and feared that a communist revolution would reduce them to the level of the working classes
- the Catholic Church, which saw a communist revolution as a major threat; Mussolini, formerly an atheist, went out of his way in 1921–22 to court the support of the papacy
- the royal family. Mussolini abandoned his earlier republican views. The King, while not giving open approval to Mussolini, helped to bring him to power by refusing to allow the army to be used against him.

Don't underestimate Mussolini. He created the Fascist Party and gained power in three years.

Mussolini himself played an important part. Not only did he found the Fascist Party and gain it a foothold in parliament, but he also provided leadership. At this stage in his career he had presence and the ability to project himself both by his oratory and his journalistic skills.

Fascist ideas

Fascism had no coherent philosophy. Mussolini's changing political views (he was a socialist and a republican before the war) suggest that his main aim was simply to get power. Fascism did, however, have some basic ideas.

- It stood for strong, centralised government (the name Fascist was derived from an ancient Roman symbol of authority).
- It placed great emphasis on the cult of the leader: Fascist propaganda depicted Mussolini (Il Duce) as a hero.
- It taught the subordination of the interests of the individual to the state.
- It was anti-democratic (hence a one-party state) and anti-communist.
- It aimed for economic self-sufficiency (autarchy).
- It emphasised national pride.

11.3 Mussolini's Italy

After studying this section you should be able to:

- *analyse the political structure of Fascist Italy*
- *discuss the effectiveness of the methods adopted by Mussolini to control opinion*
- *explain the relations between Mussolini and the Catholic Church*
- *explain the economic policies adopted by Mussolini and assess their success*
- *discuss the effects of Fascist policies for the Italian people*

LEARNING SUMMARY

The Fascist State

OCR	M3
WJEC	M2
NICCEA	M2

 Mussolini seems to have believed in his own propaganda about his unique abilities.

At the heart of the Fascist state was Mussolini – Il Duce (the leader). Much emphasis was placed on the cult of the Duce. Mass rallies were organised to glorify Mussolini and the media were harnessed to propaganda. With the power to make laws by decree, he was a dictator. He alone appointed ministers, and he was personally in charge of a number of ministries. Since all other parties were abolished, the electoral system was changed in 1928 so that electors could only accept (or, in theory, reject) a list 400 candidates drawn up by the Fascist Grand Council.

The Grand Council itself was the centrepiece of Mussolini's **Corporate State**. It consisted of representatives from each of the corporations Mussolini set up to organise workers and employers. In 1938 the Chamber of Fasces and Corporations replaced the Chamber of Deputies (Parliament). It had little real power, however. It only met when Mussolini summoned it. He played off its members against one another and made sure that it did what he wanted. Thus Mussolini ensured that his authority was not challenged by the Fascist Party. No party élite grew up.

The system was not, however, a thoroughgoing dictatorship like that of Hitler or Stalin. Much of the existing machinery of government remained in operation. At local level the prefects continued to be in charge and the local Party officials were subordinated to them. The monarchy, the army and the police all remained. In central government Mussolini's reforms simply made the administration more complicated and less efficient.

> Mussolini's Italy was a totalitarian state but his dictatorship was less repressive than those of Germany and the USSR. His secret police and the Special Tribunal for the Defence of the State were less active and less ruthless than similar institutions in other dictatorships.
>
> KEY POINT

The control of opinion

Much effort was devoted to developing the cult of the Duce through the media and education, but with only partial success. Newspapers and books were strictly censored and the radio was state-controlled. The media churned out government propaganda. The government regarded the film industry as important and tried to regulate it to serve its propaganda purposes, but its control was limited. Similarly the Ministry of Popular Culture failed to impose its ideas of Fascist culture in the spheres of literature, music and art.

Education and youth.

Education was closely supervised. University teachers had to take an oath of loyalty to Mussolini. Schoolteachers had to be party members. Textbooks were rewritten to glorify the Fascist state. State interference in education intensified from 1936 when textbooks became a state monopoly. Even so, it was not wholly effective, especially in universities, where the historian Croce and others continued to criticise the regime. The indoctrination of the young was also pursued through fascist youth groups which encouraged hero-worship of Mussolini and glorified war. Members often became enthusiastic fascists but 40 per cent of Italy's youth did not join them.

Anti-Semitism

Anti-Semitism was not a part of fascist ideology at first, but in 1938 Mussolini reversed his previously tolerant attitude to the Jews. Decrees were issued prohibiting inter-marriage between Jews and non-Jews and removing Jews from important positions. This was probably because Mussolini wished to compete with Hitler by emphasising Italy's racial purity. It was unpopular and was condemned by the Pope.

Church and State

One of Mussolini's successes was the **Lateran Treaty** (1929). The Papacy had refused to recognise the State of Italy since 1870. Mussolini realised the value of the support of the Catholic Church. By the Treaty he recognised the Vatican City as a sovereign state and paid for lands taken from the Papal States during the process of unification before 1871. Catholicism was recognised as the official state religion. Bishops and priests were to receive state salaries and religious education was made compulsory in schools.

> Overall, Mussolini's dictatorship was not very efficient in improving Italy's administration or in imposing cultural and educational conformity. **KEY POINT**

The economy

OCR — M3
WJEC — M2
NICCEA — M2

The Corporate State

The central feature of Mussolini's economic policy was the creation of the Corporate State. Corporations were set up for each industry or occupation. They replaced trade unions, which were abolished, and consisted of representatives of employers and workers. In 1926 thirteen corporations were set up under a Minister of Corporations. In 1934 they were reorganised into twenty-two corporations and in 1938 the whole system was tied into the political structure when the Chamber of Deputies was replaced by a Chamber of Fasces and Corporations. The aim of the Corporate State was to replace the capitalist system, in which employers and labour were often in conflict, with a system of co-operation. Strikes were therefore forbidden and the Corporations were empowered to draw up labour contracts and settle labour disputes. It was, however, an inefficient system. It favoured the employers, with whom the government was closely allied. The labour contracts were, therefore, often weighted against the workers.

> Notice how complicated the system was.

> Nor did it prevent industrial unrest in the 1930s.

> Note the emphasis on state intervention in the economy.

The other main features of Mussolini's economic policies were as follows.

- Public works schemes were introduced to reduce unemployment. Motorways, blocks of flats, sports stadiums and schools were built. Railways were electrified. But many projects were not completed and a lot of money disappeared through corruption.
- Government subsidies were provided to develop industry. In 1933 the IRI (Institute for Industrial Reconstruction) was set up. Industrial production increased: iron and steel production was doubled, as was production of hydroelectric power. But Italy still remained industrially weaker than the other European great powers, with low productivity and high costs.
- A programme of land reclamation was started, the most famous result being the draining of the Pontine Marshes near Rome.

> This was only partly Mussolini's fault. Italy's economy was relatively weak before he came to power.

129

- In the 'Battle for Grain', farmers were subsidised to produce more wheat. The aim was self-sufficiency. Wheat production doubled between 1922 and 1939. But to achieve this, land which would have been better suited to dairy or fruit farming was given over to wheat. Agriculture remained backward and consequently the south remained poverty-stricken.
- Mussolini regarded maintaining the value of the lira as a matter of national prestige. Unfortunately it was revalued at too high a level in 1926 and this led to a loss of exports. Even before the Great Depression many workers suffered wage cuts as a result. The Depression made matters worse: unemployment rose and Mussolini tried to defend the lira by wage cuts. Standards of living fell and discontent grew. In 1936 he finally accepted a devaluation.
- Mussolini believed that a strong Italy needed a bigger population. Large families were encouraged by payment of child benefits and bachelors faced extra taxation. In spite of this the birth rate fell.

> The Italian economy remained comparatively weak in the 1930s. It was slow to recover from the Great Depression.

KEY POINT

The social effects of Fascist policies

Industrialists, big landowners and some of the middle classes benefited from Fascist policies. The Corporate State favoured industrialists, as did government subsidies to industry in the 1930s. The landed gentry were helped by policies which made it difficult for agricultural workers to leave the land and therefore kept agricultural wages down. Many of the middle classes benefited from the expansion of the civil service. Those working in private enterprises, however, did not do so well in the Depression years.

In this respect Fascist Italy compared well with other industrialised countries.

The working classes were worse off. Real wages declined, food prices rose and there was high unemployment, especially in the 1930s. Agricultural workers fared even worse than urban workers, with a fall in real wages of up to 40 per cent in the 1930s. The working classes did, however, benefit from improvements in welfare provision. Pensions and unemployment benefits were increased, more schools were built and medical care was improved.

Finally, the status of women was significantly lowered. Because of Mussolini's obsession with raising the birth rate, the state discouraged women from seeking employment.

11.4 Foreign affairs

After studying this section you should be able to:

- *explain the development of Mussolini's foreign policy*
- *assess how far he was successful in making Italy great*
- *analyse his relationship with Hitler*
- *account for his overthrow in 1943 and subsequent execution*

LEARNING SUMMARY

Foreign policy 1922–39

OCR ▶ M3
NICCEA ▶ M2

Fascism was nationalistic and aimed to make Italy great. It was to be expected that Mussolini would pursue an aggressive foreign policy. He had an early success in the Corfu Incident (1923), when he gained compensation from Greece for the murder of an Italian general on an international commission surveying the border between Greece and Albania. He did this by bombarding Corfu and refusing to recognise the competence of the League of Nations in the matter. In 1924 he gained further prestige in Italy by seizing Fiume. His foreign policy over the next ten years was mainly directed towards counteracting French influence in Eastern Europe and especially Yugoslavia. In the process he made Albania virtually an Italian protectorate.

> Compare this with Hitler's seizure of Austria in 1938.

The rise of Hitler presented Mussolini with a problem. He regarded it as vital to preserve an independent Austria as a buffer between Italy and Germany. When Nazis tried to seize control in Austria in 1934 and murdered the Chancellor, Dollfuss, he moved troops to the Austrian frontier. Hitler abandoned his plans to unite Austria with Germany, at least for the time being. This success boosted Mussolini's prestige. In the following year he joined Britain and France in the Stresa Front to condemn German rearmament.

The Ethiopian War

> Mussolini aimed to divert social unrest by a prestigious victory.

The turning point in Mussolini's foreign policy came in 1935 when he invaded Ethiopia. Italians had felt since the late nineteenth century that they had not got their fair share of colonies in the 'Scramble for Africa'. They had tried unsuccessfully to take over Ethiopia in 1896. Mussolini had already tried to establish economic domination there. He now saw the conquest of Ethiopia as the answer to Italy's economic problems and as a way of boosting his regime at a time when unrest was growing because of the effects of the Great Depression. The diplomatic situation seemed favourable. Britain and France were anxious to keep on good terms with Italy because of their concern about the growing strength of Germany. Mussolini thought they would therefore accept the Italian conquest of Ethiopia without much protest.

> The Hoare-Laval Pact demonstrated how keen Britain and France were to keep on good terms with Mussolini.

The Italian armies had little trouble in taking over Ethiopia, though in the process they used poison gas. The real importance of the episode lay in its effects on Italy's relations with Britain, France and Germany and on the League of Nations. The League declared Italy an aggressor and imposed sanctions, but coal, steel and – most importantly – oil were excluded. The sanctions therefore had little effect on Italy's war effort. The failure to impose effective sanctions was largely because Britain and France were not prepared for war and, as Mussolini had calculated, were anxious to maintain good relations with Italy. For the same reasons they allowed Italy free passage through the Suez Canal, which they controlled. They even proposed, in the Hoare-Laval Pact, to allow Mussolini to keep two-thirds of Ethiopia, but public outrage in Britain and France forced the withdrawal of this plan.

1 Nothing was done to stop Italy completing the conquest of Ethiopia.

2 The League of Nations had been shown to be ineffective.

3 Even the mild sanctions which had been applied angered Mussolini. He withdrew from the League and drew closer to Germany, which had not applied the sanctions.

Mussolini and Hitler, 1936–39

Between 1936 and 1939 Mussolini's relations with Hitler became closer.

- In October 1936 he reached an understanding with Hitler which came to be known as the Rome–Berlin Axis.
- When the Spanish Civil War broke out both Italy and Germany gave military assistance to Franco. Italy's contribution, however, was the greater and it was a serious drain on its military resources. Moreover, Italian involvement widened the breach with Britain and France and increased Mussolini's dependence on Germany.
- In 1937 Italy joined Germany and Japan in the Anti-Comintern Pact.
- When Germany took over Austria in the *Anschluss* (March 1938), Mussolini accepted it without question – a complete reversal of the policy he had pursued in 1934 and one which damaged his prestige in Italy.
- His role at the Munich Conference in September 1938, when he seemed to have played a key part, revived his popularity a little.
- In April 1939, following Hitler's take-over of the rest of Czechoslovakia, Mussolini imitated his aggression by sending troops into Albania. This was unnecessary as Italy already had economic control over Albania. Its main effect was to demonstrate that Italy's armies were not prepared for a full-scale war.
- Although Mussolini made the 'Pact of Steel' with Hitler in May 1939, he stayed out of the Second World War in September.

> Mussolini could not have stopped the *Anschluss* but many Italians thought he should have protested.

> This attempt to keep up with Hitler suggests why he declared war on Britain and France in 1940.

It became increasingly obvious between 1936 and 1939 that Mussolini was the junior partner in the relationship with Hitler.

The fall of Mussolini

> Consider whether Mussolini's regime would have survived if he had stayed out of the war.

By the middle of 1940 Mussolini was convinced that Hitler would win the war and wanted to make sure that Italy would share the spoils. He entered the war in June 1940, just before the fall of France. The war was a disaster for Italy. In 1940 Italian troops invaded Greece and advanced from Libya into Egypt. On both fronts they were driven back and had to be rescued by the Germans. Most of the navy was destroyed by Allied bombing. British troops captured all of Italy's African colonies. The war was unpopular in Italy. Civilian morale quickly dropped as a result of military disasters, food shortages and Allied bombing of Italian cities. In July 1943 Allied troops invaded Sicily from North Africa.

In the same month Mussolini was overthrown and imprisoned. The Fascist Grand Council turned against him and persuaded the king to dismiss him even before the Allied troops crossed to the mainland, which they did in August.

> Mussolini as head of a German puppet government.

The new government surrendered to the Allies in September 1943 but German troops still occupied much of Italy. The Germans captured Mussolini four days later and set him up as the head of a puppet government in northern Italy. It took until April 1945 for the Allies to push the Germans back over the Alps. Mussolini himself was captured by Italian partisans and executed on 28 April 1945.

You should be able to explain the significance of each of these dates.

KEY POINT

Mussolini was directly responsible for Italy's defeat. He went to war in 1940 knowing that Italy could not sustain a prolonged war. The Italian armed forces were ill-equipped and had not made good the losses suffered in the invasion of Ethiopia and the Spanish Civil War. Italy's industrial base was much inferior to that of Britain, let alone the USA.

KEY DATES

1923	Corfu Incident
1935–36	Conquest of Ethiopia
1936	Rome–Berlin Axis
1936–38	Spanish Civil War
1937	Anti-Comintern Pact
1939	Invasion of Albania; Pact of Steel
1940	Declaration of war against Britain and France
1943	Allied invasion of Sicily; Mussolini overthrown, captured by Germans and set up as head of a puppet government
1945	Execution of Mussolini

Sample question and model answer

The consolidation of Mussolini's power.

(a) Explain how Mussolini consolidated his hold on power from 1922 to 1925. [15]

This question requires clear explanation of a sequence of events, showing how they are linked.

- He persuaded parliament to grant him dictatorial powers for a year. This enabled him to place Fascists in key positions in local government and the police.
- The Acerbo Law (1923) provided that the party that gained most votes in a general election should have two-thirds of the seats in the Chamber of Deputies. Violence by the blackshirts helped to ensure that the Fascists and their allies achieved this in the 1924 election.
- The murder of Matteotti nearly brought Mussolini down, but the king refused to dismiss him. This resulted in the Aventine Secession, which left Mussolini in complete control of parliament.
- In 1925 all other parties were banned, non-Fascists removed from the government and opposition newspapers taken over.
- In December 1925 Mussolini became responsible to the king and not to Parliament, and the king's right to appoint or dismiss ministers was taken away. Thus Mussolini was effectively dictator.

(b) Why was there so little opposition to the establishment of a Fascist dictatorship in Italy? [15]

The question requires analysis of support for Mussolini –

Parliamentary government had virtually broken down between 1918 and 1922. There was widespread violence. Many important groups, including landowners, industrialists and the middle classes, began to see Mussolini as a bulwark against a communist revolution. The Catholic Church also saw communism as a threat. Parliament granted Mussolini dictatorial powers in 1922 because MPs saw a strong leader as better than the growing anarchy of 1918–22. In this they probably reflected public opinion. The king, in inviting him to be Prime Minister, was probably right in thinking this was what majority opinion wanted. The main group which

– as well as the opposition.

could have opposed Mussolini were the socialists, but they were divided between democratic socialists and communists.

Practice examination questions

1 Read the following source and answer the questions which follow.

Source

From *The March on Rome* by D. Mack Smith

The 'march on Rome' was a comfortable train ride, followed by a petty demonstration, and all in response to an express invitation from the monarch.

(a) What was the 'march on Rome'? [5]

(b) Explain why King Victor Emmanuel III invited Mussolini to form a government in October 1922. [7]

(c) 'The experience of the years 1918–22 demonstrated that parliamentary democracy was incapable of providing Italy with effective government.' How far do you agree or disagree with this statement? [18]

2 (a) Explain the appeal of fascism to Italians in the 1920s. [10]

(b) Assess the success of Mussolini's economic policies. [20]

Chapter 12

Germany, 1918–45

The following topics are covered in this chapter:

- The Weimar Republic
- The rise of Hitler, 1930–33
- Nazi Germany, 1933–39

12.1 The Weimar Republic

After studying this section you should be able to:

- account for the establishment of the Weimar Republic
- explain the Weimar constitution
- explain the challenges that the Weimar Republic faced
- account for the currency crisis of 1923 and assess its significance
- explain why the period 1924–29 is called the 'Golden Era of Weimar'

LEARNING SUMMARY

The establishment of the Weimar Republic, 1919–20

AQA	M1, M3
EDEXCEL	M2
OCR	M3
WJEC	M1

Be sure you understand why German nationalists regarded the members of the provisional government as 'the November criminals'.

The November Revolution

In November 1918 the German Empire collapsed in defeat. The generals in command of the army on the Western Front said they could no longer prevent the allied forces advancing into Germany. The navy in Kiel mutinied. The civilian population faced starvation. Germany asked for an armistice. In the November Revolution, the Kaiser abdicated and a provisional government was set up under a Social Democrat, Ebert. In January 1919 a National Assembly was elected which met at Weimar and drew up a new constitution.

> The German people were totally unprepared for defeat. When the armistice was signed, the German armies were still in France and the people did not realise how desperate the military situation was. The generals did not disillusion them.
>
> **KEY POINT**

The Weimar constitution

The main features of Germany's government under the Weimar constitution were:

- The President was elected by the people for a term of office of seven years. His most important function was to appoint the Chancellor, but he also had emergency powers to suspend the constitution and rule by decree. These powers became very important in the early 1930s.
- The Chancellor was normally the leader of the largest party in the Reichstag.
- The Reichstag, elected every four years by universal suffrage and proportional representation, controlled taxation and legislation.
- The Reichstag consisted of representatives of the provinces and had only limited delaying powers.

> The Weimar constitution was highly democratic. Its weakness lay in the system of proportional representation, which had the result that no single party ever gained a majority and therefore all governments were coalitions. As a result there were frequent changes of government.
>
> **KEY POINT**

The circumstances in which the Weimar Republic was set up were not favourable. Many Germans believed that the defeat was caused by a 'stab in the back' by socialists. They argued that the November Revolution had caused the surrender rather than the other way round.

The Republic was further handicapped by being blamed for the Treaty of Versailles. The provisional government only accepted the treaty with great reluctance when it realised that there was no alternative. The treaty was bitterly resented by most Germans because:

> Make sure you can elaborate these points if necessary.

- of the way it was drawn up (the 'diktat');
- of the extensive losses of territory (14 per cent of Germany's land area and all its colonies);
- of the heavy reparations (fixed in 1921 at £6 600 million);
- of the severe limits on the size of the armed forces;
- most of all, the 'War Guilt' clause.

Challenges from Right and Left

At the end of the war, the communists hoped to seize power, as the Bolsheviks had done in Russia a year earlier. During the November Revolution, soviets sprang up all over Germany. An Independent Socialist republic was set up in Bavaria and in January 1919 the Spartacists (communists) attempted a revolution in Berlin. The provisional government had to use the army and the Freikorps – bands of anti-socialist ex-soldiers – to regain control. There was street fighting in Berlin and the Spartacist leaders, Karl Liebknecht and Rosa Luxemburg, were murdered. In Bavaria there was also civil war.

> The Spartacist Rising.

> The Kapp Putsch.

In 1920 in the Kapp Putsch members of the Freikorps attempted to seize power. The putsch was badly organised and soon brought to an end by a general strike in Berlin. Ominously, however, the army refused to come to the aid of the government and few of those responsible for the putsch were punished.

> **KEY POINTS**
> 1 These challenges showed that some Germans were prepared to overthrow democracy by force.
> 2 The government had not been able to overcome its enemies by using its own armed forces.

The currency crisis of 1923

AQA	M1, M3
EDEXCEL	M2
OCR	M3
WJEC	M1
NICCEA	M1

> The French government thought Germany was trying to wriggle out of paying what it owed.

Germany faced severe economic problems at the end of the war with high unemployment and high inflation. The unexpectedly large reparations bill presented in 1921 made matters worse. To pay the reparations, the government printed paper money, resulting in further inflation. In 1923 it defaulted on its reparations payments. France responded by occupying the Ruhr. Passive resistance in the Ruhr brought Germany's greatest industrial area to a standstill. By November 1923 hyperinflation left the mark worthless.

The crisis was defused by Stresemann, who became Chancellor in August 1923. He called off the campaign of passive resistance and dealt effectively with communist attempts in various parts of Germany to take advantage of the situation. In 1924 a new currency, the Rentenmark, was introduced and the Dawes Plan scaled down the annual payments of reparations. The French then withdrew from the Ruhr.

> Hitler's first abortive attempt to seize power.

The crisis also led to the **Beer Hall Putsch** in Munich, when Hitler tried to seize control of the Bavarian government as a prelude to a march on Berlin. However, the army remained loyal to the government, even though General Ludendorff supported Hitler. The rising was suppressed and Hitler was imprisoned.

The 'Golden Era' of Weimar, 1924–29

AQA	M1, M3
EDEXCEL	M2
OCR	M3
NICCEA	M1

> It was also a period of vibrant cultural activity in Germany.

After the troubles of the early 1920s, the period 1924–29 saw Germany emerge into an era of relative stability and prosperity. The economy recovered. With a stable currency, industry entered a period of expansion. Unemployment decreased and living standards rose. The basis of this prosperity was, however, rather shallow, as it depended heavily on foreign loans, beginning with an American loan as part of the Dawes Plan of 1924. The Dawes Plan also reduced Germany's reparations payments and the Young Plan of 1929 rescheduled them over a period of 59 years. Both these plans were negotiated for the Germans by Stresemann, who was Foreign Minister from 1923 to 1929.

> The Locarno Treaties.

Stresemann also restored Germany's position among the great powers. By the Treaties of Locarno (1925) Germany accepted the 1919 frontiers with France and Belgium. They were also guaranteed by Britain and Italy, which gave France greater security. Moreover, unlike the Treaty of Versailles, the Locarno Treaties were negotiated by Germany, not dictated. Treaties were also signed between Germany, Poland and Czechoslovakia, but these did not include guarantees of Germany's eastern frontiers. The restoration of Germany to its position among the great powers was recognised in 1926 when it was admitted to the League of Nations and made a permanent member of the Council of the League. In 1928 it was a signatory of the Kellogg-Briand Pact to outlaw war as an instrument of policy.

> Also the Nationalist Party, led by the press baron Hugenberg after 1928, was strongly anti-Weimar.

Politically, too, there was relative stability. Coalitions came and went but they were all different combinations of moderate parties. In the elections of 1924 and 1928 the extremists gained relatively small numbers of seats. There were, however, some worrying features of the political scene. Despite their small numbers, extremists of right and left were an unsettling influence, engaging in regular street battles.

It proved to be unfortunate that the 1925 presidential election was won by Hindenburg. Though he was much respected as the former German commander on the Western Front in the First World War, he was authoritarian in outlook and had little faith in democracy. He was not the man to defend the Weimar Republic in the crisis which Germany faced in the early 1930s. It was also unfortunate that in 1929, just before Germany was hit by the effects of the Great Depression, Stresemann died.

> You should be able to explain the significance of each of these dates.

1918	November Revolution; armistice
1919	Spartacist rising; Weimar constitution; Treaty of Versailles
1920	Kapp Putsch
1923	Currency crisis; Stresemann Chancellor, then Foreign Minister; Beer Hall Putsch; Hitler imprisoned
1924	Dawes Plan
1925	Locarno Treaties
1926	Germany admitted to the League of Nations
1928	Kellogg-Briand Pact
1929	Young Plan; death of Stresemann

KEY DATES

12.2 The rise of Hitler, 1930–33

The rise of the Nazi Party

AQA · M1
EDEXCEL · M1
OCR · M3
NICCEA · M1

Hitler joined the German Workers' Party in 1919. By 1921 he was its leader and the party had been renamed the National Socialist Party. Hitler quickly became known because of his oratorical gifts, which he used to attack Jews and Communists and to promise the restoration of national pride. Some of the distinctive features of Nazism date from this period – the swastika badge, the use of songs and slogans, the brown shirt uniform of the Sturm-Abteilung (SA), Hitler's private army led by Captain Röhm. Röhm was one of the early recruits to Nazism, as were Goering, Hess and Himmler.

Hitler set out his main ideas in the form of an autobiography of 'My Struggle'.

In the early 1920s the National Socialist Party was one of a number of extremist groups opposed to the Weimar Republic. The currency crisis of 1923 brought a rapid increase in its membership, which prompted Hitler to embark on an attempt to seize power by force – the Beer Hall Putsch (see page 136). The putsch was a rather pathetic failure, but Hitler's subsequent trial gained him national publicity. While in prison afterwards he wrote *Mein Kampf*. After the failure of the putsch, he decided to seek power through elections.

The Nazi Party also gained some respectability by its association with Hugenberg's Nationalist Party in campaigning against the Young Plan.

Support for the Nazis declined after 1924. In the December 1924 elections they won only 14 seats and in 1928 only 12. Nevertheless, there were important developments between 1924 and 1930. Hitler consolidated his hold over the party. Party organisation was greatly strengthened: in each district cells of party extremists were set up under the control of 'gauleiters' appointed by Hitler. The SA was gaining recruits and was conducting an increasingly bitter and violent campaign against communist gangs. The cult of Hitler as the leader developed as he proclaimed the need for strong leadership to save Germany from a Jewish-socialist conspiracy. In 1930, with the Weimar system falling into crisis, his message appealed to many Germans and the Nazis gained 107 seats in the Reichstag.

> Before 1930 the Nazi Party was no more than a small extremist fringe organisation.

KEY POINT

Hitler's beliefs and policies

AQA · M1
EDEXCEL · M1
OCR · M1, M3
WJEC · M2
NICCEA · M1

Hitler's racial theories were based on Social Darwinism which had been popularised in Germany by Houston Stewart Chamberlain. He believed that some races were inherently superior to others. In the highest category were the Aryan races, of which the Germans were the purest example. This was the basis for Hitler's anti-semitism. He believed that the Jews were polluting other races (especially the Germans) by inter-marriage. He accused the Jews of causing the Russian Revolution and of stabbing the German army in the back in 1918. He seems to have believed stories of a Jewish conspiracy to dominate the world.

Hitler's racial theories provided the basis for his nationalist policies – the overthrow of the Treaty of Versailles and the union of all German peoples in a Greater Germany. They also provided a justification for his demand for 'lebensraum' – living space for the Germans, which could only be acquired by conquests in Eastern Europe and Russia. Other important features of Hitler's political outlook were hostility to communism and to democracy. He saw the democracy of the Weimar Republic as a source of weakness and believed that for Germany to regain its greatness it needed a strong leader or Führer.

> Nazi ideas were racist, anti-semitic, nationalist, anti-communist and anti-democratic.
>
> **KEY POINT**

All these ideas appeared in *Mein Kampf*. So too did Hitler's ideas about propaganda and especially the value of the 'big lie'. He made particularly effective use of the myth of 'the stab in the back', which he exploited by labelling the politicians who took over when the Kaiser abdicated 'the November criminals'. The Nazis' propaganda machine was run from 1929 by Goebbels.

Another example was the idea that there was a Jewish conspiracy to dominate the world.

None of Hitler's ideas were original but the policies he advocated appealed to many sections of German society.

- Nazism drew its greatest support from the middle classes. The political weakness of the Weimar Republic led many of the middle classes to look for an alternative to the democratic parties, especially since they feared that weak government might lead to a communist revolution.
- Shopkeepers were attracted by Hitler's promise to help them compete with department stores.
- Peasant farmers were won over by pledges to reduce interest on agricultural debts.
- The working classes on the whole remained loyal to the Socialist Party, but the socialist element in the Nazi programme, which amounted to little more than vague promises of land reform and an attack on profiteering, did win some working-class support.
- Nazism appealed to the nationalist and anti-semitic strands in German society.
- It made a strong impact on the young and particularly young males.
- Support for the Nazis was stronger among Protestants than Catholics.

It was the Great Depression which transformed the Nazi Party into the largest party in the Reichstag. Many of the middle classes, frightened by the growing support for the Communists in the early 1930s, turned to Hitler because of his extreme anti-communist views. Industrialists also saw him as a bulwark against 'red revolution' and began to finance the Nazis. The SA gained recruits from among the unemployed because it offered food, accommodation and a small wage.

> One of the strengths of National Socialism was that it appealed to people from a variety of social backgrounds.
>
> **KEY POINT**

The Crisis of Weimar, 1930–33

AQA	M1, M3
EDEXCEL	M1
OCR	M3
NICCEA	M1

The Wall Street crash affected Germany particularly badly because it led to the withdrawal of the American loans which had financed the recovery after 1924. Unemployment shot up to 4 million in 1931 and 6 million in 1932.

In 1930 the coalition between the Social Democrats, the Centre Party and the People's Party collapsed because of disagreements about measures to deal with the budget deficit. President Hindenburg appointed Brüning, leader of the Centre Party, as Chancellor. Unable to get a majority in the Reichstag, Brüning used the President's emergency powers to force through his proposed expenditure cuts. On the streets the Communists and Nazis were increasingly turning to political violence. In September 1930 a general election was called. Brüning hoped the violence of the extremists would increase support for the moderate parties, but instead the instability of the Weimar system led many to turn to the extremes. The Nazis gained 107 seats and the Communists 77. With the moderate parties at odds with each other and no party willing to co-operate with the Nazis or the Communists, it was impossible to construct a government with a majority. Brüning had to continue to rely on the President's emergency powers.

> In other words the Weimar constitution became unworkable, since the Chancellor was supposed to command a majority in the Reichstag.

In 1930 the Weimar Republic ceased to be a functioning democracy.	**KEY POINT**

As the economic crisis worsened in 1931 and 1932, violence continued and confidence in the government ebbed away. The sequence of events in 1932–33 was complicated.

- In April the growing strength of National Socialism was clearly demonstrated in the Presidential elections. Although Hindenburg was re-elected, Hitler gained 37 per cent of the votes in the second ballot.
- In May Hindenburg, on the advice of General Schleicher, dismissed Brüning and appointed Papen in his place.
- In July the Nazis won 230 seats in the Reichstag elections, thus becoming the biggest party. The Communists also did well, winning 89 seats.
- Papen invited Hitler to join his cabinet, but Hitler was not willing to accept any position other than that of Chancellor, and Hindenburg would not agree to this.
- Papen therefore called a second general election in November. This time the Nazis lost 2 million votes and 34 seats, while the Communists made substantial gains. Papen was still unable to gain a majority and resigned.
- Hindenburg then appointed Schleicher as Chancellor. He too failed to put together a coalition with a majority in the Reichstag.
- Papen, resenting the way Schleicher had replaced him, did a deal with Hitler: Hitler would become Chancellor of a coalition government with only three Nazis and Papen as Vice Chancellor. Hindenburg believed that Papen would be able to keep Hitler under control and agreed.
- On 30 January 1933 Hitler was appointed Chancellor.

> The extremist parties, both of which opposed the Weimar system, had more than half the seats in the Reichstag between them.

> Hindenburg despised Hitler as an upstart 'Bohemian corporal'.

Hitler came to power by manipulation of the parliamentary system, which he then proceeded to destroy.	**KEY POINT**

Why did the Weimar Republic fail?

AQA   M3
OCR   M3
NICCEA   M1

- It was handicapped from the start because it was born of defeat in war and had to accept humiliating terms at Versailles. Nationalist opinion could not forgive the politicians who had set up the republic in these circumstances.
- Proportional representation led to unstable coalitions. In the end it was impossible to form a government which commanded a majority in the Reichstag. This instability discredited democracy.
- The political leaders had no experience of democracy because under the constitution of the Empire Chancellors had been responsible to the Emperor and not the Reichstag.
- The government had to rely on former servants of the Empire as civil servants, judges, teachers and, most importantly, army officers.

- Anti-democratic parties (Communists, Nationalists and National Socialists) had much support. They were responsible for much violence, which the government failed to control.
- The mainstream political parties failed the republic. The Socialists were more concerned with fighting their battle with the Communists than with saving democracy. The Centre Party under Brüning was happy to connive at the undermining of democracy by the use of the President's emergency powers. The Liberals lost the middle-class support on which they depended.
- The Weimar Republic faced two severe economic crises. It survived the currency crisis of 1923 and there was then a period of relative prosperity. But the second crisis – the Great Depression – stretched the loyalty of the middle classes to breaking point.
- Hindenburg's political outlook was authoritarian and anti-parliamentary. He was happy to allow democracy to wither through the use of his emergency powers. In the crisis of 1932 he turned to men of an equally anti-democratic outlook – Papen and Schleicher.
- The manoeuvrings of the politicians in 1932 created the opportunity for Hitler to gain power by legal means. Papen especially was foolish to believe that he could control Hitler.

12.3 Nazi Germany, 1933–39

After studying this section you should be able to:

- *explain how Hitler established his dictatorship*
- *discuss the nature of the Nazi state*
- *evaluate Nazi policies on education, youth and the churches*
- *account for the success of Hitler in gaining control over the army*
- *discuss the persecution of the Jews*
- *assess the Nazis' economic policies and their social effects*

LEARNING SUMMARY

The consolidation of Hitler's power

AQA	M3
OCR	M1, M3
WJEC	M2, M3
NICCEA	M1

This cannot be regarded as a genuinely free election, yet the Nazis still did not win an overall majority.

So Hitler had used the Weimar constitution to set himself up as a dictator.

Hitler's first aim as Chancellor was to secure his hold on power. He began by calling another general election in March 1933. Nazi propaganda used the Reichstag fire to whip up anti-communist feeling. Hitler made effective use of the radio to project his image. The SA made violent attacks on their opponents during the campaign. Even so, the Nazis only gained 44 per cent of the votes. With the support of the Nationalist Party Hitler had a bare majority. He needed a two-thirds majority to change the constitution. He secured this by arresting the Communist deputies under an emergency law issued after the Reichstag fire and by doing a deal with the Catholic Centre Party: in return for their support he would allow them to continue to control their schools.

On 23 March the **Enabling Law** was passed. This gave Hitler dictatorial powers. He then dissolved all other political parties and took over control of all branches of national activity.

Be sure you understand why Hitler thought it was so important to carry out a purge of the Nazi party.

The Night of the Long Knives

The only remaining sources of potential opposition were the army and the radical wing of the Nazi Party itself. Röhm, the leader of the SA, wanted Hitler to introduce a more socialist programme. He also wanted to absorb the army into the SA. Hitler could not afford to alienate the army; the alternative was to eliminate Röhm and

141

destroy the influence of the SA. On 30 June 1934 (the Night of the Long Knives) Röhm was murdered and some 400 others – old enemies or potential dissidents – were removed. The SA survived but with little influence. The SS (Schutzstaffel), which had played the leading part in the Night of the Long Knives, became ever more powerful.

> **KEY POINT**
>
> In August 1934 Hindenburg died. Hitler proclaimed himself President, Chancellor and Führer.

The National Socialist State

EDEXCEL ▶ M3
OCR ▶ M1, M3
WJEC ▶ M2, M3
NICCEA ▶ M1

The title of Führer (leader) expressed Nazi ideology about leadership. For members of the army it meant that they had to take an oath of personal loyalty to Hitler rather than to the state.

Totalitarianism

Nazi Germany was a totalitarian state. Its ethos was summed up in the phrase 'Ein Volk, ein Reich, ein Führer' (one people, one empire, one leader). Everything was subordinated to the good of the state. Nazi propaganda rammed home the message that the Germans would achieve their destiny as the 'master race' by their loyalty to their great Führer. A highly developed personality cult depicted Hitler as the supremely wise leader, the focus of his people's aspirations. Mass rallies at Nuremberg, using all the techniques of flags, banners, music, etc., allowed Hitler to use his rabble-rousing oratorical gifts to the full.

All organisations which might rival the Nazi Party were either abolished or absorbed into the party. The German state and the Nazi Party became synonymous. No other political parties were allowed. Trade unions were abolished and replaced by the German Labour Front. The state governments were put under the control of Nazi Reich Governors. All social organisations, down to the level of village gardening clubs, were subjected to 'Gleichschaltung' – co-ordination, which in fact meant Nazification.

Gleichschaltung (co-ordination).

In practice the Nazi state was not as highly organised and tightly controlled as these measures would suggest. Much of the existing machinery of government survived alongside the Nazi organisations. The civil service continued to function efficiently. The functions of ministers overlapped with those of Nazi Special Deputies. Alongside the new Reich Governors, each province retained its Minister-President. The Reich Governors themselves were often gauleiters – party officials responsible for running the activities of the party in their province.

> **KEY POINT**
>
> Some historians argue that competition between subordinates strengthened Hitler's authority: it was a process of divide and rule. Others claim that he was remote and indecisive and therefore the overlapping functions of the state and the party led to inefficiency.

A police state

A useful exercise would be to list the roles of the leading Nazis other than Hitler.

Nazi Germany was a police state. The Gestapo (secret police), set up in Prussia in 1933 by Goering, kept a close watch on possible opponents (communists, socialists, trade unionists) and people the Nazis disapproved of, such as the Jews, gypsies and homosexuals.

In 1936 Himmler, the head of the SS, became the police chief for the whole of Germany and the Gestapo came under his control. The SS was formed in 1925 as an élite paramilitary body within the Nazi Party. It played the leading role in the Night of the Long Knives in 1934 and from then grew in power and influence. It had its own security service (the SD) under Heydrich, who was also, under

Himmler, the head of the Gestapo. It ran concentration camps, the first of which was opened at Dachau in 1933. Through the Waffen SS, set up in 1938, it had a leading role in the army. In the Second World War it administered occupied territories and ran the extermination camps.

With the 'legal revolution' the law courts were also an instrument of Nazi coercion. Judges were appointed for their loyalty to Nazi ideas and had to undergo training in Nazi ideology.

> The combination of the SS, Gestapo and SD provided the Nazi state with the means to suppress any opposition by terror.

KEY POINT

Propaganda

Goebbels was a convinced advocate of the 'Big Lie'.

Goebbels was put in charge of a new Ministry of Propaganda in 1933. He established strict censorship of the press, books, films, and the arts. News agencies were amalgamated into one central source of 'correct information'. 'Un-German' books were burnt. The works of Jewish composers were banned. The government-controlled radio was used to good effect to spread Nazi ideas.

Education and youth

Education was particularly important. In the schools Nazi racial views were taught and textbooks in subjects such as history and biology were re-written. Teachers were required to join the Nazi Teachers' Association and were watched to ensure that they followed the party line. Universities were placed under the control of government-appointed rectors and academics who were not willing to toe the Nazi line were forced out.

All youth movements were absorbed into the Hitler Youth, which boys joined at the age of 14. From 1936 membership was compulsory. Boys were indoctrinated with nationalist and racist ideas. They took an oath to Hitler as 'saviour of our country' and were taught to look forward to their future role in military service to the Nazi state. The parallel girls' organisation, the League of German Maidens, prepared girls to serve the state as wives and mothers.

The churches

Historians continue to debate how far the churches compromised their principles in their dealings with Hitler.

The churches were bound to be a problem for the Nazis with their belief in the total subordination of the individual to the state. This was particularly true of relations with the Catholic Church, which owed loyalty to the Pope in Rome. Hitler quickly tackled this problem: in 1933 a Concordat with Rome ensured that the Catholic Church withdrew from politics in return for keeping some control over its schools. The Catholic Centre Party dissolved itself voluntarily. But relations deteriorated and in 1937 Pope Pius XI issued an encyclical criticising the Nazi regime. Some Catholic bishops and priests continued to speak out against the Nazis and many were imprisoned.

Many Protestants initially welcomed the Nazis in preference to what they regarded as the ungodly Weimar Republic. This encouraged Hitler to attempt to bring the Protestant Churches under Nazi control by amalgamating the 28 provincial Churches into a Reich Church under a Reich Bishop, Müller. The Nazification of the Reich Church, which attempted to combine Christianity with anti-semitism and Führer-worship, resulted in a split and the emergence of the Confessional Church, led by Pastor Niemoller. This was banned in 1937 and Niemoller and some hundreds of other pastors were sent to concentration camps.

> Persecution of priests and pastors ensured that the Churches did not become centres of opposition but the Churches continued to be a source of mute protest.

The army

Until 1938 the army was the most powerful institution which was not fully under Hitler's control. One of the main reasons for the Night of the Long Knives was his fear that the activities of Röhm and the SA would provoke an army coup. By removing Röhm and other SA leaders, Hitler earned the goodwill of the army. A few weeks later, in August 1934, when Hindenburg died and Hitler took the title of Führer, all members of the army were required to take an oath of personal allegiance to him. Military ideas of personal honour made it difficult for army officers to oppose Hitler after this.

As younger officers were promoted, the army became increasingly Nazified.

The Hossbach memorandum.

Between 1934 and 1938 the army was gradually brought under Nazi control. The swastika was adopted as a badge on army uniforms. Officers were given instruction in Nazi ideology. The adoption of a policy of large-scale rearmament naturally won army support. But the general staff became increasingly worried by the trend of Hitler's foreign policy. They regarded the remilitarisation of the Rhineland as risky. In November 1937, as recorded in the Hossbach memorandum, Hitler announced to his chief military advisers his plans for the expansion of Germany, which would involve attacking Austria and Czechoslovakia. Horrified by the risk of war with Britain and France, the generals protested. Hitler's response was to reorganise the command structure of the army. The War Minister, Blomberg, and the Commander-in-Chief of the Army, Fritsch, were both dismissed in 1938 on charges of personal misconduct. Hitler put the army under his direct command through the OKW.

It was, however, from the army that two attempts were made to remove Hitler. In 1938 General Beck tried to persuade the General Staff to remove him, but he received no support and resigned. In 1944 Stauffenberg placed a bomb in Hitler's conference room in East Prussia but Hitler survived.

> By 1938 the army, the last institution with a degree of independence, was under Hitler's direct control.

The Jews

EDEXCEL	M3
OCR	M1, M3
WJEC	M2, M3
NICCEA	M1

The German people seem to have approved this. How far they approved of more brutal methods, culminating in the Holocaust, is a matter of historical debate.

The Jews were singled out for special persecution as the scapegoats for all Germany's ills. They were blamed especially for the 'stab in the back', a myth which Goebbels' propaganda machine made great play with. In 1933 there was a boycott of Jewish shops and businesses. Jews were dismissed from the civil service and excluded from universities and in due course from most of the professions.

In 1935 the Nuremberg Laws deprived Jews of German citizenship and forbade them to marry 'Aryans'. Persecution intensified in 1938. Jews were banned from commerce. In November, attacks on synagogues and Jewish houses and businesses took place all over Germany (Kristallnacht – the Night of Broken Glass). This was allegedly a spontaneous outburst in retaliation for the assassination of a German embassy official in Paris by a Jew, but was largely the work of the SA. Many Jews went into exile; others ended up in concentration camps.

The 'final solution' began in 1941 with mass deportations of Jews to concentration camps. Between 1942 and 1945 some 3 to 4 million Jews died in the gas chambers.

1 Some historians claim that Hitler intended to exterminate the Jews from the start.

2 Others argue that it was only decided upon as the result of the war in the east, which closed off the possibility of mass deportation.

3 It has been argued that Hitler himself was not responsible for the Holocaust but the overwhelming majority of historians reject this view.

The economy

EDEXCEL ▸ M3
OCR ▸ M1, M3
WJEC ▸ M2, M3
NICCEA ▸ M1

Nazi economic policies had two main aims: to reduce unemployment and to revive Germany's military and industrial might. To achieve these ends economic activity was state-controlled. Wages, food prices, rents, investment and foreign exchange were all controlled. Trade unions were abolished and strikes made illegal. Farm prices were fixed so that farmers made a reasonable profit. Public works were started, financed by the state; the most famous example is the building of autobahns. Under Dr Schacht an elaborate system of exchange controls was developed, which exploited the dependence of much of Eastern Europe upon Germany as a market for food exports. Bilateral trade agreements were made with Eastern European and South American countries to boost German exports and secure essential raw materials. As a result, by 1935 exports exceeded imports.

> It does not follow that he intended to go to war in 1940.

In 1936 a Four-Year Plan was introduced with the explicit aim, stated in a memorandum from Hitler, of making Germany ready for war within four years. The basic purpose was to achieve self-sufficiency (autarky) by boosting domestic production and developing synthetic substitutes for oil and other imports. At the same time a programme of large-scale rearmament was undertaken. Under state direction industrialists produced what the Nazis thought Germany needed and, where necessary, labour was directed where it was needed.

How successful were Nazi economic policies?

The Nazis were successful in reducing unemployment to two million by 1935 and to virtually nil in 1939. Unemployment had already begun to fall before Hitler came to power and the upturn in world trade from 1934 helped to reduce it further. The public works schemes and rearmament provided the sort of stimulus advocated by Keynesian economics. Rearmament also took half a million men out of the labour market by conscription into the army. But the reduction in unemployment also owed something to more questionable aspects of the Nazi regime. The expansion of the civil service and the party organisation created jobs but both were over-staffed. The removal of political opponents and 'undesirables' to concentration camps reduced unemployment because they were not counted. Neither were Jews who had been forced out of their jobs, since they were no longer citizens after 1935.

> The reduction of unemployment was one of the reasons why the German people supported Hitler. When you have studied this paragraph, you should be able to assess how much credit he deserved for it.

In other respects, too, the success of Nazi economic policy may be doubted. Despite massive investment, synthetic substitutes for oil and rubber only produced a small proportion of Germany's needs. Agriculture failed to meet its targets and Germany continued to depend on food imports. Although there was some economic growth, it was not fast enough to pay for the massive cost of rearmament. By 1939 Schacht, as President of the Reichsbank, was warning of the danger of runaway inflation.

> Some historians argue that by 1939 war was the only answer to Germany's economic problems. A short, successful war would win 'lebensraum' – land in Eastern Europe, which would supply Germany's food needs and thus free foreign exchange to buy the raw materials required by its industry.

KEY ISSUE

The response of the German people to Nazism

EDEXCEL ▸ M3
OCR ▸ M1, M3
WJEC ▸ M2, M3
NICCEA ▸ M1

- Industrialists saw Hitler as a bulwark against communism. They welcomed the abolition of trade unions. Big business grew at the expense of smaller businesses. It profited from rearmament and from the war effort. In return it provided much of the money to finance the Nazi party.
- The middle classes, who had lost so much under the Weimar Republic, were impressed by Hitler's success in restoring prosperity, in warding off the threat of communist revolution and in rebuilding national pride.
- The working class were pleased by the drop in unemployment, by rent controls and by the benefits offered by the Strength through Joy organisation, such as subsidised holidays. On the other hand wages only increased slowly and in many industries there was a drop in real wages. Hours of work were generally longer.
- Farmers were won over by fixed prices for their products and by a law which made farms hereditary estates. On the other hand this meant that many peasant farms remained small; agriculture was inefficient and peasant incomes low. The standard of living of agricultural workers was low and many migrated to the towns in search of better paid work.

Nevertheless, the Nazis enjoyed much support among women because they stressed the importance of the family.

- The status of women suffered. The Nazis taught that their function was to serve the state by producing children. Women were eased out of professional positions and the civil service. In the later 1930s, however, labour shortages created a demand for women workers in agriculture and industry. In line with their racial theories, the Nazis passed a law enforcing compulsory sterilisation of people with hereditary diseases.

Successive plebiscites gave over 90 per cent approval for Hitler's policies and, although intimidation may have exaggerated support for the Nazis, there is little evidence of serious discontent and much evidence of general approval.

> Hitler was popular in the 1930s, even though Nazi Germany was a totalitarian police state. The three main reasons for this were:
> - the Nazis reduced unemployment and restored prosperity
> - they established strong and stable government, in contrast to the last years of the Weimar Republic
> - Hitler's foreign policy made Germany the greatest power in continental Europe again.

KEY POINT

You should be able to explain the significance of each of these dates.

1933	Hitler was appointed Chancellor; Enabling Law
1934	Night of the Long Knives; death of Hindenburg; Hitler Führer, President and Chancellor
1935	Nuremberg Laws
1938	Kristallnacht (Night of the Broken Glass)
1939	Outbreak of Second World War

KEY DATES

Sample question and model answer

The consolidation of Hitler's power

Study the following sources and then answer the questions which follow.

source 1

From Hitler's 'Appeal to the German People', drawn up on 31 January 1933 and broadcast the next day

It is an appalling inheritance which we are taking over. The task before us is the most difficult which has faced German statesmen in living memory. But we have unbounded confidence, for we believe in our nation. Farmers, workers and the middle class must unite to contribute the bricks wherewith to build the new Reich. Germany must and will not sink into Communist anarchy.

source 2

From a report in *The Times*, March 1933

The 'seizure of power' by Herr Hitler's government is almost complete. Bavaria, Baden, Württemberg and Saxony are virtually governed by Nazi dictators or Reich commissioners with almost unlimited powers. The smaller states have been forcibly converted into Hitlerite citadels. In Prussia the council elections have gone in favour of the Nazi-Nationalist combination. The 'purging' of the police and the civil service is still continuing, but this is no more than an incident in the swift advance of the government of the Reich to power over its states and citizens.

source 3

A Nazi poster of 1933 entitled 'The field marshal and the corporal'. The caption reads, 'Fight with us for Peace and Equal Rights'

source 4

From *My Part in Germany's Fight* by Joseph Goebbels, 1935

February 3, 1933. I talk over the beginning of the election campaign in detail with the Leader. The struggle is a light one now, since we are able to employ all means of the state. Radio and Press are at our disposal. The Leader is to speak in all towns having their own broadcasting station. We transmit the broadcast to the entire people and give listeners a clear idea of all that occurs at our meetings.

I am going to introduce the Leader's address, in which I shall try to convey to listeners the magical atmosphere of our huge demonstrations.

Sample question and model answer (continued)

From *Hitler* by Ian Kershaw, 1998

[Hitler was no] 'mere' accident in the course of German history. Without the unique conditions in which he came to prominence he would have been nothing. The impact on the German people of war, revolution and national humiliation, and the acute fear of Bolshevism in wide sections of the population, gave Hitler his platform. He exploited the conditions brilliantly. More than any other politician of his era, he was the spokesman for the unusually intense fears, resentments and prejudices of ordinary people not attracted by the parties of the Left or anchored in the parties of political Catholicism. And more than any other politician of his era, he offered such people the prospect of a new and better society – though one seeming to rest on 'true' German values with which they could identify. The vision of the future went hand in hand with the denunciation of the past in Hitler's appeal.

(a) Study source 3. Why, according to Goebbels, was it easy to convey the Nazi message to the German people in February 1933? [3]

Explain the value of control of radio (a new medium).

The Nazis had control of the radio and the press after Hitler became Chancellor.

(b) Study source 2. Use your own knowledge to explain why *The Times* drew attention to the appointment of Reich commissioners and to the council elections in Prussia. [4]

The Weimar constitution was federal, so each German state had its own government. To consolidate their grip on Germany the Nazis therefore had to gain control over the government of each state.

(c) Study source 1. How useful is this source as evidence of the ways in which Hitler appealed to the German people? [5]

Assessment of usefulness means 'What does it tell me?' and 'How reliable is it?'

Source 1 is Hitler's own appeal to the German people on appointment as Chancellor. He uses exaggerated language to describe the problems he inherits and skilfully appeals to nationalist and anti-communist sentiments.

(d) Study sources 3 and 4. What does a comparison of these sources reveal about the ways in which the Nazis consolidated their position in Germany after Hitler was appointed Chancellor? [6]

Be sure to compare.

Both sources are evidence about the use of propaganda. Source 3 seeks to associate the Nazis with the army and the pre-1918 Empire and to appeal to the desire for stability and harmony between the classes and to German nationalism. This is all conveyed in the visual imagery. Source 3 – by Hitler's Minister of Propaganda – highlights other methods: the use of radio and the press, huge demonstrations with their 'magical atmosphere'. Comparison shows the range of propaganda weapons used.

(e) Study all the sources. Using these sources and your own knowledge, explain why Hitler was able to establish a Nazi dictatorship in Germany in 1933. [12]

Own knowledge.

The contemporary sources show Hitler's personal contribution through rhetoric, the use of propaganda, the gaining of control over state governments, the police and the civil service. Source 5 adds a historian's perspective, noting the importance of the history of Germany since 1918 and Hitler's skilful exploitation of its impact on the people. Other important factors are the breakdown of the Weimar constitution, shown in the political history of 1930–33, the use of violence, the miscalculation of Papen and Hindenburg in believing that Hitler could be used for their purposes, the Reichstag fire and the Enabling Law.

Practice examination questions

1 (a) How did the Weimar Republic overcome threats to its survival between 1919 and 1923? [15]

   (b) Why was the period 1924–29 one of comparative stability? [15]

2 (a) Identify and explain the main weaknesses of Germany's political system under the Weimar constitution. [10]

   (b) How successful were the Nazis from 1933 to 1939 in solving Germany's economic problems? [20]

3 Study the following source and then answer the questions which follow.

From *Youth in the Third Reich* by A. Klonne, 1982

What I liked about the Hitler Youth was the comradeship. I was full of enthusiasm when I joined the Jungvolk at the age of ten. What boy isn't fired by being presented with high ideals such as comradeship, loyalty and honour?

The partnership of our camps was a scale model of Hitler's partnership of the whole people and it was completely successful. We were allowed to excel in our own particular way but we took pains to be both co-operative and self-reliant. However, when I became a leader the negative aspects became obvious. I found the compulsion and requirement of absolute obedience unpleasant. It was preferred that people should not have a will of their own and should totally subordinate themselves.

   (a) What, according to this source, were the author's feelings about being a member of the Hitler Youth? [5]

   (b) In what ways did the Nazis try to mould the outlook of young people? [7]

   (c) How successful were the Nazis in eliminating opposition to their regime between 1933 and 1939? [18]

Chapter 13

Soviet Russia, 1917–53

The following topics are covered in this chapter:

- *Lenin, 1917–24*
- *Stalin's dictatorship, 1924–41*

- *The Second World War and the Cold War*

13.1 Lenin, 1917–24

After studying this section you should be able to:

- *explain how Lenin established the Communist state in Russia*
- *account for the defeat of the Whites in the Civil War*
- *discuss War Communism and the New Economic Policy*
- *assess Lenin's achievements*

LEARNING SUMMARY

The consolidation of Bolshevik power

AQA	M3
EDEXCEL	M2
WJEC	M2
NICCEA	M3

Continuing the war had been one of the chief mistakes of the Provisional Government. For Lenin the survival of the Bolshevik regime was the top priority, whatever the cost.

Lenin took several crucial decisions in the early days of Bolshevik rule in order to fulfil the promises of 'land, peace and bread' and 'all power to the soviets'.

- Land was confiscated from the crown, the Church and the landowners and redistributed to the peasants.
- The Constituent Assembly, which met in January 1918, was immediately dissolved by Red Guards because the elections had left the Bolsheviks in a minority. The All-Russian Congress of Soviets then considered Lenin's proposals for the constitution.
- The Peace of Brest-Litovsk was made with Germany and Austria (March 1918). The terms imposed by Germany were extremely harsh. Russia surrendered Poland and the Baltic States to Germany, recognised Finland and the Ukraine as independent and agreed to pay huge reparations. Despite the severity of the terms, Lenin insisted that there was no alternative to accepting it.
- War Communism was instituted. Industry and the banks were nationalised. Private trade was forbidden. Peasants were made to sell all surplus grain to the state at fixed prices.

> Lenin later claimed that War Communism was an emergency measure to deal with the crisis, but it is more likely that it was an attempt to introduce doctrinaire communist ideas. By 1921 he realised that it did not work.
>
> **KEY ISSUE**

Lenin was ruthless in dealing with opponents. In December 1917 he set up the Cheka (secret police) which instituted the 'Red Terror'. The first victims were the leaders of the other political parties. Over 140 000 people had been executed by February 1922 when the Cheka was replaced by the OGPU. By then Lenin was satisfied that all opposition had been suppressed.

The Bolshevik Party re-named itself the Communist Party.

In July 1918 the new Soviet constitution was introduced. Russia became the Russian Soviet Federated Socialist Republic. Supreme power was nominally given to the All-Russian Congress of Soviets, but this only met for about one week each year. The Congress elected an Executive Committee, which in turn elected the ten members of the Council of People's Commissars (ministers). Almost all the Commissars were members of the Politburo of the Communist Party, which was where real power lay. No other political parties were allowed.

At the end of the Civil War there was a further constitutional change. Pre-revolutionary Russia was a multi-national state. The danger that some of the nationalities would break away in the Civil War was overcome by the Red victory. To incorporate them into the new Soviet system, the Union of Soviet Socialist Republics was set up in 1922. This was a federation of republics, of which Russia was the most important.

> The Soviet system of government was described by Lenin as 'democratic centralism'. Essentially this meant that the state was subordinated to the Communist Party in both the USSR and the constituent republics.
>
> **KEY POINT**

The Civil War, 1918–20

AQA	M3
EDEXCEL	M2
WJEC	M2
NICCEA	M3

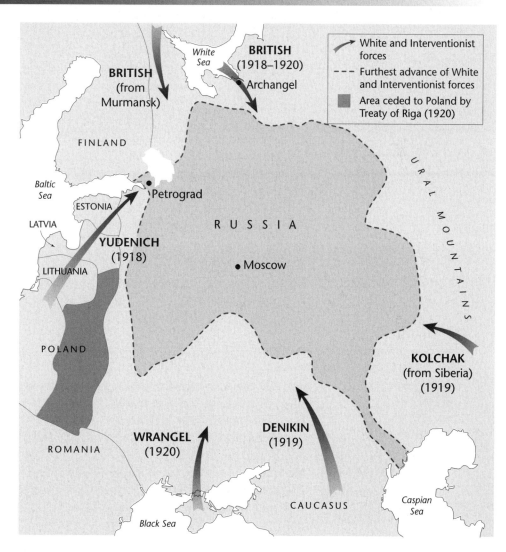

The Russian Civil War, 1918–20

Lenin had seized power by force and it was not surprising that this provoked counter-revolution and civil war. Nor was it surprising that there was foreign intervention in the Civil War. Foreign powers feared that the example of the Russian Revolution would be followed by the workers elsewhere. The founding of the Third Communist International by the Bolsheviks in 1919, with the purpose of promoting world revolution, gave substance to this fear. Britain and France were angry at Russia's desertion of the Allied cause and worried that the armaments they had supplied to Russia might fall into German hands. France, which had substantial investments in Russia, was also angered by Lenin's repudiation of all foreign debts.

The Civil War raged from 1918 to 1920. The Whites (counter-revolutionaries) attacked from three main directions. From the south they were led by Denikin and then by Wrangel. Kolchak attacked from the east and Yudenich from the Baltic towards Petrograd. Foreign forces landed at Archangel and Murmansk in the north and in the Crimea and the Caucasus in the south. A Japanese force went into Siberia from Vladivostok. For a time much of Siberia and southern Russia was under White control but by 1920 the Bolsheviks had overcome most of the White forces. Then Russia was attacked by Poland, which, with French aid, succeeded in taking over a substantial part of White Russia and the Ukraine, leaving 3 million Russians in Poland (Treaty of Riga, 1921). The remaining White forces in central Asia and the Far East were mopped up in 1921–22.

Why did the Communists (Reds) win the Civil War?

Advantages of the Reds.

- The Red Army was united under a single command, that of Trotsky, who created an efficient fighting machine by sheer personal dynamism. By the end of the Civil War the Red Army numbered over 5 million men.
- The Communists controlled the main cities and the railways. They therefore had the advantage of internal communications.
- The Russian peasants feared that the Whites would return the land to the landlords.
- Foreign intervention enabled the Communists to pose as Russian patriots.

Weaknesses of the Whites.

- The Whites were not united in their aims. Some were Tsarists, others wanted a republic.
- The Whites also lacked co-ordination. This was partly a matter of geography – transport and communication between the White forces was difficult.
- The foreign supporters of the Whites were half-hearted. They had other priorities – ending the Great War in 1918, working out the peace settlement in 1919.

> **KEY POINT**
>
> The Communists seized power in 1917 but they were not fully in control of Russia until 1921.

The New Economic Policy

AQA M3
EDEXCEL M2
WJEC M2
NICCEA M3

A class of prosperous peasants emerged as a result – only to be destroyed by Stalin's collectivisation policies.

By 1921 the economy was on the verge of collapse, partly because of the strain of seven years of foreign and civil war, but also because of War Communism. Since the government took all surplus agricultural produce, the peasants stopped producing more than they needed for themselves. The result was famine, aggravated by droughts in 1920–21. There were widespread disturbances. The most serious was the naval mutiny at Kronstadt in 1921, which convinced Lenin that a change was needed. The New Economic Policy allowed the peasants to sell their surplus produce on payment of a tax of a percentage of the crop. It also restored private trading through 'Nepmen'. All major industrial installations, however, remained under state control, as did banking, transport and foreign trade. Economic recovery was delayed by continuing famine and financial crisis, but by the time of Lenin's death things were improving.

> **KEY POINTS**
>
> 1 The New Economic Policy was a retreat from pure communism and a compromise with capitalism.
> 2 By the time of Lenin's death in 1924 the Russian economy was beginning to recover as a result.

Lenin's achievements

AQA	M3
EDEXCEL	M2
WJEC	M2
NICCEA	M3

- Lenin played a crucial role in 1917 in the overthrow of the Provisional Government, persuading his colleagues to seize power and planning how to achieve it.
- His immediate decisions about the land and the peace with Germany were crucial in enabling the Bolsheviks to hold on to power.
- With the help of Trotsky and the Red Army he held the new communist state together through the Civil War.
- His decision to replace War Communism by the New Economic Policy was realistic, even though it involved compromising the basic economic principles of Marxism.
- He made a start on social reform with decrees providing free education and a National Insurance scheme.
- He achieved some foreign recognition for the Communist government in Russia, including the resumption of full diplomatic relations with Germany by the Treaty of Rapallo (1922).

But

- He was completely ruthless: millions of Russians died in the civil war and the great famine of 1920–21, and thousands more were victims of the secret police.
- The new Russian state which he created was a totalitarian police state. It had a vast bureaucracy, meshed with the Communist Party.
- Unfortunately he had made no arrangements for choosing his successor and this allowed Stalin to take over eventually.

> Did Lenin lay the foundations for Stalinism? Some historians argue that Stalinism was a direct consequence of the totalitarian system created by Lenin. Others claim that Lenin used terror in response to a critical situation and would later have modified it if he had lived.
>
> **KEY ISSUE**

13.2 Stalin's Dictatorship, 1924–41

After studying this section you should be able to:

- *account for Stalin's rise to power*
- *evaluate Stalin's policies of industrialisation and the collectivisation of agriculture*
- *explain the purges of the 1930s*
- *discuss the political, social, educational and cultural aspects of life in the Soviet Union in the 1930s*
- *explain Soviet foreign policy in the 1930s*

LEARNING SUMMARY

Rise to power

AQA	M1, M3	WJEC	M2
EDEXCEL	M2	NICCEA	M3
OCR	M3		

This was crucial because it enabled him to manipulate the Politburo against his enemies.

Stalin, a Georgian whose father had been a serf, became Commissar for Nationalities in 1917 and General Secretary of the Communist Party in 1922. This position enabled him to build up a power base. Membership of the Party at local level was carefully controlled by the Secretariat, i.e. Stalin. The local parties elected the Party Congress, from which the Central Committee and the Politburo were drawn. Thus Stalin controlled promotion within the Party.

Shortly before he died, Lenin advised the Communist Party to remove Stalin from the post of General Secretary, but the Central Committee ignored this. Kamenev and Zinoviev, who were jealous and mistrustful of Trotsky, joined Stalin in the Triumvirate. This isolated Trotsky, who was forced to resign as Commissar for War in 1925. There was a complicated power struggle in 1926–27. Stalin allied himself to Bukharin, who advocated continuing with the New Economic Policy, while Kamenev and Zinoviev joined forces with Trotsky to demand that it should be abandoned. At the Party Congress in 1927 Stalin triumphed. Trotsky, Kamenev and Zinoviev were removed from the Politburo. In 1929 Trotsky was sent into exile. In the same year Stalin changed his views about the New Economic Policy. When Bukharin and his 'rightist' colleagues protested, they too were removed from the Politburo. Stalin was left as undisputed dictator.

> The struggle for power between Stalin and Trotsky was both a clash of personalities between a Georgian peasant and a middle-class intellectual and a conflict of principles. Trotsky stood for 'permanent revolution' and Stalin for 'socialism in one country'.

KEY POINT

Why did Stalin win the battle for the succession to Lenin?

'Permanent revolution' meant promoting revolution elsewhere in Europe so as to ensure the survival of communism in Russia.

- He displayed great political skill in out-manoeuvring his rivals.
- As General Secretary he had built up solid support in the Party Congress.
- 'Socialism in one country' had more appeal than 'permanent revolution' to Russians, who simply wanted peace and prosperity after the hardships of the First World War and the Civil War. It also appealed to Russia's national pride and self-reliance.
- The case for 'permanent revolution' had been seriously weakened by the failure of attempts at communist revolution in the west, especially the Spartacist Rising in Germany in 1919.
- Trotsky, who was in many ways the obvious successor to Lenin, was mistrusted. He was regarded as too clever, too western in his ways of thought and too inclined to think he was right and the Party wrong. He was suspect because he had been a Menshevik until 1917. He had great intellectual and organisational abilities but lacked political skill.

Economic policy ('Socialism in one country')

EDEXCEL M3
OCR M3
WJEC M2
NICCEA M3

The Five-Year Plans

'Socialism in one country' implied building up Russia's strength and this meant industrialisation. Stalin embarked on a series of **Five-Year Plans**. Targets were set for all major industries, to be achieved by a mixture of rewards and punishments. The first Five-Year Plan (1928–32) concentrated on heavy industry. The second (1933–37) allowed for some limited production of consumer goods but the third (1938–42) returned to the emphasis on heavy industry (and also, in view of the approach of war, armaments). The result of these plans was a remarkable rate of growth, which transformed Russia into a major industrial power, though it is questionable how efficient the new industries were. Between 1928 and 1941 coal and steel production quadrupled. Great new industrial areas were developed in the Urals and Siberia.

This was the foundation for Russia's war effort between 1941 and 1945.

Success was achieved by using the power of the state to put great pressure on the workforce. Conditions for the workers were very poor with low wages, poor housing in the new industrial towns, direction of labour and ruthless discipline in the factories. But there were also incentives: pay differentials and medals for outstanding workers (Stakhanovites). The emphasis on heavy industry meant that the Russians saw little benefit in terms of availability of consumer goods. Low wages meant that living standards fell, though by the mid-1930s workers began to see some benefits in education, health care and holidays with pay. Government propaganda stressed that the sacrifices were in a patriotic cause.

Since foreign loans were not available to Communist Russia, the capital needed for industrialisation had to be raised by Russia itself. This is why wages were held down. Government control of the economy allowed it to cut labour costs to the minimum and plough back all surpluses. But it was also vital to earn foreign exchange to pay for imports of foreign machinery. The success of the Five-Year Plans therefore depended on agriculture, since Russia's principal export was grain. Grain was also required to feed the growing industrial towns at the lowest possible cost.

The collectivisation of agriculture

For Stalin agriculture presented two problems. Firstly, there were 24 million separate peasant farms, many of them too small to use modern agricultural machinery. Secondly, the richer peasants (kulaks), who had profited from the New Economic Policy, wanted high prices for their produce. In any case, the rise of a class of prosperous peasants, who owned their own land, was an affront to communist ideology.

Stalin's solution was collectivisation. In 1929 he decreed that all farms should be collectivised within three years. The kulaks resisted by burning their crops and slaughtering their cattle. Between 1929 and 1932 there was virtual civil war in the countryside, resulting in famine in 1932–33. Ultimately Stalin triumphed: by 1939, 97 per cent of all land had been collectivised. Along with the provision of agricultural machinery by motor tractor stations, this enabled Russian agriculture to produce record grain harvests in the late 1930s. Even so, it remained relatively inefficient. The number of livestock did not recover until the 1950s. The human cost of it all was enormous. A minimum of 10 million kulaks were killed, died in the famine or were deported to Siberia.

> Low agricultural productivity was a real problem, which could only be solved by creating bigger farms. Whether collectivisation was the way to do this quickly is more controversial.

> **KEY ISSUES**
> 1 Some historians claim that Stalin's industrialisation enabled Russia to defeat Germany in the Second World War and to emerge as a superpower afterwards.
> 2 Another view is that the foundation for Russian industrial strength was laid by the Tsars and that Stalin merely built on it. On this view, faster progress would have been made by different methods.

The purges

OCR ▸ M3
WJEC ▸ M2
NICCEA ▸ M3

> Trotsky, in exile in Mexico, was murdered by a Russian agent in 1940.

> Purges are a common feature of single-party dictatorships. What was extraordinary about Stalin's purges was their scale.

In the mid-1930s Stalin set about destroying all possible opposition to his rule. The murder of the Communist Party boss in Leningrad, Kirov, by a young Communist dissident in December 1934 sparked off the purges. In 1935 Zinoviev and Kamenev were arrested and imprisoned; in 1936 after a show trial they were executed on the evidence of their own confessions. Another show trial in 1938 removed Bukharin and Yagoda, the head of the NKVD (secret police). All the possible rivals to Stalin were liquidated: all the living members of Lenin's politburo except Stalin himself and Trotsky (in exile); the Chief of the General Staff, Marshal Tukhachevsky; and about two-thirds of the senior officers in the army. About 300 000 lesser people were shot and 7 million sent to labour camps in Arctic Russia and Siberia (the gulags). Many were condemned on the basis of confessions which were clearly false.

There have been many explanations for the purges. Some historians lay the emphasis on Stalin's paranoid personality. Others think that he saw the elimination of the entire generation of Bolsheviks of Lenin's time as the only way to ensure that there would be no threat to his position in the future. Another theory is that he wanted to make sure there would be no internal rivals in a position to profit from any external disaster such as defeat in war. Whatever the explanation, most of the victims presented only an imaginary threat.

> The purges left Stalin in total control of a terrorised population, but they also deprived Russia of many of its best brains, slowed down its industrial growth and weakened the army, which lost more officers in the purges than in the Second World War.
>
> **KEY POINT**

Stalin's Russia

EDEXCEL ▸ M2, M3
OCR ▸ M3
WJEC ▸ M2
NICCEA ▸ M3

Nominally the USSR was a democracy. The Constitution of 1936 provided for all citizens over 18 to elect by secret ballot the Supreme Soviet. This apparently democratic constitution had some propaganda value for Stalin: it was applauded by left-wing sympathisers of the Soviet Union in the west. However, there was only one party to vote for. Real power lay with the Communist Party and within the Party with its Secretary, Stalin. Stalin's control over the Party was further strengthened by the purges. High office demanded unquestioning loyalty.

The Soviet Union was a police state. Guarantees of individual liberty in the constitution were meaningless, as the purges demonstrated. There was strict censorship of the press. There was no freedom of speech and little freedom of movement. Lenin's secret police, the Cheka, had been abolished in 1922 but its place had been taken by the OGPU, which Stalin used to enforce collectivisation. In 1934 the OGPU was merged with the NKVD (People's Commissariat for Internal Affairs), which became notorious as the instrument by which Stalin carried out the purges.

> The secret police.

The USSR was also a totalitarian state. The influence of the state was felt in all areas of Russian life. All forms of opposition or disagreement were suppressed. Although there were over a hundred national groups within the USSR and 12 nominally separate republics, the national minorities were suppressed. Jews were regarded with particular disfavour and often persecuted. The government tried to diminish the influence of the Orthodox Church by closing churches and persecuting the priests.

> Totalitarianism.

> Stalin's rule was a ruthless dictatorship, more repressive than the Tsarist autocracy.
>
> **KEY POINT**

Education

Education was closely supervised to ensure that Marxist doctrines of the class struggle and the dictatorship of the proletariat were inculcated. In both schools and universities teachers were required to accept unquestioningly Stalinist ideology, a combination of nationalist and Marxist ideas which portrayed the Soviet Union under its great leader as the epitome of 'all patriotic and progressive forces'. It was strongly anti-religious. The educational system did, however, succeed in its foremost aim: illiteracy was almost eradicated. It also made it possible for working-class children to enter higher education, though in the 1930s Stalin moved away from favouring working-class applicants to selecting those with the best qualifications.

> This was a considerable achievement and should be set against the fact that education was used for indoctrination.

Soviet culture

Cultural life was state controlled. Writers, artists and musicians were required to produce works of 'socialist realism'. Stalin defined this as 'National in form, Socialist in content'. Practitioners of the arts, scholars and intellectuals all had to be careful to

It also meant producing works which were readily accessible to ordinary Russians and which portrayed Russia as happy, successful and progressive.

produce what was acceptable to the state for fear of their lives. This meant glorifying the Soviet state and above all Stalin. Stalin became the object of an extraordinary personality cult. Propaganda portrayed him as the great leader who cared for his people and on whom everything depended. Everywhere there were statues or portraits of him.

The family

Policy towards the family changed in the 1930s. Under Lenin divorce and abortion became easy. By the 1930s family breakdown was becoming a serious problem. Stalin therefore made divorce more difficult and abortion illegal. Emphasis was placed on strict sexual morality.

The nature of the Soviet state makes it difficult to know how much suppressed discontent there was.

In spite of everything, Stalin seems to have enjoyed much support among the Russian people. They accepted the sacrifices as the means to make Russia great and prosperous. Stalin appealed both to their desire for better conditions and to their sense of Russian nationalism. And in the second half of the 1930s his policies did seem to be slowly paying dividends. Literacy was increasing, standards of living were at last beginning to rise and social services were improving.

> Propaganda portrayed Stalin as the great leader who was concerned for his people and on whom almost everything depended. In spite of his brutal methods, he enjoyed much support.
>
> **KEY POINT**

Foreign policy

OCR M3

Stalin was not even consulted about the fate of Czechoslovakia. He was correct in thinking that Britain and France were unsure whether Nazi Germany was a greater threat to the world than Soviet Russia.

For much of the inter-war period the USSR was isolated from international diplomacy. In the mid-1930s Stalin began to take more interest in European affairs, joining the League of Nations (1934) and sending forces to fight in the Spanish Civil War. At first he was not alarmed by the rise of Hitler, thinking his regime would not last. When he realised his error he tried to improve relations with the west. In the end, however, he came to the conclusion that the western powers would not help Russia in the event of a German attack. The policy of appeasement, which reached its climax at Munich, reinforced this view. He therefore decided to seek an agreement with Germany.

The German–Soviet Pact (1939) bought him time and enabled him to regain the territory lost to Poland at the Treaty of Riga in 1921. Stalin went on to attack Finland. Despite unexpectedly stiff resistance by the Finns, Russia gained territory in Karelia. It also annexed the Baltic states. Relations with Germany deteriorated but Stalin was convinced that Hitler would not attack Russia while still at war in the west. He was completely taken by surprise when Hitler launched Operation Barbarossa in June 1941.

You should be able to explain the significance of each of these dates.

1922	Stalin Secretary General of the Communist Party	
1924	Death of Lenin	
1925	Fall of Trotsky	
1927	Kamenev and Zinoviev expelled from the Politburo	
1928	First Five-Year Plan	
1929	Collectivisation decree	**KEY DATES**
1933	Second Five-Year Plan	
1935	Purges begin with arrest of Kamenev and Zinoviev	
1938	Third Five-Year Plan	
1939	Nazi–Soviet Pact	
1941	German invasion of Russia	

13.3 The Second World War and the Cold War

After studying this section you should be able to:

- *account for the victory of Russia in the war against Germany, 1941–45*
- *account for the development of the Cold War in Eastern Europe after 1945*
- *assess the record of the Soviet Union in the last years of Stalin's dictatorship*

LEARNING SUMMARY

The Great Patriotic War

 OCR M3

The military history of the war fell into two phases. In the first phase (1941–42) the Germans advanced deep into Russia. There were three main lines of attack: against Leningrad in the north, towards Moscow in the centre and through the Ukraine in the south. By the end of the year Leningrad was besieged and the Germans had almost reached Moscow, which the Russians successfully defended. In the south, Kiev, Odessa and the Crimea had been captured, except for Sebastopol, which was under siege. Only the Russian winter halted the German advance.

In 1942 the main German offensive was in the south. In September they attacked Stalingrad, the key to Russia's links with the Caucasus and its oil reserves. This was the limit of their advance. In February 1943 the combination of the Russian winter and over-extended supply lines forced the Germans at Stalingrad to surrender.

This was the turning point of the war.

In the second phase (1943–45) the Russian armies pushed the Germans back. In July 1943 Marshal Zhukov won the massive tank battle at Kursk. In November Kiev was liberated and early in 1944 Leningrad. In the second half of 1944 the Red Army advanced into Eastern Europe, occupying Romania, Bulgaria and Poland. In March 1945 Russian troops entered eastern Germany, reaching Berlin in April.

Why was the USSR victorious?

But it can be argued that it allowed the bulk of the German forces to be withdrawn from the Caucasus.

Part of the explanation lies in German mistakes, especially Hitler's refusal to allow a retreat from Stalingrad. The rapid advance of the German armies left them with over-extended lines of communication. By the brutal treatment of the Russians in German-occupied territory Hitler threw away the chance to turn them against Stalin's dictatorship.

Stalin himself played a great part. The personality cult which had developed around him helped to provide a focus of leadership, which he used to great effect to mobilise Russian patriotism. He set up the State Defence Committee in 1941 to organise and co-ordinate the war effort. He reorganised the army and promoted able officers. Unlike Hitler, he did not interfere in the detail of military strategy.

Stalin's apologists would argue that this achievement justified the methods used in the Five-Year Plans.

Russia's industrial strength, together with massive aid from the USA and Britain, enabled it to equip its vast army. Industrialisation in the 1930s underlay this. Industrial plants east of the Urals, e.g. Magnetogorsk, produced quantities of aircraft and tanks. The State Defence Committee also organised a massive transfer of industrial plant from the war zone to Siberia and Central Asia. In the latter years of the war the USSR was producing more military equipment than Germany and of better quality.

> The cost of the war to Russia was enormous. Overall the USSR lost 23 million dead, including 3 million who died as prisoners of war in German hands. 5 million people were homeless.

KEY POINT

The Cold War

OCR ▸ M3

The future of Poland was the first major cause of dissent between the Allies. The Russians had set up a Communist-dominated government, which had started to expel Germans living east of the Oder–Neisse line.

They were also, of course, occupying eastern Germany (except for the western sectors of Berlin).

The war temporarily transformed Russia's relations with the west. When the USA entered the war in 1942, the Grand Alliance of the USA, Britain and the USSR was formed. The leaders of the three countries met at three major conferences: Teheran (1943), Yalta (February 1945) and Potsdam (July–August 1945). It was, however, a somewhat uneasy alliance between the capitalist western powers and Communist Russia. Stalin accused the USA and Britain of failing to take the pressure off Russia in 1943 by postponing the invasion of France. He was always suspicious that the western powers would ultimately try to overthrow Communism in Russia. He therefore wanted a Communist-controlled Eastern Europe as a buffer against the perceived threat from the west.

At the end of the war Russian troops occupied Poland, Romania, Bulgaria and Hungary. In all these states Stalin set up People's Democracies including both Communists and non-Communists. The Communists soon took control and established one-party states. Yugoslavia and Albania also had Communist governments. Thus by 1946 Churchill was able to speak of an Iron Curtain across Europe. Only Czechoslovakia, with a coalition government under a Communist prime minister, was not fully under Communist control by then. A Communist coup in 1948 completed Soviet control of Eastern Europe.

Both sides felt threatened by the other.

This was preceded by Cominform (1947), through which Russia controlled the European Communist parties, both in Eastern Europe and in France and Italy.

To the USA and the Western European powers this looked like a Communist threat to the whole of Europe. Because of this, the USA began to strengthen its ties with the states of Western Europe. This simply reinforced Stalin's fears and he tightened his control over the Eastern European satellite states. In 1949 he set up Comecon to co-ordinate their economies and direct their trade towards Russia. The Soviet military presence in Eastern Europe was built up to a total of 5.5 million troops by the early 1950s.

During Stalin's last years, the Cold War flared up twice, in the Berlin blockade of 1948–49 and the Korean War of 1950–53.

Stalin's last years, 1945–53

OCR ▸ M3

The major task facing Russia in 1945 was reconstruction. The fourth and fifth Five-Year Plans rebuilt Russian industry. By 1950 the USSR was the world's second biggest industrial power. Particular attention was given to the development of a nuclear industry. By 1949 the USSR had an atomic bomb. Much of the new industry was east of the Urals so as to keep it as far away as possible from any threat from the west.

You should now revise your work on Stalin by comparing Russia in 1953 with Russia in 1924.

Politically Stalin's last years were marked by a renewal of the repression of the 1930s: censorship, an omnipresent secret police (under Beria), persecution of the Church, anti-semitic tendencies, and state pressure on the arts and universities.

After 1945 Stalin returned to the policies of the 1930s. Russia was ruled by a savagely repressive dictatorship and its people were isolated from the rest of the world. But it was also one of the two superpowers.	**KEY POINT**

You should be able to explain the significance of each of these dates.

1941	Operation Barbarossa begins	**KEY DATES**
1943	Stalingrad	
1945	Russian armies capture Berlin; surrender of Germany; Yalta Conference	
1948	Communist coup in Czechoslovakia	
1948–49	Berlin Blockade	
1950–53	Korean War	
1953	Death of Stalin	

Sample question and model answer

Source

Industrialisation

Read the following source and then answer the questions which follow.

From *Beyond the Urals* by John Scott, 1943. Scott was an American engineer working in Russia.

I was going to be one of the many who cared not to own a second pair of shoes, but who built the blast furnaces which were their aim. I would wager that Russia's battle of ferrous metallurgy alone involved more casualties than the battle of the Marne. All during the thirties the Russian people were at war. At Magnetogorsk I was precipitated into a battle. I was deployed on the iron and steel front. Tens of thousands of people were enduring the most intense hardships in order to build blast furnaces, and many of them did it willingly, with boundless enthusiasm, which infected me from the day of my arrival.

(a) What, according to this source, was the author's attitude towards Stalin's programme of industrialisation? [3]

Quote from the source to explain this. →

Enthusiastic, because he saw what hardship the Russian people were prepared to accept to bring about industrialisation. Regarded it as a battle – prepared to share the hardship.

(b) How did Stalin carry out a policy of industrialisation? [7]

The question calls for a full description of the Five-Year Plans. →

The Five-Year Plans set targets for all major industries, to be achieved by a mixture of rewards and punishments. The Five-Year Plans concentrated on heavy industry and, in the later 1930s, armaments. Consumer goods had low priority. Methods used included direction of labour and ruthless discipline in the factories, but also pay differentials and medals for outstanding workers (Stakhanovites).

(c) What was the impact of Stalin's attempts in the 1930s to industrialise the Soviet Union? [15]

Impact on economic growth – →

- The economic impact. The Five-Year Plans produced a remarkable rate of growth, which transformed Russia into a major industrial power. Between 1928 and 1941 coal and steel production quadrupled. Great new industrial areas were developed in the Urals and Siberia.

– on the workers →

- Conditions for the workers were very poor with low wages and poor housing in the new industrial towns. There were few consumer goods. By the mid-1930s workers began to see some benefits in education, health care and holidays with pay. Government propaganda stressed that the sacrifices were in a patriotic cause. The source shows the propaganda was successful.

– on the agricultural sector. →

- To pay for industrialisation, agricultural production had to be increased. Hence the programme of collectivisation, which led to millions of deaths among the peasants (kulaks) as well as a terrible famine in 1932–33.

Practice examination questions

1 (a) In what ways did Lenin attempt to consolidate Bolshevik rule in Russia in 1917–18? [15]

(b) Why did the Bolsheviks win the Civil War? [15]

2 (a) Explain how Lenin tackled Russia's economic problems between 1917 and 1924. [15]

(b) Why did Stalin emerge victorious from the struggle for power in the Soviet Union after the death of Lenin in 1924? [15]

3 Read the following source and then answer the questions which follow.

From *From Lenin to Stalin* by V. Serge

I am convinced that at the end of 1934, just at the moment that Kirov was murdered, the Politburo was entering upon a policy of normality and relaxation. The shot fired by Nikolayev (the assassin) ushered in an era of panic and savagery.

(a) In the context of the Soviet Union in the 1930s, explain 'Politburo'. [3]

(b) Why did the murder of Kirov lead to 'an era of panic and savagery'? [7]

(c) Assess the results for Stalin and the Soviet Union of the purges in the years 1934 to1939. [15]

(adapted from NEAB, 1999)

Practice examination answers

1 (a) It traced its history back to eighteenth-century parliamentary reform movements, which had been boosted in the 1790s by the French Revolution.

    (b) Demobilisation at the end of the war and the end of wartime contracts caused distress. The industrial revolution caused displacement of some workers by machines and harsh conditions in factories and towns. Enclosure caused distress among the rural poor.

    (c) The Spa Fields Riots, the March of the Blanketeers and Peterloo were no real threat (e.g. Peterloo was an over-reaction to a peaceful meeting). The Pentrich Rising and the Cato St Conspiracy were revolutionary in intention, but their chances of success were limited. The government's fears were probably exaggerated. Was political disturbance caused more by economic distress than revolutionary ideas? What chance did uncoordinated radical movements have of overthrowing a repressive government?

2 (a) Repressive policies, e.g. use of spies, were relaxed. Six Acts not enforced. Combination Acts repealed.

    (b)• Peel reformed the penal code and abolished the death penalty for over 100 offences. Gaols Act (1823) introduced improvements. Set up the Metropolitan Police in 1829.
      • Huskisson moved towards free trade: reduced import duties, relaxed Navigation Laws, secured passing of Reciprocity of Duties Act, introduced sliding scale for Corn Laws.

    (c) Reforms of Peel and Huskisson together with repeal of the Combination Acts (1824), repeal of Test and Corporation Acts (1828) and Catholic emancipation (1829) are their chief claim to be called liberal. But note that repeal of Combination Acts was followed by an Amending Act which effectively deprived trade unions of right to strike and repeal of Test and Corporation Acts merely replaced annual Indemnity Acts.

      Three big issues demonstrate limits of their liberalism:
      • Catholic emancipation was only accepted by Wellington and Peel because they judged that civil war in Ireland was the alternative; and it split the Tory Party.
      • They had no thought of repealing the Corn Laws.
      • They were totally opposed to parliamentary reform.

3 (a) He favoured it because it would give the middle classes more political influence and strengthen the ties between middle and upper classes. Thus it would strengthen the constitution (implicitly against threats from below).

    (b) Under-representation of the industrial areas of the north and the midlands, over-representation of the south. Rotten and pocket boroughs. Large industrial towns not represented. County franchise excluded many middle-class men whose property was not freehold. Borough franchise was anomalous and outdated – often excluded many of the middle classes.

    (c) Opposition came from Tories, especially in the Lords, where they had a majority. The first Bill was defeated at the committee stage in the Commons and the second in the Lords. Factors which helped to bring about the passing of the Bill were:

- Support of the electorate in the general election of 1831.
- Agitation in the country. Riots in Nottingham and Bristol, mass support for Attwood's Birmingham Political Union. Fears of revolution if the Bill was not passed. 1830 revolutions in Europe were fresh in people's memories.
- Middle classes joined with working classes in the agitation – threatened to withdraw money from the banks and to refuse to pay taxes.
- The disunity of the Tories. Although they opposed the Bill, Wellington was unable to form a government when the king asked him to.
- The king agreed to create enough new peers to overcome the opposition in the Lords. He did not need to.

4 (a) • Peel's acceptance of the Reform Act and of the need to appeal to the new electorate. Tamworth Manifesto offered a policy of reforming proven abuses.
- The declining popularity of the Whigs. After 1835 they passed few reforms, disappointing their radical supporters. Poor financial management led to budget deficits. Their church reforms antagonised Anglican opinion.

(b) • Free trade budgets produced trade revival, reduced unemployment, reduced cost of living.
- Income tax turned budget deficit into surplus.
- Mines Act tackled worst abuses in mines.
- Factory Act limited working hours of women and children. Both Acts were disappointing to radicals and humanitarians.
- Bank Charter Act – important in creating a stable currency and banking system and in development of London as a financial centre.
- Companies Act.
- Repeal of the Corn Laws. Major symbolic step in move to free trade. But it split the party.

Chapter 2 England, 1846–86

1 (a) • His personal popularity and reputation for upholding British interests and standing up to foreign countries as Foreign Secretary 1830–41 and 1846–51.
- Successful conclusion of Crimean War, support for Italian unification and pursuit of British interests in China enhanced his popularity.
- Domination of Whigs/Liberals. Gladstone's acceptance of office under Palmerston in 1859 brought together Whigs and Peelites in the first genuinely Liberal ministry.

(b) • The split in the Conservative Party in 1846 proved irreversible. The Peelites moved from supporting Russell's ministry via participating in Aberdeen's coalition to joining the Whigs in Palmerston's Liberal ministry in 1859.
- The limited appeal of Conservative policies to the electorate. Opposition to free trade lost them the election of 1847. Liberals benefited from the association of mid-Victorian prosperity with free trade. The Conservatives had nothing to set against Palmerston's popularity as the promoter of British interests abroad. Reform Act of 1867 did not benefit them until 1874.
- Weak leadership. When the party split in 1846 most of the ministers followed Peel. The only outstanding figure who remained was Disraeli, who was distrusted because of his background and character.

2 (a) • Social reform. Ideas about the 'two nations'. Manchester and Crystal Palace speeches. A paternalistic approach – the rich looking after the poor and thus winning working-class support for the monarchy and aristocracy.
   • Imperialism. Hoped to develop the empire as a powerful economic and political unit which would sustain Britain as a great power in competition with Germany and the USA. Imperialism would harness mass support to the Conservatives and the monarchy through appeal to patriotism.

 (b) • Balkan Crisis. Safeguarded British interests in Near East by checking Russian advance towards Dardanelles and breaking up 'big' Bulgaria. Bolstered Turkey. Acquired Cyprus. Thus achieved main objectives. Congress of Berlin secured 30 years of peace for Europe. But Bulgaria turned out not to be a Russian satellite, so perhaps a 'big' Bulgaria would have been in British interests.
   • Suez Canal shares. Typical Disraelian opportunism. Safeguarded route to India. But led to further involvement in and eventual occupation of Egypt.
   • Creation of title of Empress of India. Good symbolic move.
   • Zulu and Afghan Wars. Disraeli drawn in by 'forward' policies of men on the spot. Both wars eventually successful but at high cost in loss of life. A factor in election defeat in 1880.

3 (a) Ireland was ruled by coercion, i.e. the normal course of law was suspended.

 (b) Reason given is fear that Home Rule will lead to a demand for independence. Useful as indication of one ground for opposition but language suggests it over-states the case. But this also shows the issue aroused strong passions.

 (c) Gladstone favours self-government on the grounds that the only alternative is continued coercion. Bright opposes it because it is unacceptable to protestants in Ireland and especially to Ulster. He distrusts the Irish nationalist party in parliament, whereas Gladstone accepts the demands of Irish nationalism.

 (d) Sources 2 and 4 suggest that their tactics have alienated English opinion. Source 2 attacks the Irish party for lacking 'justice and wisdom'. Source 4 refers to the 'violence' of Irish MPs and the Phoenix Park murders. Source 3 implicitly takes the same line ('disloyal Ireland'). Source 1, however, shows that Gladstone accepts the demands of 'Irish nationality'. The ongoing violence in Ireland, culminating in the Phoenix Park murders, led many Englishmen to think that the Irish were unfit to govern themselves, as Morley says. But it also convinced Gladstone that Home Rule was the only way forward. Thus Parnell's tactics played a great part in Gladstone's decision to introduce the Home Rule Bill, but also were a main reason for its rejection.

Chapter 3 Foreign affairs, 1815–1902

1 (a) Protection of Britain's trading interests. Maintaining the balance of power, which meant keeping a suspicious watch on France and Russia. Maintenance of peace by regular meetings (Congresses). Non-intervention in the internal affairs of smaller countries. Canning also supported liberal or constitutional regimes – but only if it was not contrary to Britain's interests.

 (b) • Congress of Verona – Canning opposed intervention in Spain and thus helped to undermine the Congress System.
   • Portugal and South America – promoted British trade, prevented intervention by Spain and France (thus maintaining balance of power) and promoted constitutional governments.

- Greece – the big problem. Victory for the rebels would upset balance of power in Russia's favour, but British opinion supported the Greeks. So he intervened jointly with Russia so as to keep control over the situation. A successful strategy but after his death Wellington reversed it.

2 (a) Upholding British prestige. Maintaining peace (if necessary by the use of British power, but preferably by diplomacy). The balance of power – particularly suspicious of France and Russia. British trading interests. Britain's naval supremacy. Sympathy for constitutional governments and nationalist aspirations. But above all pragmatic in pursuing national interest – 'no eternal allies and no perpetual enemies'.

(b) • Italy. He helped to ensure that Parma, Modena and Tuscany were able to unite with Piedmont and gave moral support to Garibaldi. But Britain's role was relatively minor because Palmerston's suspicion of France prevented him co-operating with Napoleon III over Italy.
- USA. Two relevant issues: the seizure of two Southern agents from the *Trent* and the failure to prevent the *Alabama* putting to sea and attacking Northern shipping. Palmerston's handling of the first was unnecessarily provocative. In the second Palmerston and Russell refused to accept that they were in the wrong.
- Schleswig-Holstein. Palmerston threatened war in support of Denmark but was out-manoeuvred by Bismarck, who realised that he was bluffing.

Chapter 4 The Edwardian age

1 (a) Tariff reform is the major reason. Other factors included lack of social reform, the Education Act of 1902, the Taff Vale Case and the Chinese labour scandal.

(b) • Suffragettes. Increasing militancy, culminating in 1913 in a campaign of arson and violence, leading to imprisonment, hunger strikes and the Cat and Mouse Act. The government could not give in to violence but was unable to stop the militants' campaign.
- Industrial unrest. Wave of strikes 1910–14 – railwaymen, miners, dockers. Government response firm – sometimes too strong (troops at Tonypandy). Unrest caused by unemployment and falling real wages. Also syndicalist ideas. Triple Alliance (1913) threatened possible general strike. Historians differ as to how near Britain came to industrial chaos.
- Ireland. Under the Parliament Act, the Home Rule Bill became law in 1914. Ulster prepared to resist: role of Carson, formation of Ulster Volunteers – matched by Irish Volunteers. Bonar Law encouraged resistance. Asquith was indecisive. Curragh Mutiny indicated government could not rely on army. This was the most serious threat – Ireland on verge of civil war in 1914.

2 (a) • Conservative majority in the Lords.
- Rejection of 1893 Home Rule Bill.
- Rejection of Liberal government bills by Lords after election of 1906: Education Bill, Plural Voting Bill, Licensing Bill.
- 1909 budget – taxes on rich to pay for Dreadnoughts and pensions. Land value tax particularly resented by landowners.
- Rejection of budget by Lords unprecedented. Raised issue of powers of hereditary house against elected house in a democracy.

(b) • General election (1910): Liberals returned with Labour and Irish support. Lords accepted budget.
   • Constitutional Conference – broke down over issue of Lords' power to block Home Rule. Asquith, dependent on Irish support, could not accept.
   • Second general election on issue of reform of the Lords. Same result.
   • King agreed to create enough peers to pass Parliament Act if necessary. Lords accepted the Act – enough peers stayed away.
   • State terms of the Act.

3 (a) The meeting set up the Labour Representation Committee with the aim of forming a distinct Labour group in parliament. The name was changed to Labour Party in 1906, but it was uncertain in 1900 whether it would survive.

(b) Various organisations grew up in the late nineteenth century to further labour interests and/or socialist ideas: the SDF, Fabians, ILP, trade unions. Had different ideas about what they wanted to achieve – a socialist society, moderate social reform, improved wages and conditions. Also differed about methods. Liberal and Conservative Parties had working-class wings, which competed with Labour for members. There were also a few Lib-Labs – working-class MPs: some trade unionists thought this better than a separate party. Problems of creating a national organisation from scratch and raising funds.

(c) Conservatives paid little attention to the LRC. Their refusal to reverse the Taff Vale judgement helped to strengthen trade union support for the LRC. This and electoral pact with Liberals enabled it to win 29 seats in 1906. Liberals passed Trade Disputes Act, which was largely Labour's work. Miners' union supported Labour from 1909. Labour won 42 seats in 1910. Persuaded Liberals to start payment for MPs and reverse Osborne judgement. But still seemed more like a radical wing of the Liberals than a separate party in 1914.

4 (a) Avoiding alliances with commitments to war. Britain relied on the navy for defence rather than allies.

(b) Explain why by 1900 isolation was beginning to seem dangerous. Approaches to Germany were rebuffed and the expansion of the German navy seemed threatening. Britain's first alliance was with Japan (1902). France felt less secure with only Russia as an ally after Japan's victory over Russia and was willing to clear up colonial disagreements with Britain.

(c) The dates refer to the German Naval Law and the Agadir Crisis. The main issues are the naval race, Germany's attitude to the Boer war, the failure of Chamberlain's attempts to make an alliance with Germany, the effects of the Ententes on Anglo-German relations and the two Morocco crises. Each of these soured relations. The navy was particularly important to Britain. Note the importance of William II's Weltpolitik.

Chapter 5 The inter-war years

1 (a) The May Committee proposed a cut in unemployment pay as part of a package to stop the run on sterling.

(b) Useful as a precise record of events by one close to the centre. As a diary entry on the day it does not try to answer charges of betrayal which were made later. Useful on role of the king, Baldwin and Samuel in influencing MacDonald. Naturally, it takes a favourable view of MacDonald. Fails to mention his lack of consultation with Labour colleagues – see Source 3.

(c) The case against MacDonald is that he failed to consult his colleagues, who were shocked and believed his behaviour was due to love of office. Source 3 – by a Labour minister who followed MacDonald – supports this. He was also accused of giving way to royal flattery (Sources 1 and 4). Labour bitterness was compounded by the disastrous 1931 election result. The case for MacDonald is that a coalition was an appropriate response to such a serious crisis. Source 2 supports this. Sources 1 and 4, especially 4, suggest that he was not so much 'seduced by royal flattery' as pressed by the king, whose role was crucial. Source 1 says he expected this would ruin his political career.

2 (a) Wheatley Housing Act. MacDonald's conduct of foreign affairs – restoring relations with the USSR, role in Dawes Plan and Geneva Protocol.

(b) • They were minority governments, dependent on Liberals and therefore restricted in how far they could pursue genuinely Labour policies.
   • 1924 ministry was tainted by suspicion, especially among middle-class voters, that Labour really aimed for a socialist revolution. Hence the importance of the Zinoviev letter.
   • 1931 financial crisis presented Labour with problems it could not handle and which split the ministry.

3 (a) The key word in the source is 'revolutionary'. Explain how the article justified this charge and what conclusions it drew from it.

(b) The coal owners proposed a wage cut, which the mineworkers rejected. Throughout the subsequent negotiations the miners expected the support of other unions because of the Triple Alliance. A strike was averted by a government subsidy to the industry while awaiting the report of the Samuel Commission. When it reported, both sides rejected its proposals. A miners' strike followed and the miners turned to the TUC for support. Mindful of the collapse of the Triple Alliance in 1921, the TUC ordered a general strike.

(c) The government was prepared for the strike and maintained essential services. Through the *British Gazette* it put over its case, portraying the strike as a challenge to the authority of parliament. The TUC was less well prepared; its leaders became afraid that it would lead to violence, possibly revolution, and that they would lose control to extremists. They were also worried by the charge that the strike was illegal. They seized the opportunity to end the strike offered by the Samuel compromise.

Chapter 6 Post-war Britain 1945–64

1 (a) • The Conservatives were blamed by voters for unemployment and appeasement in the 1930s.
   • Labour's manifesto offered full and enthusiastic implementation of the Beveridge Report. It seemed more likely to create a fairer society.
   • Labour leaders had gained experience in the wartime coalition.

(b) • Post-war economic recovery – see the model answer on page 82.
   • The establishment of the welfare state – the National Health Service and National Insurance scheme. Remarkably successful in that both have survived in main principles for over 50 years.
   • Nationalisation. Explain which industries were nationalised. Success was debatable. Railways and mines were clearly not thriving under private ownership but nationalisation did not solve their problems. Iron and steel nationalisation was controversial and was reversed by the Conservatives. Management of publicly-owned industries proved a long-term problem.

2 (a) • Electoral reaction against continuing austerity, shortages and controls (rationing, national service).
- The revival of the Conservative Party.
- Divisions in the Labour Party, especially over health service charges.
- The government seemed tired, especially after the 1950 election, when it had only a small majority.
- Attlee's decision to call an election was unnecessary.

(b) • Increased living standards, for which the Conservatives got the credit. End of controls and austerity. Housing drive.
- Disunity of the Labour Party, especially over nuclear disarmament (to which it was for a time officially committed) and 'socialism', particularly further nationalisation.
- The political skill of Macmillan, who revived the morale of the Conservatives after Suez and enabled it to win a third election. He was also the first politician to make effective use of television.

Chapter 7 France, 1814–75

1 (a) • Tried to restore the *ancien régime*. The divisions in post-revolution France (republicans, Bonapartists, moderate royalists, Ultras) made this dangerous.
- Early mistakes: compensation for émigré nobles, the ancient religious form of coronation, increased privileges for the Church, tighter press censorship.
- Appointment of the extreme Ultra Polignac as chief minister in 1829 provoked a clash with the Chamber of Deputies, but a general election produced an even more hostile Chamber.
- Instead of backing down, Charles issued the Ordinances of St Cloud.
- Economic hardship caused discontent among working classes in Paris.

(b) • Foreign policy was unpopular. He avoided war because of expense and because unsure of support for his regime. Seen as subservient to Britain, e.g. in Belgium and the Mehemet Ali affair. Scored diplomatic victory in Spanish Marriages affair, but this was short-lived and deprived him of British sympathy in 1848. But unpopular foreign policy was not enough to cause his overthrow.
- Other reasons for unpopularity were:
  - Louis Philippe's uninspiring personality.
  - Lack of a political base: he was asked to become king in 1830 as a compromise acceptable to moderate royalists and republicans, but never had the enthusiastic support of either.
  - In the 1840s under the influence of Guizot the regime became increasingly corrupt, inefficient and illiberal.
  - Perhaps most important, economic change led to widespread distress but the regime did little to tackle the consequent social problems.

2 (a) • 1859 amnesty to political opponents, followed in 1860 by moves towards 'Liberal Empire'. During the 1860s press censorship was relaxed and trade unions were legalised. In 1867 ministers were required to answer questions in parliament. A parliamentary opposition developed.
- In 1869 a new constitution gave the Assembly power to propose laws and vote on the budget. A ministry representing the majority in the Assembly was formed in January 1870.
- But Napoleon still retained considerable powers, including the power to change the constitution, subject to a plebiscite.

(b) • The essential background is the political divisions in France: royalists, republicans, Bonapartists, socialists.
  • The role of Thiers. His prestige after negotiating with Bismarck, suppressing the Commune and organising the payment of the indemnity. Although a royalist, by 1875 he concluded that republic was the least divisive solution and persuaded the Assembly of this.
  • The effects of the Commune – a warning of how divisive a restored monarchy would be.
  • Although royalists had a majority in the Assembly, they were divided between the Bourbon and Orléans claimants.
  • The Comte de Chambord ruined his cause by demanding the restoration of the Bourbon flag – a symbol of a royalist reaction.

Chapter 8 Russia, 1825–1917

1 (a) Serfdom, which tied the vast majority of the population to the nobility and thus to the Tsardom.

(b) Explain details of the new system. Comment on the small size of peasant holdings, the communal liability for redemption payments and the difficulty of leaving the village.

(c) • Emancipation did away with the most backward feature of Russian society. But it also created new problems: communal liability for redemption payments meant peasants were tied to the mir. Agriculture remained backward.
  • Zemstva. A small step towards representative government, though the franchise was heavily weighted in favour of gentry.
  • Education. Greater freedom for universities. Censorship relaxed. Some expansion of school education, but illiteracy was still widespread.
  • Reform of justice. Jury system introduced. But did not apply to political cases.
  • Increasing repression after 1863. Alexander refused to consider a parliament.
  • Conclusion. Alexander's reforms were partial because they were designed to preserve the autocracy rather than genuinely liberalise Russia. So they did not fulfil the high hopes with which his reign had begun.

2 (a) • The revolutionaries were not united, so eventually the Tsar was able to split the liberals from the socialists with the October Manifesto. There was no central leadership: the strikes and peasant uprisings were spontaneous and not organised.
  • The army and navy for the most part remained loyal. This enabled the Tsar to revert to repression once he had regained the upper hand.

(b) • The First World War exposed the inefficiency of the regime. The armies were ill-equipped and the transport system could not cope with supplying them. Consequently there were heavy defeats and morale plummeted. Since the Tsar took command of the armies, he was personally blamed.
  • The legacy of 1905. The Tsarist regime never really regained the loyalty of the people after Bloody Sunday, nor did it learn the lessons of 1905. Attempts to modernise Russia and bind the people to the regime by the Dumas were undermined by the Tsar's reluctance to allow a democratic franchise or to give the Dumas real power.
  • The sufferings of the civilian population triggered the revolution. By 1917 food was so short that there were food riots in Petrograd.

3 (a) Both say peasants were disaffected. Source 3 claims they were hostile to the dynasty in February, while Source 4 suggests it was after the fall of Nicholas that they realised that the Tsardom did not matter to them. But Source 3 is about peasants who had been drafted into the army, whereas Source 4 is about those who remained in their villages.

(b) Farmborough was there at the time. Being English, she had no obvious axe to grind. But since she was at the front in Galicia, what she says about events in the cities is what she has learnt from newspapers rather than seen. But she had first-hand knowledge of growing discontent among the soldiers.

(c) Source 1 shows that a perceptive observer realised that the Tsarist system was in danger before the war. He predicts accurately what the effect of the war will be. Source 5, the historians' view, takes the same line: the war did not cause the overthrow of the Tsar but brought together the underlying discontents. The ideas given in the answer to Question 2 (b) above suggest the interrelation between the effects of the war and other factors.

Chapter 9 The unification of Italy

1 (a) If Garibaldi conquered Naples, he could then go on to attack the Papal States. Rome had been protected by French troops since 1848, so this could lead to war with France. Austria, a Catholic state, might also intervene.

(b) It identifies two obstacles: the disunity of Italians and the armies of the King of Naples ('the Bourbon'), Austria and the Pope.

(c) Source 2 shows that Garibaldi's aim was to bring Naples and Sicily into a kingdom of Italy under Victor Emmanuel. The 'boot' refers to the shape of Italy on the map. The caption suggests that Garibaldi is pressing the king to use force to gain control of the whole of Italy. Source 4, written after the campaign in Naples was completed, shows that Garibaldi had achieved his aim but that for the people of Naples he was the real hero. They felt little loyalty to the new king.

(d) As well as the events focused on in the documents, the answer should refer to the defence of the Roman Republic in 1848, which played an important part in arousing Italian patriotism. Explain the expedition to Sicily and Naples and show that it forced Cavour to go further than he intended and to send Piedmontese troops into the Papal States in order to keep control over Garibaldi. Garibaldi's ability as a military leader and his European reputation were important. Thus he played a key role in achieving a united kingdom of the whole of Italy, rather than just of Northern Italy as Cavour wished.

2 (a) • The military strength of Austria – 1848 demonstrated that no Italian state could match this, not even Piedmont.
  • Lack of common purpose between revolutionary leaders in different parts of Italy, partly reflecting their different visions of a united Italy: Mazzini wanted a republic, Gioberti a federation headed by the Pope, Charles Albert a kingdom of North Italy under Piedmont.

(b) • The strengthening of Piedmont by Cavour between 1852 and 1859 – see the model answer on page 105.
  • The intervention of France led to the defeat of Austria and thus to the annexation of Lombardy by Piedmont (and subsequently of Parma, Modena, Tuscany and the Romagna, through plebiscites made possible by the defeat of Austria).
  • The role of Garibaldi in conquering Naples and Sicily and forcing Cavour to intervene. This in turn led to the invasion of the eastern Papal States, and the union of Naples, Sicily, Umbria and the Marches with northern Italy.

Chapter 10 The unification of Germany

1 (a) Refers to the struggle with the Catholic Church. The main attack came in the May Laws of 1873–75.

(b) The North German Confederation was predominantly Protestant. The South German states were Catholic. Bismarck feared Catholics would have divided loyalties. This fear was heightened by the ultramontanism displayed in the First Vatican Council in 1870.

(c) Not very successful. The Kulturkampf was abandoned, partly in order to concentrate on attacking the Socialists. The anti-Socialist law failed to prevent the continuing growth of the Socialist Party and lapsed after Bismarck's fall. He got his way in his quarrel with the Liberals over tariffs, but only by abandoning the Kulturkampf and allying with the Catholic Centre Party.

2 (a) The main aim was peace. This entailed preventing a war of revenge by France. A war on two fronts would be particularly dangerous. Therefore France must be kept isolated. It followed that Germany must maintain good relations with both Austria and Russia.

(b) Achieved a close alliance with Austria, but it was difficult to reconcile this with good relations with Russia, since Russian and Austrian interests clashed in the Balkans, especially in the crisis of 1875–78. In the Congress of Berlin Bismarck backed Austria, but this created the risk of driving Russia into an alliance with France. Explain the agreements he made between 1879 and 1887 to deal with this problem: the Dual Alliance with Austria; the Dreikaiserbund; the Triple Alliance with Austria and Italy; the Reinsurance Treaty with Russia. He succeeded in keeping France isolated, but it was doubtful whether the complex web of agreements was sustainable in the long run.

3 (a) Background: 1893 Franco-Russian alliance; 1904 Anglo-French Entente. Anglo-Russian Entente (1907) completed the Triple Entente.

(b) • William II's Weltpolitik – navy needed to make Germany a world power.
 • Role of Tirpitz – argued navy was needed to support Germany's position as a colonial power and to compete in international affairs with Britain.
 • Navy League whipped up enthusiasm for Tirpitz's programme.

(c) Give details of the crises and comment on each. Germany had a legitimate interest in Morocco, but in the Moroccan Crisis (1905–06), the Kaiser's real aim was to break up the Anglo-French Entente. This backfired – Britain supported France. In Bosnia (1908) Germany backed Austria (as one would expect) but Serbia was embittered and, because Germany virtually threatened war, Russia was thwarted. In the Agadir Crisis (1911) Germany's interest was legitimate but sending a gunboat to Agadir was provocative to Britain. The result was to strengthen ties between Britain and France. In the Balkan Wars (1912–13) Germany supported Austria, insisting that Serbia should not gain Albania, but worked with Britain to achieve a negotiated peace (Treaty of London) and again co-operated with Britain to prevent the Second Balkan War escalating. Overall the view seems justified except in relation to the Balkan Wars.

Chapter 11 Italy, 1919–45

1 (a) Mussolini's seizure of power in 1922. Fascists from all over Italy were to descend on Rome. Mussolini stayed in Milan until the king summoned him.

(b) The underlying reason was the breakdown of parliamentary government. The specific circumstances of 1922 included a general strike, the weakness of Facta's government in handling it, the prominence of the fascists in tackling the socialists during the strike and the march on Rome. The attitude of the king was important – he refused to allow Facta to use the army against the fascists.

(c) Outline main features of Italian politics. Parliament was managed before the war by transformism, which meant bribery and patronage. Regional differences, especially between north and south, worked against formation of national parties. Further splits were caused by differences of opinion about Italy's entry into the war. After the war Socialists were unwilling to co-operate with any other party; also they split into Socialists and Communists. Result: five governments between 1918 and 1922. Thus governments were unable to cope with post-war problems: weakness of the economy, inflation, disappointment over the peace treaties, growth of paramilitaries of both right and left.

2 (a) It stood for strong, centralised government, with emphasis on the cult of the leader, in contrast to the virtual breakdown of parliamentary government after 1918. It was anti-Communist at a time when landowners, industrialists and the middle classes were all alarmed by the threat of communist revolution. It emphasised national pride at a time when Italians were dissatisfied with their country's performance in the war and with the peace terms.

(b) • The Corporate State was supposed to produce co-operation between employers and labour. Strikes were forbidden.
  • The government intervened actively in the economy. It funded public works – most famously the draining of the Pontine Marshes. Industrial output was promoted by the Institute for Industrial Reconstruction, and subsidies.
  • The 'Battle for Grain' doubled wheat production. But dairy or fruit farming would have been more suited to some areas.
  • But there were many weaknesses. The Corporate State was cumbersome and inefficient; in practice it favoured employers against workers. There was much corruption. Italy remained industrially weaker than the other great powers. Agriculture remained backward. The south remained poverty-stricken.
  • The lira was overvalued, leading to a loss of exports.

Chapter 12 Germany, 1918–45

1 (a) Identify and explain the threats: the Spartacist Rising, the Kapp Putsch, the currency crisis and French occupation of the Ruhr, the Beer Hall Putsch. The Spartacists were overcome by the army and the freikorps, but there was serious fighting in Berlin. Kapp was overcome by a general strike in Berlin; the army refused to intervene. The currency crisis was overcome by Stresemann, who ended passive resistance and negotiated the Dawes Plan. The Beer Hall Putsch failed because the police and the army (except for Ludendorff) remained loyal.

(b) Examine economic, diplomatic and political reasons. The new currency and the Dawes Plan produced comparative prosperity. Stresemann's diplomacy restored Germany's international position and produced better relations with France. The French withdrew from the Ruhr and the Locarno Treaties guaranteed the Versailles settlement of Germany's western borders. With the return of prosperity, extremist parties gained few seats in the Reichstag. The mainstream parties worked together reasonably well in a series of coalitions.

2 (a) • The Weimar Republic lacked support among the German people. It was born of defeat in war and therefore unwelcome to nationalist opinion. The currency crisis of 1923 undermined middle-class support.
  • Proportional representation resulted in an endless series of coalitions. After 1930 it was impossible to form a government with a majority in the Reichstag, so Brüning had to use the president's emergency powers.
  • The system relied on former servants of the Empire – civil servants, judges and, above all, army officers – who had no faith in democracy.
  • Political leaders had no experience of democracy because under the Empire ministers were not responsible to the Reichstag.
  • Anti-democratic parties (Communists, Nationalists and National Socialists) had much support.

(b) • Unemployment was virtually eliminated, partly by revival of world trade, partly by Nazi policies – public works (e.g. autobahns), rearmament, expansion of the civil service and the party organisation. Jews who had been forced out of their jobs and political opponents in concentration camps were not counted as unemployed.
  • The state controlled wages, food prices, rents, investment and foreign exchange. Trade unions were abolished and strikes made illegal. Farm prices were fixed so that farmers made a reasonable profit.
  • Exports were boosted by Dr Schacht's manipulation of exchange rates and trade agreements with Eastern European and South American countries.
  • In 1936 a Four-Year Plan was introduced. The aim was self-sufficiency (autarky) by boosting domestic production and developing synthetic substitutes for oil and other imports. But production of synthetics was disappointing and agriculture failed to meet its targets. Economic growth was not fast enough to pay for rearmament and by 1939 there was a danger of runaway inflation.

3 (a) Mixed. He liked the comradeship and the sense of belonging to a co-operative community. But he disliked the demand for absolute obedience and subordination.

(b) • Education. Nazi racial views were taught and textbooks rewritten. Teachers had to toe the party line.
  • Hitler Youth. Compulsory membership. Inculcated Nazi ideas, especially the cult of the leader, prepared boys for military service. But also provided normal youth activities such as camps.
  • League of German Girls. Parallel organisation – prepared girls to be wives and mothers – their function, according to Nazi ideas.

(c) • Children and young people. Education directed towards indoctrination. Youth movements reinforced this but also offered enjoyable youth activities. Universities under strict control. Impossible to measure success but probably considerable.
  • The Churches. Much support for Nazis among Protestants at first, but setting up of the Reich Church divided them. The Confessional Church

(banned in 1937) produced some of the most outspoken and courageous opponents of Nazism. But the majority conformed. So did most Catholics. At first difficulties were smoothed over by the Concordat, but the Pope issued a critical encyclical in 1937. Some priests were imprisoned. But on the whole Catholic opposition very muted.

- The Jews. Explain boycotts of Jewish businesses, the Nuremberg Laws and Kristallnacht. Some Jews emigrated, others sent to concentration camps. Jewish population suffered considerable persecution.

Chapter 13 Soviet Russia, 1917–53

1 (a) He tried to provide 'land, peace and bread'. Land was confiscated and redistributed to the peasants. The Peace of Brest-Litovsk was accepted despite the severity of the terms. War Communism was instituted. Opposition was dealt with ruthlessly. The Cheka (secret police) instituted the 'Red Terror'. The first victims were leaders of other political parties. The Constituent Assembly was immediately dissolved because the elections left the Bolsheviks in a minority.

   (b) • The Red Army: the dynamism of Trotsky turned it into an efficient fighting machine, numbering over 5 million men by 1920.
   - The Communists controlled the main cities and the railways and had the advantage of internal communications.
   - The Russian peasants feared that the Whites would return the land to the landlords.
   - The Whites were not united in their aims and lacked co-ordination. Communication between the White forces in different areas was difficult.
   - The foreign supporters of the Whites were half-hearted and their intervention enabled the Communists to pose as Russian patriots.

2 (a) • In 1918 War Communism was instituted – as an emergency measure, Lenin later claimed. Industry and the banks were nationalised. Private trade was forbidden. Peasants had to sell surplus grain to the state at fixed prices.
   - War Communism combined with civil war caused economic chaos. Peasants refused to grow any surplus grain and famine resulted, causing widespread unrest by 1920. The Kronstadt Mutiny made Lenin realise War Communism was not working.
   - The New Economic Policy, 1921. A retreat from communist principles. Peasants were allowed to sell their surplus produce on payment of a tax. Private trading was restored through 'Nepmen'. But major industrial plants, banking, transport and foreign trade remained under state control.
   - The economy began to recover but only slowly because of continuing famine and financial crisis.

   (b) • His political skill. As General Secretary before Lenin's death, he had built up solid support in the Party Congress. He then proceeded to out-manoeuvre all his rivals, playing off Kamenev and Zinoviev against Trotsky and then Bukharin against all of them.
   - 'Socialism in one country' appealed to ordinary Russians' desire for peace and prosperity after the hardships of the First World War and the Civil War. It also appealed to their national pride.
   - 'Permanent revolution', by contrast, suggested continuing struggle. In any case Communist revolution in the west seemed unlikely in the later 1920s.

- Trotsky's weaknesses. He lacked political skill and was regarded as too clever and too arrogant.

3 (a) The political bureau of the Communist Party. Since the party controlled the government, the Politburo was effectively the central organ of government.

(b) Kirov was an old associate of Stalin – but as the party leader in Leningrad also a possible rival. His murder was probably arranged by Stalin and provided him with the excuse to remove all possible rivals. He saw the elimination of the entire generation of Bolsheviks of Lenin's time as the only way to ensure that there would be no threat to his position in the future.

(c) Stalin was left virtually unchallengeable. All the Old Bolsheviks (associates of Lenin) were liquidated, along with all other possible rivals. The army chief and about two-thirds of the senior officers in the army were removed. Millions of less important people were either shot or sent to labour camps. Russia became a state based even more on terror. The purges eliminated a large proportion of the relatively small class of educated people, slowed down industrial progress and weakened the army, with disastrous results in the first two years of the war.

Index